BABY KNITS *from* NORWAY

65 CHARMING MODERN HEIRLOOMS TO KNIT FOR NEWBORNS AND TODDLERS

Hanne Andreassen Hjelmås & Torunn Steinsland
CREATORS OF
KlompeLOMPE

PHOTOGRAPHY BY HANNE ANDREASSEN HJELMÅS

SCHIFFER CRAFT
4880 Lower Valley Road • Atglen, PA 19310

Other Schiffer Craft Books by the Authors:

Knitting for Little Sweethearts, ISBN 978-0-7643-5627-8

All-Year-Round Knitting for Little Sweethearts: 68 Patterns for Everyday, Parties, and Special Times, ISBN 978-0-7643-6507-2

Summer Knitting for Little Sweethearts: 40 Nordic-Style Warm Weather Patterns for Girls, Boys, and Babies, ISBN 978-0-7643-6606-2

Winter Knitting for Little Sweethearts: 46 Nordic-Style Patterns for Girls, Boys, and Babies, ISBN 978-0-7643-6844-8

Originally published as *Klompelompe Nye Favoritter Til Baby* by J. M. Stenersens Forlag AS, Oslo © 2023 by Hanne Andreassen Hjelmås and Torunn Steinsland
Translated from the Norwegian by Carol Huebescher Rhoades

Library of Congress Control Number: 2026932941

Designed by Anne Vines
Cover design by Lindsay Hess
Photography by Hanne Andreassen Hjelmås
Type set in Alexandria

ISBN: 978-0-7643-7246-9
ePub: 978-1-5073-0764-9
Printed in China

10 9 8 7 6 5 4 3 2 1

MIX
Paper | Supporting responsible forestry
FSC www.fsc.org FSC® C104723

Published by Schiffer Craft
An imprint of Schiffer Publishing, Ltd.
4880 Lower Valley Road
Atglen, PA 19310
Phone: (610) 593-1777; Fax: (610) 593-2002
Email: Info@schifferbooks.com
Web: www.schifferbooks.com

For our complete selection of fine books on this and related subjects, please visit our website at www.schifferbooks.com. You may also write for a free catalog.

Schiffer Publishing's titles are available at special discounts for bulk purchases for sales promotions or premiums. Special editions, including personalized covers, corporate imprints, and excerpts, can be created in large quantities for special needs. For more information, contact the publisher.

Contents

Abbreviations

KNITTING

as est	as established, that is, continue in pattern
BO	bind off (= British cast off)
CC	contrast color (pattern color)
cm	centimeter(s)
CO	cast on
dpn(s)	double-pointed needle(s)
g	grams
k	knit
k2tog	knit 2 together = right-leaning decrease; 1 stitch decreased
k3tog	knit 3 together = right-leaning decrease; 2 stitches decreased
kf&b	knit into front and then back of same stitch: Knit into front of stitch but do not slip stitch off needle, knit into back of same stitch and slip original stitch off needle = 1 st increased.
m	meter(s)
M1R	Make 1 Right = with left needle, lift strand between two stitches from back to front and knit into front loop = 1 stitch increased; right-leaning increase.
M1L	Make 1 Left = with left needle, lift strand between two stitches from front to back and knit into back loop = 1 stitch increased; left-leaning increase. M1L is the default increase unless otherwise specified.
M1p	Make 1 purl = lift strand between two stitches onto left needle and purl into back loop = 1 st increase; stitch is twisted
MC	main color (background color)
mm	millimeters
p	purl
pm	place marker
psso	pass slipped stitch(es) over
rem	remain/remaining
rep	repeat(s)
rnd(s)	round(s)
RS	right side
sl	slip
slm	slip marker
ssk	(sl 1 knitwise) 2 times, insert left needle into sts and knit together through back loops = left-leaning decrease; 1 stitch decreased
st(s)	stitch(es)
tbl	through back loop
WS	wrong side
wyb	with yarn held in back
wyf	with yarn held in front
yd(s)	yard(s)
yo	yarnover
-	repeat the sequence between asterisks
#-#r	epeat the sequence between hash marks

CROCHET

ch	chain
sc	single crochet (= British double crochet)
sl st	slip stitch

PICK UP

In this book, "pick up" uses stitch loops from an I-cord and "pick up and knit" creates new stitches along an edge.

Pick up: Insert right needle tip into stitch loop from back to front and lift loop onto needle. (See photos on page 15.)

Pick up and knit: Insert right needle tip into stitch loop from front to back, yarn around needle and draw through loop for a knit stitch.

About the Videos

In many of the projects we point you to our videos in case you want extra help. The videos are available on the English-language page of our website: www.klompelompe.no/en/

Choose to view English subtitles using the CC button.

Where It All Began

The Klompelompe journey began with two small babies on their way into the world and two pregnant friends with the same due date. We were both in love with handcrafts and had been knitters for a long time but these small babies caused our love of knitting to increase considerably.

We had noted that there weren't many well-designed clothes for boys, especially caps, and so we designed the Kjekka and Pilot caps. Both of these were classics that fit well. The caps became popular, but, in the meantime, after countless hours of knitting, we realized that we couldn't continue producing all the knitwear ourselves. The patterns were the key to this challenge, because people wanted to make our baby garments with their own hands.

Now, many books later, we've developed our company's line by adding designs and patterns for older children and adults. Still, we wanted to return to our starting point of knitting for babies. Even if neither of us now have small babies, there is always something special about making small and sweet garments to keep a new body warm. In this collection we've enjoyed designing both simple basic garments and more advanced pieces featuring, for example, multicolor patterns and steeks.

Knitting a layette set—traditionally, baby's very first set of clothing—is, to us, especially wonderful. Just think about having the opportunity to make a layette set for a new little treasure! Making garments to dress the little one for the first trip home—so lovely. The designs here are arranged in layettes in all variations and levels of difficulty. Each set includes several garments, so you can choose what you like best for your little one's set. And don't forget baby blankets! They are a must.

We hope you'll be inspired to make garments for your own or a loved one's baby with the designs gathered here.

Hanne & Torunn

Mini-Ruffle Layette Set

Mini-Ruffle Mohair Cardigan

Soft and sweet, this ruffled cardigan ties at the neck. It pairs beautifully with any dress.

SKILL LEVEL: 2

SIZES: 0–1 (3, 6–9 months; 1, 2, 3 years)

FINISHED MEASUREMENTS
Chest: Approx. 19 (20¾, 23¾, 25¾, 27¾, 29¾) in [48.5 (52.5, 60.5, 65.5, 70.5, 75.5) cm]
Total Length: Approx. 8¾ (9½, 10¾, 11½, 12¾, 13¾) in [22 (24, 27, 29, 32, 35) cm]

YARN: Sandnes Garn Klompelompe Tynn Merinoull [CYCA #1 – fingering, 100% fine Merino wool, 191 yd (175 m) / 50 g] + Sandnes Garn Tynn Silk Mohair (fine silk mohair) [CYCA #0 – lace, 57% mohair, 28% silk, 15% wool, 232 yd (212 m) / 25 g]

YARN COLORS AND AMOUNTS
Tynn Merinoull, Color 4032: 100 (100, 100, 100, 150, 150) g, Tynn Silk Mohair, Color 3511: 50 (50, 50, 50, 50, 75) g

NEEDLES: U.S. sizes 1.5 and 4 (2.5 and 3.5 mm): 16 and 32 in (40 and 80 cm) circulars

GAUGE: 20 sts on larger size needles with 1 strand of each yarn held together = 4 in (10 cm).
Adjust needle size to obtain correct gauge if necessary.

The sweater begins at the top with the tie cord and neck edging. The sweater is worked throughout with 1 strand of each yarn held together.

Tynn Merinoull, color 2650
Tynn Silk Mohair, color 3511

YOKE
With 1 strand pf each yarn held together and smaller size circular, CO 3 sts and knit an I-Cord 22¾ (23¾, 24½, 25¼, 26, 26¾) in [58 (60, 62, 64, 66, 68) cm] long.

Pick up the center 61 (65, 69, 71, 73, 75) sts along the cord. With larger size circular, knit 1 row, purl 1 row.

The yoke is shaped with M1 increases, M1R on right side of raglan stitch and M1L on left side of raglan stitch (see Abbreviations on page 4 and video at klompelompe.no/en/).

Next Row (RS): K10 (11, 12, 13, 13, 14), M1, k1 (raglan st), M1, k8, M1, k1 (raglan st), M1, k21 (23, 25, 25, 27, 27), M1, k1 (raglan st), M1, k8, M1, k1 (raglan st), M1, k10 (11, 12, 13, 13, 14) = 8 sts increased.

Purl 1 row.

Short Rows to raise back neck: Continue with raglan increases as est until 5 sts rem; turn. Purl until 5 sts rem; turn. Knit with raglan increases as est until 3 sts before previous turn; turn. Purl until 3 sts before previous turn; turn. Knit with raglan increases as est to end of row.

Increase as est on every RS row a total of 10 (11, 14, 16, 18, 20) times = 141 (153, 181, 199, 217, 235) sts.

Next Row (RS): Knit to and including raglan st, place the 28 (30, 36, 40, 44, 44) sleeve sts on holder, CO 6 sts for underarm, knit to raglan st, place the 28 (30, 36, 40, 44, 44) sleeve sts on holder, CO 6 sts for underarm, knit to end of row = 97 (105, 121, 131, 141, 151) sts rem for body.

Pm on each side of each set of 6 underarm sts.

Continue back and forth in stockinette. After 1 in (2.5 cm), increase 1 st on each side of the 6 underarm sts at each side = 4 sts increased across.

Increase the same way every 1 in (2.5 cm) a total of 3 (4, 4, 5, 6, 7) times.

Continue in stockinette until body (from shoulder) measures 8 (8¾, 9¾, 10¾, 11¾, 13) in [20 (22, 25, 27, 30, 33) cm] and next row will be on RS. CO 3 sts.

Change to smaller size needle and BO with I-Cord bind-off. (see video at klompelompe.no/en/) as follows:

K2, k2tog tbl, place the 3 sts back on left needle; rep *-* until all sts are bound off.

RUFFLE ON LOWER EDGE
With RS facing and larger size circular, pick up each st along backmost st row of I-Cord bind-off, all the way across.

Purl 1 row on WS.

Next Row (RS): *K1, M1*; rep *-* until 1 st rem, k1.

Purl 1 row, knit 1 row.

BO purlwise on next row.

SLEEVES
Beginning at center of one underarm, pick up and knit 3 sts, pick up and knit 1 st in gap between underarm and armhole, knit the 28 (30, 36, 40, 44, 44) held sleeve sts, pick up and knit 1 st in gap between underarm and armhole, pick up and knit 3 sts to center of underarm = 36 (38, 44, 48, 52, 52) sts total. Join and pm for beginning of round at center of underarm.

Knit around in stockinette until sleeve measures 4¼ (5¼, 6, 6¾, 8¼, 9½) in [11 (13, 15, 17, 21, 24) cm].

Knit 1 rnd, decreasing 6 (8, 10, 14, 16, 14) sts evenly spaced around = 30 (30, 34, 34, 36, 38) sts rem.

Change to smaller size circular and bind off with I-cord bind-off (but, do not cast on 3 sts first).

Seam I-Cord, joining last row with cast-on row.

RUFFLE ON LOWER EDGE OF SLEEVE
With RS facing and larger size circular, pick up each st along backmost st row of I-Cord bind-off, all the way around. Knit 1 rnd.

Next Rnd: *K1, M1*; rep *-* around.

Knit 2 rnds. BO knitwise on next rnd.

FRONT BANDS
With RS facing and smaller size circular, *pick up and knit 3 sts for every 4 rows*; rep *-* along front edge. Cut yarn and begin again on RS. CO 3 sts. Bind off with I-Cord BO as before.

Work opposite front edging the same way.

FINISHING
Weave in all ends neatly on WS.

Dampen sweater and lay flat, patted out to finished measurements and with ruffles arranged to lie nicely, on a towel until completely dry.

Mini-Ruffle Mohair Soakers

Soakers are a great item to have in baby's wardrobe. With a leotard, tights, and soakers, your baby will be well-dressed for everyday and parties alike.

SKILL LEVEL: 2

SIZES: 0–1 (3, 6–9, 12, 18, 24 months)

YARN: Sandnes Garn Klompelompe Tynn Merinoull [CYCA #1 – fingering, 100% fine Merino wool, 191 yd (175 m) / 50 g]
+ Sandnes Garn Tynn Silk Mohair (fine silk mohair) [CYCA #0 – lace, 57% mohair, 28% silk, 15% wool, 232 yd (212 m) / 25 g]

YARN COLORS AND AMOUNTS
Tynn Merinoull, Color 2650: 50 (50, 50, 50, 50, 100) g
Tynn Silk Mohair, Color 3021: 25 (25, 25, 25, 25, 50) g

NEEDLES: U.S. sizes 1.5 and 4 (2.5 and 3.5 mm): 16 and 32 in (40 and 80 cm) circulars

GAUGE: 20 sts on larger size needles with 1 strand of each yarn held together = 4 in (10 cm).

Adjust needle size to obtain correct gauge if necessary.

The soakers are worked from the waist down. They are knitted in the round on a circular needle with 1 strand of each yarn held together throughout.

With 1 strand of each yarn held together and smaller size circular, CO 80 (88, 92, 96, 100, 104) sts. Join, being careful not to twist cast-on row; pm for beginning of rnd. Work 12 rnds in k1, p1 ribbing.

CO 3 sts and then bind off with I-cord bind-off: *K2, k2tog tbl, place the 3 sts back on left needle*; rep *-* around.

Seam ends of I-cord, joining last rnd with cast-on row.

With larger size circular, pick up each st along backmost row of sts on I-cord all the way around (see photo on page 15) = 80 (88, 92, 96, 100, 104) sts.

Knit 1 rnd.

Next Rnd: *K4, M1*; rep *-* around = 100 (110, 115, 120, 125, 130) sts.

Knit around in stockinette until piece measures 5¼ (5½, 5¾, 6, 6⅛, 6¼) in [13 (14, 14.5, 15, 15.5, 16) cm].

Lengthen back with German short rows (see video at komppelompe.no):

K20; turn. P40; turn.
K45; turn. P50; turn.
K55; turn. P60, turn.
Knit to end of rnd.

Continue around in stockinette until piece measures 5½ (6, 6⅛, 6¼, 6½, 6¾) in [14 (15, 15.5, 16, 16.5, 17) cm] down the front. BO 1 st on sizes 6–9 and 18 months.

Work the center 28 (30, 30, 34, 36, 36) sts back to the back and place remaining sts on a holder.

BACK
The first row is on RS.

K2tog, knit until 2 sts rem, k2tog tbl.

Decrease the same way on every RS row until 16 sts rem.

On next RS row, BO rem sts.

FRONT
Knit the center 22 (24, 24, 26, 28, 30) sts of the front and place rem 25 (28, 30, 30, 30, 32) sts on a holder. The first row is on RS.

K2tog, knit until 2 sts rem, k2tog tbl.

Decrease the same way on every RS row until 16 sts rem.

Work 4 rows in stockinette, binding off on 4th row.

Seam Crotch

With smaller size circular, pick up and knit sts for leg edging. Begin where you seamed crotch. Pick up and knit 3 sts for every 4 sts.

Work held sts: *K1, k2tog*; rep *-* until 1 st rem, k1, pick up and knit 3 sts for every 4 sts.

CO 3 sts and BO with I-Cord bind-off (see video at komppelompe.no).

RUFFLE
With larger size circular, pick up sts along I-cord in same sts where you picked up previously. Knit 1 rnd.

Next Rnd: *K1, M1*; rep *-* around.

Knit 4 rnds. BO on next rnd.

FINISHING
Weave in all ends neatly on WS.

Block soakers by laying them flat, patted out to finished measurements, on a damp hand towel until completely dry.

Mini-Ruffle Mohair Bonnet

A special extra-soft bonnet with a sweet ruffle.

SKILL LEVEL: 2

SIZES: preemie (0–3, 3–6, 6–12 months, 1–2 years)

YARN: Sandnes Garn Klompelompe Tynn Merinoull [CYCA #1 – fingering, 100% fine Merino wool, 191 yd (175 m) / 50 g] + Sandnes Garn Tynn Silk Mohair (fine silk mohair) [CYCA #0 – lace, 57% mohair, 28% silk, 15% wool, 232 yd (212 m) / 25 g]

YARN COLORS AND AMOUNTS
Tynn Merinoull, Color 2650: 50 (50, 50, 50, 50) g
Tynn Silk Mohair, Color 3021: 25 (25, 25, 25, 25) g

NEEDLES: U.S. sizes 1.5 and 2.5 (2.5 and 3 mm): 16 and 32 in (40 and 80 cm) circulars

GAUGE: 22 sts on larger size needles with 1 strand of each yarn held together = 4 in (10 cm).

Adjust needle size to obtain correct gauge if necessary.

The bonnet is worked back and forth on a circular needle with 1 strand of each yarn held together throughout.

With 1 strand of each yarn held together and smaller size circular, CO 67 (77, 81, 83, 87) sts. Work 4 rows in k1, p1 ribbing.

CO 3 sts and then bind off with I-cord bind-off (see video of technique at kompelompe.no):

K2, k2tog tbl, place the 3 sts back on left needle; rep *-* across.

With larger size circular, pick up each st along backmost row of I-cord (see photo on page 15) = 67 (77, 81, 83, 87) sts.

Work back and forth in stockinette until piece measures 3¼ (4, 4¼, 4¾, 5¼) in [8 (10, 11, 12, 13) cm].

Pm, join sts and begin knitting in the round, decreasing 4 (5, 1, 3, 7) sts evenly spaced on the first rnd.

Knit 3 rnds.

SIZES 3–6, 6–12 months, 1–2 years only:

Next Rnd: *K8, k2tog*; rep *-* around.

Knit 2 rnds.

ALL SIZES:

Next Rnd: *K7, k2tog*; rep *-* around.

Knit 2 rnds.

Next Rnd: *K6, k2tog*; rep *-* around.

Knit 1 rnd.

Next Rnd: *K5, k2tog*; rep *-* around.

Knit 1 rnd.

Next Rnd: *K4, k2tog*; rep *-* around.

Knit 1 rnd.

Next Rnd: *K3, k2tog*; rep *-* around.

Knit 1 rnd.

Next Rnd: *K2, k2tog*; rep *-* around.

Knit 1 rnd.

Next Rnd: *K1, k2tog*; rep *-* around.

Next Rnd: *K2tog*; rep *-* around.

Cut yarn and draw ends through rem sts; tighten.

RUFFLE

Pick up the same sts along I-cord as those you picked up for cap.

With larger size needle, knit 1 row on RS.

Purl 1 row.

Next Row: *K1, M1*; rep *-* until 1 st rem, k1.

Purl 1 row, knit 1 row. On WS, BO purlwise.

NECK EDGING

With smaller size circular, pick up and knit 2 sts for every 3 sts*; rep *-* across.

Place sts on a holder.

With smaller size circular, CO 3 sts and knit an I-cord 8 in (20 cm) long (see video of technique at kompelompe.no). Work I-cord BO over held sts until 3 sts rem. On WS: bind off purlwise.

End with another 8 in (20 cm) I-cord.

FINISHING

Weave in all ends neatly on WS.

Block by laying cap between two damp towels until completely dry.

Mini-Ruffle Socks

The I-cord around the ankle ensures that these socks will fit exceptionally well. Knit the smallest size with U.S. size 1.5 (2.5 mm) and they will fit little preemie feet perfectly.

SKILL LEVEL: 2

SIZES: 0–1 (3, 6, 9–12, 18–24 months, 2–3 years)

YARN: Sandnes Garn Klompelompe Tynn Merinoull [CYCA #1 - fingering, 100% fine Merino wool, 191 yd (175 m) / 50 g]

YARN COLORS AND AMOUNTS
Color 1013: 50 (50, 50, 50, 50, 50) g

NEEDLES: U.S. sizes 1.5 and 2.5 (2.5 and 3 mm): 32 in (80 cm) circular for magic loop

GAUGE: 27 sts on larger size needles = 4 in (10 cm).
Adjust needle size to obtain correct gauge if necessary.

The socks are worked cuff down in the round on a magic loop circular needle (see video at klom pelompe.no/en/).

With smaller size circular, CO 36 (40, 40, 44, 48, 48) sts. Join to work in the round; pm for beginning of rnd.

Work 20 (22, 24, 26, 28, 30) rnds k1, p1 ribbing.

Knit 1 rnd.

Bind off with I-cord bind-off (see video of technique at kompelompe.no): *K2, k2tog tbl, place the 3 sts back on left needle*; rep *-* around.

Seam to join first and last I-cord ends.

With larger size circular, pick up sts on backmost row of I-cord, beginning on opposite side of round begun last. Knit 1 rnd, adjusting stitch count to 30 (30, 34, 34, 38, 42), by decreasing 6 (10, 6, 10, 10, 6) sts evenly spaced around.

HEEL

Rows are turned with German short rows (see video of technique at klompelompe.no/en/).

Knit until 6 (6, 8, 8, 10, 10) sts rem; turn. Purl until 6 (6, 8, 8, 10, 10) sts rem; turn.

Continue working short rows with 1 less st before previous turn until you have 8 sts between the turns.

Knit to end of rnd.

Knit until 10 (10, 12, 12, 14, 14) sts rem; turn.

Purl until 10 (10, 12, 12, 14, 16) sts rem; turn.

Continue working short rows, turning 1 st after previous turn until you again have 4 (4, 6, 6, 8, 8) sts. Knit to end of rnd.

On all sts around: Knit 11 (13, 15, 19, 23, 27) rnds.

Decrease as follows:

Size 2–3 years:
K8, k2tog, k1, k2tog tbl, k8; rep *-* around.
Knit 1 rnd.

Sizes 18–24 months and 2–3 years:
K7, k2tog, k1, k2tog tbl, k7; rep *-* around.

Sizes 6 (9–12, 18–24 months and 2–3 years:
K6, k2tog, k1, k2tog tbl, k6; rep *-* around.

ALL SIZES:
K5, k2tog, k1, k2tog tbl, k5; rep *-* around.
Knit 1 rnd.

Next Rnd: *K4, k2tog, k1, k2tog tbl, k4*; rep *-* around.
Next Rnd: *K3, k2tog, k1, k2tog tbl, k3*; rep *-* around.
Next Rnd: *K2, k2tog, k1, k2tog tbl, k2*; rep *-* around.
Next Rnd: *K1, k2tog, k1, k2tog tbl, k1*; rep *-* around.

Cut yarn and draw end through rem sts; tighten.

RUFFLE

With larger size circular, pick up the same sts you picked up previously along I-cord. Knit 1 rnd.
Next Rnd: *K1, M1*; rep *-* around.
Knit 1 rnd.
BO purlwise on next rnd.

Make second sock the same way.

FINISHING

Weave in all ends neatly on WS.

Block by laying socks between two damp towels until completely dry.

Color 4344

Simple Pixie Cap

Simplest is often best and will be the most worn. This cap fits well and can be embellished with embroidery if you like.

SKILL LEVEL: 1

SIZES: 1–3 (3–6, 6–9 months, 1–2, 3–4 years)

YARN: Sandnes Garn Klompelompe Merinoull [CYCA #3 – DK/light worsted, 100% Merino wool, 114 yd (104 m) / 50 g]

YARN COLORS AND AMOUNTS
Color 1013: 50 (50, 100, 100, 100) g

NEEDLES: U.S. sizes 2.5 and 4 (3 and 3.5 mm): 16 and 32 in (40 and 80 cm) circulars

NOTIONS for embroidered version: embroidery hoop, piece of water-soluble Vlieseline interfacing, embroidery needle

GAUGE: 22 sts on larger size needle = 4 in (10 cm).
Adjust needle size to obtain correct gauge if necessary.

With smaller size circular, CO 71 (77, 83, 83, 89) sts. Work 4 rows back and forth in k1, p1 ribbing. Change to larger size needle.

Purl 1 row and *at the same time* increase 3 sts evenly spaced across. Increase with M1p (see Abbreviations on page 4) = 74 (80, 86, 86, 92) sts.

Continue back and forth in stockinette until piece measures 5¼ (5½, 6, 6¼, 6¾) in [13 (14, 15, 16, 17) cm]. On next RS row, work German short rows: Knit until 10 sts rem; turn. Sl 1st st and tighten so st flips and 2 legs appear on needle (= double st/DS), purl until 10 sts rem; turn and DS as before. Knit until 3 sts before previous DS; turn and DS. Purl until 3 sts before previous DS; turn and DS. Continue, each time turning 3 sts before previous DS and, at beginning of next row, DS, until you've turned a total of 4 times on each side. Knit to end of row.

Divide piece in two and hold with RS facing RS. Using a third needle, join the two halves with 3-needle bind-off: K2tog joining 1st st on each needle, *k2tog joining front st on each left needle; pass 2nd st on right needle over first st*; rep *-* across. Turn work with RS out.

NECKBAND
With smaller size needle, pick up and knit 1 st in every other st along neck edge.

Work 3 rows k1, p1 ribbing.

Next Row: K4, BO in k1, p1 ribbing until 4 sts rem, k4.

On each side: Make an I-cord with the 4 sts (see video of technique at kompelompe.no). The cord should be about 8 in (20 cm) long.

FINISHING
Weave in all ends neatly on WS.

Block by laying cap between two damp towels until completely dry.

EMBROIDERY
Trace the design onto water-soluble interfacing such as Vlieseline.

Stretch the interfacing over the knitted fabric in an embroidery hoop or with pins. Embroider with the same yarn as for the cap.

Dampen or rinse the cap until it is dissolved. Do not iron!

Mini-Ruffle Playsuit

Sweet ruffles and fine shaping make this garment lovely for both everyday wear and parties.

SKILL LEVEL: 2

SIZES: preemie (0–1, 1–3, 6, 9, 12, 18 months, 2 years)

FINISHED MEASUREMENTS
Chest: Approx. 16¾ (18½, 19¾, 21½, 23¼, 24¼, 26¼, 27¼) in [42.5 (47, 50, 54.5, 59, 61.5, 66.5, 69) cm]
Total Length: Approx. 15½ (17, 19¼, 22, 23¼, 24½, 26½, 28¼) in [39 (43, 49, 56, 59, 62, 67, 72) cm]

YARN: Sandnes Garn Klompelompe Tynn Merinoull [CYCA #1 – fingering, 100% fine Merino wool, 191 yd (175 m) / 50 g]

YARN COLORS AND AMOUNTS
Color 4331: 150 (150, 200, 200, 250, 250, 300, 300) g

NEEDLES: U.S. sizes 1.5 and 2.5 (2.5 and 3 mm): 16 and 32 in (40 and 80 cm) circular

NOTIONS: 8 (8,8, 10, 10, 10, 12, 13) buttons, ⅝ in (15 mm) in diameter; crochet hook U.S. D-3 (3 mm) to make button loop

GAUGE: 27 sts on larger size needles = 4 in (10 cm).
Adjust needle size to obtain correct gauge if necessary.

The playsuit begins at the neck with an I-cord edging (see video of technique at klompelompe.no/en/).

The yoke is shaped with M1 increases, M1R on right side of raglan stitch and M1L on left side of raglan stitch (see Abbreviations on page 4 and video at klompelompe.no/en/).

With smaller size circular, CO 4 sts. Make an I-cord 9 (9½, 9⅝, 10, 10½, 10¾, 11½, 11¾) in [23 (24, 24.5, 25.5, 26.5, 27.5, 29, 30) cm] long.

Change to larger size circular.

Pick up 71 (74, 76, 79, 83, 86, 92, 95) sts along I-cord. Knit 1 row, purl 1 row.

Next Row: K12 (13, 13, 14, 15, 16, 17, 18), M1, k1 (raglan st), M1, k9 (sleeve sts), M1, k1 (raglan st), M1, k25 (26, 28, 29, 31, 32, 36, 37), M1, k1, (raglan st), M1, k9 (sleeve sts), M1, k1 (raglan st), M1, k12 (13, 13, 14, 15, 16, 17, 18).

Purl 1 row.

Raise back neck with German short rows (see video at klompelompe.no/en/):

Work as est with raglan increases until 6 sts in on front; turn, purl back.
Work as est with raglan increases until 9 sts in on front; turn, purl back.
Knit 1 row as est with raglan increases; turn.
Purl until 6 sts in on front; turn.
Knit 1 row as est with raglan increases; turn.
Purl until 9 sts in on front; turn.
Knit 1 row as est with raglan increases; turn.
Purl 1 row.

Increase as est on every RS row until you've increased a total of 8 (8, 9, 9, 10, 10, 11, 11) times.

Now, join to work in the round and pm for beginning of rnd.

Continue increasing as est on every other rnd until you've increased a total of 13 (15, 17, 19, 21, 22, 24, 25) times = 175 (194, 212, 231, 251, 262, 284, 295) sts.

Knit 1 rnd.

Next Rnd: Knit to and including raglan st, place sleeve sts on holder, CO 5 sts for underarm, knit to and including raglan st, place sleeve sts on holder, CO 5 sts for underarm, knit to end of rnd = 115 (126, 136, 147, 159, 166, 180, 187) sts rem for body.

Pm on each side of the 5 underarm sts at each side.

Continue around in stockinette.

After 1¼ in (3 cm), M1 on each side of the 5 underarm sts at each side.

Increase the same way every 1¼ (1¼, 1¼, 1½, 1½, 2, 2, 2) in [3 (3, 3, 4, 4, 5, 5, 5) cm] a total of 3 (3, 3, 3, 4, 4, 4, 5) times = 127 (138, 148, 159, 175, 182, 196, 207) sts.

Continue around in stockinette until piece, as measured down center back is 9¾ (10¾, 11¾, 13½, 14, 14½, 15¾, 16½) in [25 (27, 30, 34, 35.5, 37, 40, 42) cm] long.

On next rnd, decrease 1 (0, 0, 1, 1, 0, 0, 1) st.

Shape back with German short rows (see video at klompelompe.no/en/).

K20; turn. P40; turn. K43; turn. P46; turn. K49; turn. P52; turn.

SIZES 9, 12, 18 MONTHS AND 2 YEARS:
K55; turn. P58; turn.

SIZES 18 MONTHS AND 2 YEARS:
K61; turn. P64; turn.

ALL SIZES:
Knit 1 rnd.

Pm on each side of the 8 center sts at front and back.

On next rnd, M1 on each side of the 8 sts at center front and back.

Increase the same way on every 3rd rnd a total of 5 times.

On next rnd, BO the 8 sts at center front and back and work each leg separately, working back and forth = 65 (71, 76, 81, 89, 93, 100, 105) sts for each leg. Make each leg the same way.

Purl 1 row.

Next Row: K1, k2tog, knit until 3 sts rem, sl 1, k1, psso, k1.

Decrease the same way on every 4th row a total of 8 (8, 9, 9, 10, 10, 11, 11) times = 49 (55, 58, 63, 69, 73, 78, 83) sts rem.

Work back and forth in stockinette until leg measures 4 (4¾, 6, 7, 7¾, 8¼, 9, 10¼) in [10 (12, 15, 18, 19.5, 21, 23, 26) cm] and next row is on WS.

Purl 1 row, adjusting stitch count, spaced as evenly as possible across to 32 (34, 36, 36, 38, 38, 40, 40).

Change to smaller size circular and BO with I-cord bind-off.

BUTTON BAND ON LEG AND CROTCH
Note: In this section, you will pick up and knit sts, not just pick up.

Back Band: With smaller size needle, pick up and knit 3 sts for every 4 sts along each leg. Pick up and knit 1 st in each st across bound-off crotch sts. Knit 7 rows in garter stitch. BO knitwise on next row.

Front Band: Work as for back band, but make 7 (7, 7, 9, 9, 9, 11, 11) buttonholes evenly spaced along the 2nd row of band: BO 2 sts for each buttonhole and, on next row, CO 2 sts over each gap.

BUTTON LOOP ON BACK NECK
At the very top of back neck, attach yarn and ch 4. Attach ch to body with 1 sl st. Check to make sure that the button fits through the button loop before you attach the loop. Sew a button on opposite side of back neck.

RUFFLE ON LOWER EDGE
With larger size needle, pick up sts on end of front leg button band and pick up the backmost sts of I-cord all across. Omit ruffle on back button band.

Begin on RS.

Knit 1 row, purl 1 row.

Next Row: *K1, M1*; rep *-* across.

Purl 1 row, knit 1 row.

BO knitwise on next row.

RUFFLE ON NECKBAND
With larger size needle, pick up the same sts you picked up at beginning (see photo).

Begin on RS and knit 1 row tbl (= knit in back loop of each st).

Purl 1 row.

Next Row: *K2, M1*; rep *-* until 2 sts rem, k2.

Purl 1 row, knit 1 row.

Next Row (WS): BO knitwise.

SLEEVES
With larger size needle, beginning at center of the 5 underarm sts, pick up and knit 3 sts, pick up and knit 1 st in gap between underarm and armhole, knit held sleeve sts, pick up and knit 1 st in gap between armhole and underarm, pickup and knit 2 sts on underarm.

Join, pm for beginning of rnd, and knit around until sleeve measures 3½ (4¼, 5¼, 6, 6¼, 6¾, 7½, 8¾) in [9 (11, 13, 15, 16, 17, 19, 22) cm].

Knit 1 rnd, adjusting stitch count to 34 (36, 38, 40, 40, 42, 42, 44) sts.

Change to smaller size needle and BO with I-cord bind-off (see video at klompelompe.no/en/).

RUFFLE ON SLEEVE
With larger size needle, pick up backmost sts all around I-cord. Knit 1 rnd.

Next Rnd: *K1, M1*; rep *-* around.

Knit 2 rnds. BO purlwise on next rnd,

FINISHING
Weave in all ends neatly on WS. Sew buttons on leg band. Block by laying playsuit flat, patted out to finished measurements on a damp towel until completely dry.

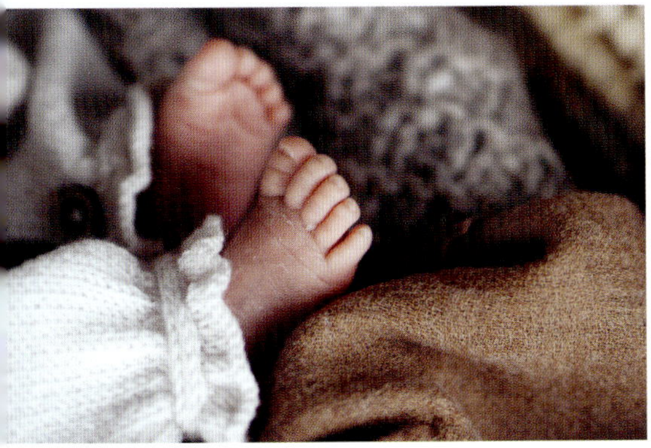
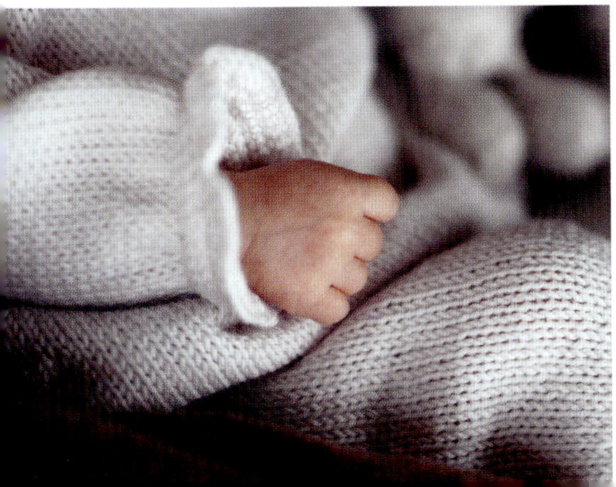

Classic Newborn Cap

A perfect cap for a newborn baby. Why not embellish it with a little embroidery?

SKILL LEVEL: 1

SIZES: preemie (0–1, 1–3, 3–6, 9–12 months, 1–2 years)

YARN: Sandnes Garn Klompelompe Tynn Merinoull [CYCA #1 – fingering, 100% fine Merino wool, 191 yd (175 m) / 50 g]

YARN COLORS AND AMOUNTS
Color 2650 or 1013: 50 (50, 50, 50, 50, 50) g

NEEDLES: U.S. sizes 1.5 and 2.5 (2.5 and 3 mm): 16 and 32 in (40 and 80 cm) circulars

NOTIONS for embroidered version: embroidery hoop, piece of water-soluble Vlieseline interfacing, embroidery needle

GAUGE: 27 sts on larger size needles = 4 in (10 cm).
Adjust needle size to obtain correct gauge if necessary.

With smaller size needle, CO 72 (78, 90, 96, 102, 108) sts. Join, being careful not to twist cast-on row; pm for beginning of rnd.

Knit around in garter ridges (1 ridge = knit 1 rnd, purl 1 rnd) for 1¼ in (3 cm).

Change to larger size needle and knit 1 rnd.

Knit around in stockinette until cap measures 3½ (4, 4¼, 4¾, 5¼, 5½) in [9 (10, 11, 12, 13, 14) cm].

Knit 1 rnd, adjusting stitch count to 72 (72, 88, 96, 96, 104) sts.

Next Rnd: *K6, k2tog*; rep *-* around.
Knit 3 rnds.
Next Rnd: *K5, k2tog*; rep *-* around.
Knit 3 rnds.
Next Rnd: *K4, k2tog*; rep *-* around.
Knit 3 rnds.
Next Rnd:*K2, k2tog*; rep *-* until 1 (1, 3, 0, 0, 1) sts rem, k1 (1, 3, 0, 0, 1 .
Knit 2 rnds.
Next Rnd: *K1, k2tog*; rep *-* until 1 (1, 0, 0, 0, 1) st rem, k1 (1, 0, 0, 0, 1).
Knit 1 rnd.
Next Rnd: *K2tog*; rep *-* until 1 (1, 0, 0, 0, 1) st rem, k1 (1, 0, 0, 0, 1) .
Knit 1 rnd.

Next Rnd: *K1, k2tog*; rep *-* until 0 (0, 2, 0, 0, 2) sts rem, k0 (0, 2, 0, 0, k2tog).

Knit around on the last 8 (8, 8, 10, 10, 11) sts for ¾ in (2 cm).
Cut yarn and draw end through rem sts; tighten.

EMBROIDERED VERSION
Trace the design onto water-soluble Vlieseline interfacing.
Stretch the interfacing over the knitted fabric in an embroidery hoop or with pins. Embroider with the same yarn as for the cap.
Dampen or rinse the cap until it dissolved. Do not iron!

FINISHING
Weave in all ends neatly on WS.
Block by laying cap between two damp towels until completely dry.

Mini-Ruffle Baby Mittens

These mittens will fit baby's hands well. We embellished them with a small ruffle.

SKILL LEVEL: 2

SIZES: 1–3 (6–9 months, 1–2, 3–4 years)
YARN: Sandnes Garn Klompelompe Merinoull [CYCA #3 - DK, 100% Merino wool, 114 yd (104 m) / 50 g]

YARN COLORS AND AMOUNTS
Color 2650 or 9871: 50 (50, 50, 50) g or leftover amount

NEEDLES: U.S. sizes 2.5 and 4 (3 and 3.5 mm): 32 in (80 cm) circular for magic loop [3 mm is used for cuff of mitten hand]

GAUGE: 22 sts on larger size needle = 4 in (10 cm).
Adjust needle size to obtain correct gauge if necessary.

The mittens are worked from the top of the hand down to the cuff, in the round.

With larger size needle, CO 6 sts. Join to knit in the round on magic loop circular (see video at klompelompe.no/en/).

Next Rnd: *Kf&b*; rep *-* around = 12 sts.
Next Rnd: *K1, kf&b*; rep *-* around = 18 sts.
Knit 1 rnd.
Next Rnd: *K2, kf&b*; rep *-* around = 24 sts.
Knit 1 rnd.
Next Rnd: *K3, kf&b*; rep *-* around = 30 sts.

SIZES 1–2 AND 3–4 YEARS
Knit 1 rnd.
Next Rnd: *K4, kf&b*; rep *-* around = 36 sts.

ALL SIZES:
Knit around in stockinette until mitten measures 2¼ (2½, 2¾, 3¼) in [5.5 (6.5, 7, 8) cm].
On next rnd, for sizes 6–9 months, 1–2 and 3–4 years, you'll knit in waste yarn for the thumbhole placement.

RIGHT-HAND MITTEN
K1. With a short length of smooth contrast color waste yarn, knit - (5, 6, 6). Slip those sts back onto left needle and knit with working yarn. Knit to end of rnd.

LEFT-HAND MITTEN

K- (9, 11, 11). With a short length of smooth contrast color waste yarn, knit - (5, 6, 6). Slip those sts back onto left needle and knit with working yarn. Knit to end of rnd.

ALL SIZES

Knit around in stockinette until mitten measures 2¾ (3¼, 3½, 4) in [7 (9, 10) cm].

Knit 1 rnd decreasing 6 sts evenly spaced around.

Change to smaller size needle. Knit 5 rnds.

WELT

Knit 1 rnd, and at *the same time* pick up and join the stitch 5 rnds down: *Count down 5 sts on back of work, lift st with left needle and knit it together with next st on needle*. Rep *-* around. If you think this is difficult, you can pick up the sts on back of work with an extra needle before you begin joining around.

Purl 1 rnd.

Work 1½ (2, 2½, 2 ¾) in [4 (5, 6, 7) cm] k1, p1 ribbing, binding off in ribbing on last rnd.

THUMB

Insert needle into - (5, 6, 6) sts below waste yarn at thumbhole and another needle into - (5, 6, 6) sts above waste yarn. Also, pick up 1 st at each side of thumbhole. Carefully remove waste yarn. Knit around in stockinette for - (1, 1¼, 1½) in [- (2.5, 3, 4) cm]. K2tog around. Cut yarn and draw end through rem sts; tighten.

RUFFLE

With larger size needle and RS facing, pick up strand between each of the purl sts of rnd just below welt. Knit 1 rnd.

Next Rnd: *K1, M1*; rep *-* around.

Knit 2 rnds.

BO purlwise on next rnd.

FINISHING

Weave in all ends neatly on WS.

Block by laying mittens between two damp towels until completely dry.

Darling Layette Set

Darling Overalls

Great overalls that fit well. These pants will be a wardrobe favorite and are perfect for wearing to nursery school.

Tip: For the overalls shown, we used Tynn Silk Mohair instead of Alpakka Følgetråd.

SKILL LEVEL: 2

SIZES: preemie (0–1, 3, 6, 9, 12, 18, 24, 36) months

YARN: Sandnes Garn Klompelompe Tynn Merinoull [CYCA #1 – fingering, 100% fine Merino wool, 191 yd (175 m) / 50 g] + Sandnes Garn Alpakka Følgetråd [CYCA #0 – lace, 100% alpaca, 437 yd (400 m) / 50 g]
Note: If you prefer, you can use Klompelompe Tynn Silk Mohair instead of Alpakka Følgetråd. In that case, you'll need a bit more yarn.

YARN COLORS AND AMOUNTS
Tynn Merinoull, Color 1013: 100 (100, 100, 100, 100, 150, 150, 150, 150) g
Alpakka Følgetråd, Color 1015: 50 (50, 50, 50, 50, 100, 100, 100, 100) g

NEEDLES: U.S. sizes 2.5 and 4 (3 and 3.5 mm): 16 and 32 in (40 and 80 cm) circulars

NOTIONS: 2 buttons, ⅝ in (15 mm) in diameter

GAUGE: 22 sts on larger size needle with 1 strand of each yarn held together = 4 in (10 cm).

Adjust needle size to obtain correct gauge if necessary.

With smaller size circular and with 1 strand of each yarn held together, CO 100 (108, 108, 116, 116, 124, 124, 130, 136) sts. Join, being careful not to twist cast-on row; pm for beginning of rnd.

Work 7 rnds in k1, p1 ribbing.

Next Rnd: Work 40 (43, 43, 46, 46, 48, 48, 51, 53) sts in k1, p1 ribbing, BO 2 sts, work 16 (18, 18, 20, 20, 24, 24, 24, 26) sts in ribbing, BO 2 sts, work 40 (43, 43, 46, 46, 48, 48, 51, 53) sts in k1, p1 ribbing.

On next rnd, CO 2 sts over each gap. Work 6 more rnds in ribbing as est = 14 rnds total in ribbing.

Change to larger size circular.

Work next rnd as follows and *at the same time* increase 0 (2, 2, 4, 4, 6, 6, 10, 4) sts evenly spaced around = 100 (110, 110, 120, 120, 130, 130, 140, 140) sts:

P1, k3, *p2, k3* rep *-* until 1 st rem, p1.

Continue as est in k3, p2 ribbing until piece measures 4 in (10 cm) for all sizes. Now lengthen back: 20 sts ribbing; turn, 40 sts ribbing; turn, 45 sts ribbing; turn, 50 sts ribbing; turn.

SIZES 12, 18, 24, 36 MONTHS:
55 sts ribbing; turn, 60 sts ribbing; turn.

ALL SIZES:
Work in ribbing around.

When piece measures 6¼ (7, 8¾, 9, 10¼, 11, 11½, 12¾, 14¼) in [16 (18, 22, 23, 26, 28, 29, 32, 36) cm], pm on each side of the center 8 sts at both back and front.

Next Rnd: Increase 1 st on each side of the 8 sts (Increase = M1 with twisted knit or twisted purl depending on pattern sequence).
Increase the same way on every 3rd rnd a total of 4 times (increase so you increase in the ribbing for the legs; do not widen the panels of 8 center sts).

Next Rnd: BO the 8 sts between markers at center front and center back.

Now work each leg separately.

Work around on leg until it measures 1¼ (1½, 2½, 3¾, 3¾, 4, 4¾, 4¾, 5½) in [3 (4, 6, 9.5, 9.5, 10, 12, 12, 14) cm]. Decrease 1 st in each purl column with p2tog.

Continue ribbing with knit over knit and purl over purl.

When leg measures 2¾ (3½, 4¼, 5¼, 5½, 6¾, 7½, 8¼, 9) in [7 (9, 11, 13, 14, 17, 19, 21, 23) cm], k2tog with first 2 sts, decrease 1 st in the opposite purl columns = 40 (44, 44, 48, 48, 52, 52, 56, 56) sts rem.

Continue as est until leg measures 3½ (4, 5½, 6¾, 7½, 8¾, 9½, 10¾, 11¾) in [9 (10, 14, 17, 19, 22, 24, 27, 30) cm].

Next Rnd: *K1, p1, k1, p1, sl 1, k2tog, psso, p1*; rep *-* until 0 (4, 4, 0, 0, 4, 4, 0, 0) sts rem, k0 (4, 4, 0, 0, 4, 4, 0, 0).

Change to smaller size needle.

Work 12 rnds in k1, p1 ribbing. BO in ribbing.

Make second leg the same way.

STRAPS
With smaller size needle, pick up and knit 19 sts across center back.

Work 18 rows in k1, p1 ribbing.

BO the center st and then work each strap separately. Continue in ribbing on one strap until it measures 7 (7, 8, 8¾, 9½, 9½, 10¼, 10¼, 10¼) in [18 (18, 20, 22, 24, 24, 26, 26, 26) cm] from row where you picked up sts. BO in ribbing. Make the other strap the same way.

FINISHING
Weave in all ends neatly on WS. Sew a button on the end of each strap. Seam crotch.

Block by laying overalls flat, patted out to finished measurements, on a damp towel until completely dry.

Darling Cap

Its perfect fit, earflaps with cables, and cute topknots will make this a favorite cap for your littlest ones.

SKILL LEVEL: 1

SIZES: 0–1 (1–3, 4–9, 12–18 months, 2–4 years)
YARN: Sandnes Garn Klompelompe Merinoull (Merino wool) [CYCA #3 - DK, 100% Merino wool, 114 yd (104 m) / 50 g]
+ Sandnes Garn Alpakka Følgetråd [CYCA #0 – lace, 100% alpaca, 437 yd (400 m) / 50 g]

YARN COLORS AND AMOUNTS
Merinoull, Color 2650: 50 (50, 50, 50, 100) g
Alpakka Følgetråd, Color 2321: 50 (50, 50, 50, 50) g

NEEDLES: U.S. sizes 4 and 6 (3.5 and 4 mm): 16 and 32 in (40 and 80 cm) circulars [ear flaps use smaller size]

GAUGE: 20 sts on gauge-size needle with 1 strand of each yarn held together = 4 in (10 cm).

Adjust needle size to obtain correct gauge if necessary.

With larger size needle and 1 strand of each yarn held together, CO 65 (70, 75, 80, 85) sts. Join, being careful not to twist cast-on row; pm for beginning of rnd.

Work around in k3, p2 ribbing for 4 (4½, 5¼, 5½, 6) in [10, 11.5, 13, 14, 15) cm].

Next Rnd: *K3, p2, k1, k2tog, p2*; rep *-* until 5 (0, 5, 0, 5) sts rem, (k3, p2) [k0, (k3, p2), k0, (k3, p2)].

Next 3 Rnds: *K3, p2, k2, p2*; rep *-* until 5 (0, 5, 0, 5) sts rem, (k3, p2) [k0, (k3, p2), k0, (k3, p2)].

Next Rnd: *K1, k2tog, p2, k2, p2*; rep *-* until 5 (0, 5, 0, 5) sts rem, (k1, k2tog, p2) [k0, (k1, k2tog, p2), k0, (k1, k2tog, p2)].

Work 3 rnds in k2, p2 ribbing.

Next Rnd: BO 10 (11, 12, 13, 14) sts in ribbing, work 8 sts ribbing, BO 18 (20, 22, 24, 26) sts ribbing, work 8 sts ribbing, BO 8 (9, 10, 11, 12) sts in ribbing.

KNOTS

Knit 5 rnds over last 8 sts.

Next Rnd: *K2, M1, k2*; rep *-*.

Knit 12 rnds.

Next Rnd: *K2, M1, k1, M1, k2*; rep *-*.

Knit 1 rnd.

Next Rnd: *K3, M1, k1, M1, k3*; rep *-*.

Knit 7 rnds.

Next Rnd: K2tog around.

Cut yarn and draw end through rem sts; tighten.

Make a knot the same way over rem set of 8 sts.

EAR FLAPS

With smaller size needle, make ear flaps with 8 (10, 12, 12, 14) center back sts in between them.

With RS facing, pick up and knit 15 (17, 17, 19, 19) sts.

Purl 1 row.

Next Row: K1, k2tog, knit until 3 sts rem, sl 1, k1, psso, k1.

Rep the previous 2 rows until 5 sts rem.

Next Row (RS): K1, sl 1, k2tog, psso, k1.

Knit an I-cord with rem 3 sts (see video at klompelompe.no/en/). When cord is 7 (8, 8, 8¾, 8¾) in [18 (20, 20, 22, 22) cm] long, cut yarn and draw end through rem sts; tighten.

Make second ear flap and cord the same way.

FINISHING

Weave in all ends neatly on WS. Seam top and make a knot with each of the tubes on top of the cap.

Block by laying cap between two damp towels until completely dry.

Darling Scarf

A quick-knit doubled scarf.

SKILL LEVEL: 1

SIZES: 0–3 (6–12 months, 1–3 years)

YARN: Sandnes Garn Klompelompe Tynn Merinoull [CYCA #1 – fingering, 100% fine Merino wool, 191 yd (175 m) / 50 g]
+ Sandnes Garn Alpakka Følgetråd [CYCA #0 – lace, 100% alpaca, 437 yd (400 m) / 50 g]

YARN COLORS AND AMOUNTS

Merinoull, Color 2650: 50 (50, 50) g

Alpakka Følgetråd, Color 2321: 50 (50, 50) g

NEEDLES: U.S. size 4 (3.5 mm): 32 in (80 cm) circular

GAUGE: 22 sts on gauge-size needle with 1 strand of each yarn held together = 4 in (10 cm).

Adjust needle size to obtain correct gauge if necessary.

Coziest Cutiepie cap: colors 2650 and 2650
Fishing Net Pullover: color 9871

SCARF CONSTRUCTION

The scarf is worked around on a long magic loop circular needle for two layers when flat. A keyhole slot holds one end of the scarf.

With gauge-size needle and 1 strand of each yarn held together, CO 30 (50, 60) sts. Join, being careful not to twist cast-on row; pm for beginning of rnd.

Work around in k3, p2 ribbing for 1½ (2¾, 3½) in [4 (7, 9) cm].

Work 1¼ (1½, 2) in [3 (4, 5) cm] in k1, p1 ribbing.

Work in k3, p2 ribbing for 8¾ (10¼, 11¾) in [22 (26, 30) cm].

Work the first 15 (25, 30) sts in k3, p2 ribbing and place rem sts on a holder.

Work back and forth in k1, p1 ribbing for 1¼ (1½, 2) in [3 (4, 5) cm]. Place sts on a holder.

Work sts originally placed on holder as follows: Work in k1, p1 ribbing for 1¼ (1½, 2) in [3 (4, 5) cm].

Return to working all sts in the round. Work around in k3, p2 ribbing for 1½ (2¾, 3½) in [4 (7, 9) cm].

BO in ribbing all around. Seam both ends.

FINISHING

Weave in all ends neatly on WS.

Block by laying scarf between two damp towels until completely dry.

Cozy Autumn Pullover

This cabled pullover is ever-so-much fun.
You'll want to knit just one more cable, and then one more ...

SKILL LEVEL: 3

SIZES: 3 (6, 9 months, 1, 2, 3 years)

FINISHED MEASUREMENTS
Chest: Approx. 19½ (21¾, 24, 24¾, 27¾, 29¼) in [49.5 (55, 61, 63, 70.5, 74) cm]
Total Length: Approx. 9¾ (11¾, 13, 13¾, 14¼, 15½) in [25 (30, 33, 35, 36, 39) cm]

YARN: Sandnes Garn Klompelompe Tynn Merinoull [CYCA #1 – fingering, 100% fine Merino wool, 191 yd (175 m) / 50 g]
+ Sandnes Garn Tynn Silk Mohair (fine silk mohair) [CYCA #0 – lace, 57% mohair, 28% silk, 15% wool, 232 yd (212 m) / 25 g]

YARN COLORS AND AMOUNTS
Tynn Merinoull, Color 2652: 100 (100, 150, 150, 150, 150) g
Tynn Silk Mohair, Color 3161: 50 (50, 50, 50, 50, 75) g

NEEDLES: U.S. sizes 2.5 and 4 (3 and 3.5 mm): 16 and 24 in (40 and 60 cm) circulars; cable needle

GAUGE: 21 sts on larger size needle with 1 strand of each yarn held together = 4 in (10 cm).

Adjust needle size to obtain correct gauge if necessary.

The pullover is worked with 1 strand of each yarn held together throughout. It begins at the center of the back and worked up to the neck and shoulders. You'll begin by working back and forth and then join at the underarms to continue in the round down to the ribbed lower edge.

With larger size circular and 1 strand of each yarn held together, CO 48 (54, 60, 64, 70, 74) sts.

Work back and forth in stockinette until piece measures 4 (4½, 5¼, 5¼, 5½, 6) in [10.5 (11.5, 13, 13, 14, 15) cm].

Next Row (RS): K17 (19, 22, 24, 27, 29), BO 14 (16, 16, 16, 16, 16), k17 (19, 22, 24, 27, 29).

Now raise back with German short rows (see video of technique at klompelompe.no/en/).

Begin at left shoulder (WS): Purl across row.

Next Row: K2tog, knit to end of row.

Purl 1 row.

Next Row: K2tog, knit until 4 sts rem; turn and purl back.

Next Row: Knit until 4 sts before previous turn; turn and purl back.

SIZES 9 MONTHS AND 1, 2, 3 YEARS:
Next Row: Knit until 4 sts before previous turn; turn and purl back.

SIZES 2 AND 3 YEARS:

Next Row: Knit until 4 sts before previous turn; turn and purl back.

ALL SIZES:

Pm innermost at neck (shoulder marker).

Work back and forth in stockinette on the outermost 2 (4, 7, 9, 12, 14) sts and in pattern following chart on rem sts.

Work 2 rows as est.

Next Row (RS): Work in pattern and stockinette until 4 sts rem; turn and purl + pattern as est to end of row.

Next Row: Work as est until 4 sts before previous turn; turn and work back.

Next Row: Work as est until 4 sts before previous turn; turn and work back.

Continue in stockinette and pattern until piece measures 2¾ (3¼, 3¼, 3¼, 3½, 4) in [7 (8, 8, 8, 9, 10) cm] from shoulder marker.

At end of row on WS, CO 1 st; turn and work 1 row in pattern and stockinette; rep *-*.

Place sts on a holder and work right shoulder.

RIGHT SHOULDER

Purl 1 row.

Knit until 2 sts rem, sl 1, k1, psso.

Purl until 4 sts rem; turn and knit until 2 sts rem, sl 1, k1, psso.

Purl until 4 sts rem before previous turn; turn and knit back.

Purl until 4 sts rem before previous turn; turn and knit back.

Purl 1 row.

Pm innermost at neck (shoulder marker).

Work in stockinette on the outermost 2 (4, 7, 9, 12, 14) sts to shoulder and in pattern following chart on rem sts.

Work 3 rows as est.

Next Row (WS): Work in pattern and stockinette until 4 sts rem; turn and work as est to end of row.

Next Row: Work as est until 4 sts before previous turn; turn and work back.

Next Row: Work as est until 4 sts before previous turn; turn and work back.

Continue in stockinette and pattern until piece measures 2¾ (3¼, 3¼, 3¼, 3½, 4) in [7 (8, 8, 8, 9, 10) cm] from shoulder marker.

Work 1 row in stockinette and pattern and, at end of row (at neck edge), CO 1 st.

Work 1 row

Work 1 row in stockinette and pattern and, at end of row (at neck edge), CO 1 st.

Cut yarn.

Begin on left side, on WS.

Work in pattern as est across, CO 14 (16, 16, 16, 16, 16) sts, work held sts. Note where you are in the pattern sequence and continue from that chart row.

Continue in pattern and stockinette until front and back are same length (fold work at shoulder markers).

When you've worked a RS row, CO 4 sts at end of row, pick up and knit 1 st in each st along cast-on edge of back and CO 4 sts at end. Now begin working in the round = 104 (116, 128, 136, 148, 156) sts total.

Continue in stockinette and pattern until sweater measures 8¼ (10¼, 11½, 12¼, 12¾, 13¾) in [21 (26, 29, 31, 32, 35) cm] from shoulder markers.

Change to smaller size circular and work 11 rnds in k1, p1 ribbing. BO in ribbing on next rnd.

SLEEVES

Begin at center of underarm. Pick up and knit 58 (64, 70, 74, 78) sts (= approx. 3 sts for every 4 sts).

Knit 1 rnd. Pm at shoulder.

Knit until 7 sts past marker, k2tog, k1; turn and purl until 7 sts past marker, p2tog, p1; turn.

Knit until 10 sts past marker, k2tog, k1; turn and purl until 10 sts past marker, p2tog, p1; turn.

Knit until 15 sts past marker, k2tog, k1; turn and purl until 15 sts past marker, p2tog, p1; turn.

Knit until 20 sts past marker, k2tog, k1; turn and purl until 20 sts past marker, p2tog, p1; turn. Purl until 30 stitches past marker, p2tog, p1; turn.

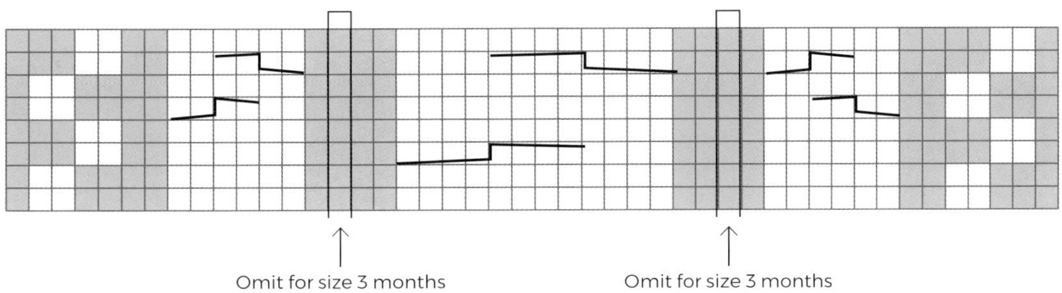

= place the 2 first sts on cable needle and hold in back of work, k2, k2 from cable needle.

= place the 2 first sts on cable needle and hold in front of work, k2, k2 from cable needle.

= place the 4 first sts on cable needle and hold in back of work, k4, k4 from cable needle.

= place the 4 first sts on cable needle and hold in front of work, k4, k4 from cable needle.

= knit on RS, purl on WS

= purl on RS, knit on WS

SIZES 9 MONTHS, 1, 2, AND 3 YEARS:
Knit until 25 sts past marker, k2tog, k1; turn and purl until 25 sts past marker, p2tog, p1; turn.

SIZES 2 AND 3 YEARS:
Knit until 30 sts past marker, k2tog, k1; turn and purl until 30 sts past marker, p2tog, p1; turn.

ALL SIZES:
Knit around.

SHOULDER AND SLEEVE SHAPING
Note: Read through this section before you begin knitting because several steps occur at the same time. The spacing for sleeve and shoulder decreases is the same for all sizes.

Knit until 7 sts before marker, k2tog, knit until 5 sts past marker, p2tog, knit to end of rnd.

Continue around in stockinette until sleeve measures 4¾ (5½, 6¼, 8, 8¾, 9½) in [12 (14, 16, 20, 22, 24) cm], and *at the same time* every 1 in (2.5 cm) down sleeve, decrease as follows: K1, k2tog, knit until 3 sts rem, sl 1, k1, psso, k1. Decrease the same way a total of 4 (5, 6, 6, 6, 7) times.

Also repeat *-* for shoulder shaping every 1½ in (4 cm) 2 (3, 3, 3, 3, 4) more times.

Knit 1 rnd, adjusting stitch count to 34 (34, 36, 36, 38, 38) sts.

Change to smaller size circular and work 11 rnds in k1, p1 ribbing. BO in ribbing on next rnd.

NECKBAND
With smaller size circular, begin neckband at center back. Pick up and knit 1 st in each st along back; pick up and knit 3 sts for every 4 sts over shoulder, pick up and knit 1 st in each st across front, pick up and knit 3 sts for every 4 sts over shoulder, pick up and knit 1 st in each st across back = 72 (80, 80, 80, 84, 88) sts total. If you don't have the correct number of sts, adjust total on next rnd.

Work 15 (17, 17, 19, 21) rnds in k1, p1 ribbing. BO in ribbing on next rnd. Fold neckband and sew down edging loosely on WS with Kitchener st.

FINISHING
Weave in all ends neatly on WS.

Block by dampening pullover and laying it flat, patted out to finished measurements, on a damp towel until completely dry.

Cozy Autumn Slippers

Sweet, warm little slippers that fit well.

SKILL LEVEL: 2

SIZES: 0–2 (3–6, 9–12, 18–24 months, 3 years)

YARN: Sandnes Garn Klompelompe Tynn Merinoull [CYCA #1 – fingering, 100% fine Merino wool, 191 yd (175 m) / 50 g]
+ Sandnes Garn Kos [CYCA #5 – bulky, 62% alpaca, 29% polyamide, 9% wool, 164 yd (150 m) / 50 g]

YARN COLORS AND AMOUNTS
Tynn Merinoull, Color 2650: 50 (50, 50, 50, 50) g
Kos, Color 2611: 50 (50, 50, 50, 50) g
Or leftovers of each yarn

NEEDLES: U.S. sizes 6 and 8 (4 and 5 mm): 32 in (80 cm) circulars; cable needle

GAUGE: 16 sts on larger size needles with 1 strand of each yarn held together = 4 in (10 cm).

Adjust needle size to obtain correct gauge if necessary.

With larger size circular and 1 strand of each yarn held together, CO 20 (24, 24, 28, 32) sts. Join and work 1 rnd in k1, p1 ribbing.

Change to smaller size circular and work 21 (21, 23, 23, 25) rnds in k1, p1 ribbing. Change to larger size needle.

Cut yarn. Place the first and last 5 (7, 7, 9, 10) sts on a holder and work the center 10 (10, 10, 10, 12) sts separately. On the first row, increase 1 (1, 1, 1, 2) sts = 11 (11, 11, 11, 14) sts

Row 1: P1, k9 (9, 9, 9, 12), p1.

Now work following the chart. Work the charted rows a total of 1.5 (2, 2.5, 3, 3.5) times.

After completing charted rows, work the next, WS, row: K1, p2tog, purl until 3 sts rem, p2tog tbl, k1.

Next Row: P1, sl 1, k1, psso, knit until 3 sts rem, k2tog, p1.

Place rem 7 (7, 7, 7, 10) sts on a holder. Cut yarn and begin again at center back.

K5 (7, 7, 9, 11), pick up and knit 5 (7, 9, 11, 13) sts along cable section, knit the 7 (7, 7, 7, 10) held sts, pick up and knit 5 (7, 9, 11, 13) sts along opposite side of cable section, k5 (7, 7, 9, 11) = 27 (35, 39, 47, 58) sts total.

Knit 2 rnds.

Now shape the sock with German short rows (see video at klompelompe.no/en/).

Next Row: K8 (10, 10, 12, 12); turn and p16 (20, 20, 24, 24). Turn and knit around.

Knit 5 (5, 5, 5, 7) rnds.

Next Rnd: K1, k2tog, k1, k2tog, k2 (6, 8, 12, 16), k2tog, k2tog, k3 (3, 3, 3, 6), k2tog tbl, k2tog tbl, k2 (6, 8, 12, 16), k2tog tbl, k1, k2tog tbl, k1.

Next Rnd: K1, k2tog, k2 (6, 8, 12, 16), k2tog, k2tog, k1 (1, 1, 1, 4), k2tog tbl, k2tog tbl, k2 (6, 8, 12, 16), k2tog tbl, k1.

On the next rnd, work sts as follows, binding off at the same time:

K1, k2tog, k0 (4, 6, 10, 14), k2tog, k3 (3, 3, 3, 6), k2tog tbl, k0 (4, 6, 10, 14), k2tog tbl, k1.

Make second slipper the same way.

FINISHING

Seam bottom of slippers and weave in all ends neatly on WS.

Block by laying slippers between two damp towels until completely dry.

Sizes 0–24 months
Right slipper

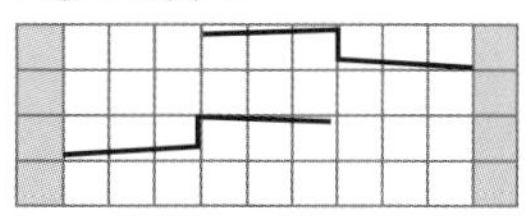

Size 3 years
Right slipper

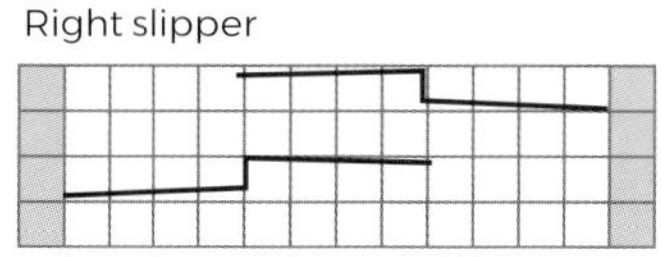

Left slipper

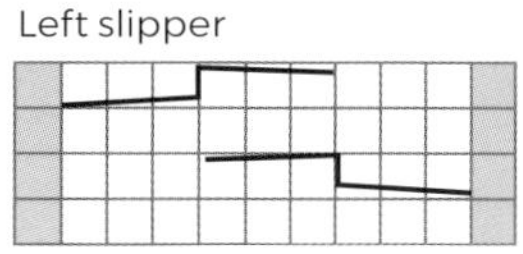

Left slipper

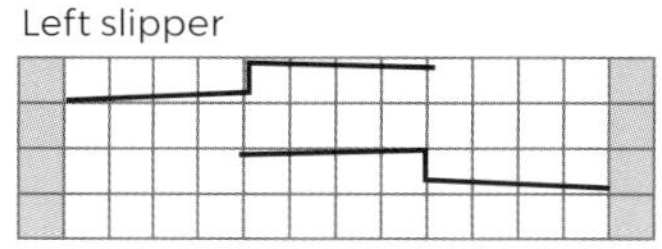

 = place the 3 sts on cable needle and hold in front of work, k3, k3 from cable needle.

 = place the 3 sts on cable needle and hold in back of work, k3, k3 from cable needle.

 = place the 4 sts on cable needle and hold in front of work, k4, k4 from cable needle.

 = place the 4 sts on cable needle and hold in back of work, k4, k4 from cable needle.

□ = knit

■ = purl

Cozy Autumn Mittens

Soft and warm mittens with cable patterning.

SKILL LEVEL: 2

SIZES: 0–1 (3, 6 months, 1–2, 3–4 years)

YARN: Sandnes Garn Klompelompe Tynn Merinoull [CYCA #1 – fingering, 100% fine Merino wool, 191 yd (175 m) / 50 g]
+ Sandnes Garn Kos [CYCA #5 – bulky, 62% alpaca, 29% polyamide, 9% wool, 164 yd (150 m) / 50 g]

YARN COLORS AND AMOUNTS
Tynn Merinoull, Color 2652: 50 (50, 50, 50, 50) g
Kos, Color 3161: 50 (50, 50, 50, 50) g

NEEDLES: U.S. sizes 6 and 8 (4 and 5 mm): 32 in (80 cm) circulars; cable needle

GAUGE: 16 sts on larger size needles with 1 strand of each yarn held together = 4 in (10 cm).

Pink mittens: colors 4032 and 4032.

Adjust needle size to obtain correct gauge if necessary.

MITTEN CONSTRUCTION
These mittens are worked in the round on a long magic loop circular (see video on klompelompe.com). Hold 1 strand of each yarn together throughout. Thumbs are worked only on the two largest sizes.

With larger size circular and 1 strand of each yarn held together, CO 20 (20, 24, 24, 28) sts.

Change to smaller size circular and work 6 (7, 8, 8, 10) rnds in k1, p1 ribbing.

Divide stitches in half either with stitch markers or on magic loop circular.

Change to larger size needle. Knit 1 rnd, increasing 3 (5, 5, 5, 5) sts evenly spaced around.

Beginning on front, continue around: k1 (2, 3, 3, 4), work following charted pattern, knit to end of rnd.

THUMBHOLE

1–2, 3–4 YEARS:
When you've worked in pattern and stockinette for ⅝ (¾) in [1.5 (2) cm], hold place for thumbhole with a short length of smooth, contrast color waste yarn as follows:

LEFT-HAND MITTEN
Work across front, knit until 5 (6) sts rem; with waste yarn, k4 (5). Slip the 4 (5) sts back onto left needle and knit with working yarn, knit to end of rnd.

RIGHT-HAND MITTEN
Work across front, k1; with waste yarn, k4 (5). Slip the 4 (5) sts back onto left needle, and knit with working yarn, knit to end of rnd.

ALL SIZES:

Continue in pattern and stockinette as est until mitten measures 4¾ (5½, 6¼, 7, 8¼) in [12 (14, 16, 18, 21) cm].

Knit 1 rnd, decreasing 3 (5, 5, 5, 5) sts evenly spaced across front of mitten.

TOP SHAPING

Decrease Rnd 1: *K2, k2tog*; rep *-* around.

Knit 1 rnd.

Decrease Rnd 2: *K1, k2tog*; rep *-* around.

Knit 2 rnds.

Decrease Rnd 3: *K2tog*; rep *-* around.

Cut yarn and draw end through rem sts; tighten.

THUMB

Insert a needle through the 4 (5) sts below waste yarn. Insert another needle through the 4 (5) sts above waste yarn. Carefully remove waste yarn. Knit 1 rnd, picking up and knitting 1 st on each side of thumbhole = 10 (12) sts around.

Knit around in stockinette until thumb measures 1⅜ (1¾) in [3.5 (4.5) cm].

Next Rnd: *K2tog*; rep *-* around. Cut yarn and draw end through rem sts; tighten.

FINISHING

Weave in all ends neatly on WS.

Block by laying mittens between two damp towels until completely dry.

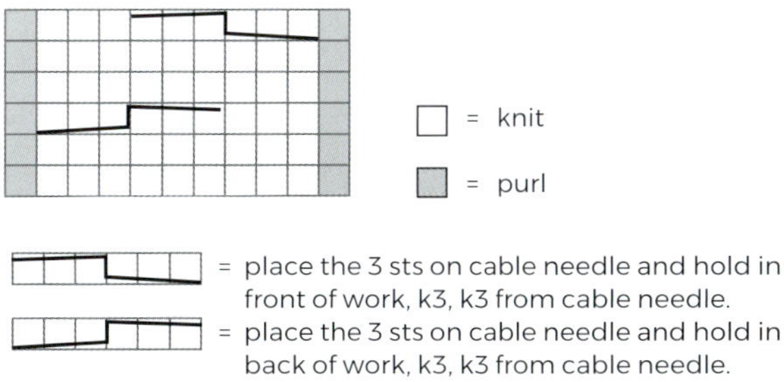

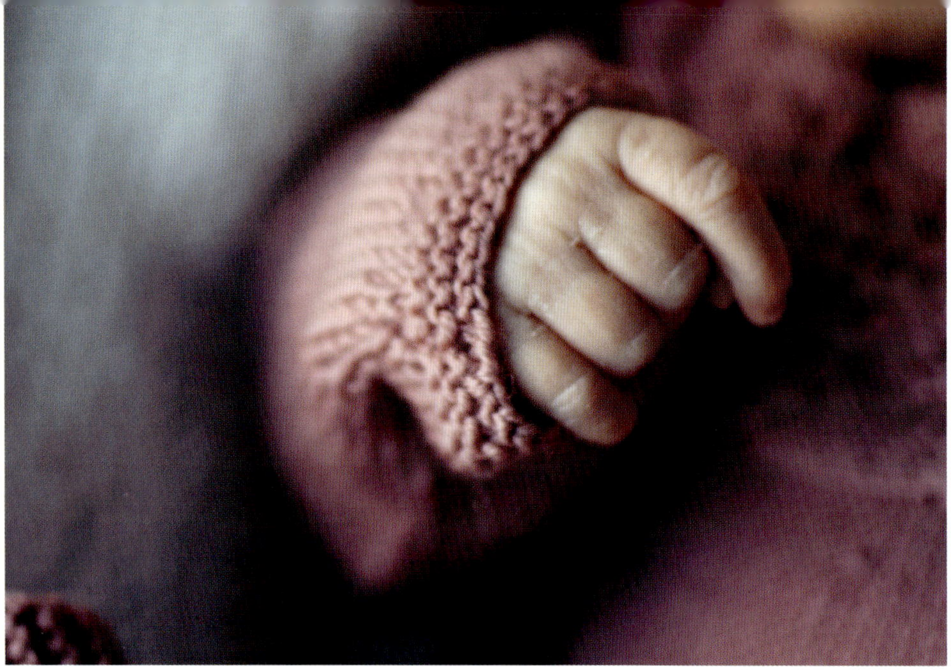

Ingebjørg's Garter-Stitch Blanket

Nothing's lovelier than wrapping a little baby in a garter-stitch blanket. This blanket is one anyone can make and it's a perfect "carry-along" project for social knitting meet-ups.

SKILL LEVEL: 1

Finished Measurements approx. 28¼ x 28¼ in (72 x 72 cm)

YARN: Sandnes Garn Klompelompe Tynn Merinoull [CYCA #1 – fingering, 100% fine Merino wool, 191 yd (175 m) / 50 g]

YARN COLORS AND AMOUNTS
Color 2652: 300 g

NEEDLES: U.S. size 6 (4 mm): 32 in (80 cm) circular

GAUGE: 23 sts on gauge-size needles = 4 in (10 cm).
Adjust needle size to obtain correct gauge if necessary.

BLANKET CONSTRUCTION
The blanket is knitted back and forth, beginning at one point.

CO 3 sts and knit 1 row.

Begin increasing with kf&b to shape blanket:

Increase Row: K1, kf&b, knit to end of row.

Rep the Increase Row (always increasing at the beginning of the row) on every row until piece measures approx. 20 in (51 cm) from cast-on or desired size (weigh the yarn to make sure you have half left so you'll have enough yarn for the entire blanket = 237 sts.
Knit 1 row.

Decrease Row: K1, k2tog, knit to end of row.

Rep the Decrease Row (always decreasing at the beginning of the row) on every row until 3 sts rem. BO knitwise.

FINISHING
Weave in all ends neatly on WS.
Block blanket by dampening it and laying it flat on a towel, patted out to finished measurements, until completely dry.

Anne Layette Set

Anne Ruffled Sweater

An amusing cardigan with ruffles and wings on a pretty silhouette.

SKILL LEVEL: 3

SIZES: 0–2 (3, 6–9 months, 1, 2, 4 years)

FINISHED MEASUREMENTS
Chest: Approx. 17¾ (19¼, 21, 22½, 23½, 25¼) in [45 (49, 53, 57.5, 59.5, 64) cm]
Total Length: Approx. 8¾ (9½, 12¼, 13, 13½, 14¼) in [22 (24, 31, 33, 34, 36) cm]

YARN: Sandnes Garn Klompelompe Tynn Merinoull [CYCA #1 – fingering, 100% fine Merino wool, 191 yd (175 m) / 50 g]

YARN COLORS AND AMOUNTS
Color 1013: 100 (150, 200, 200, 200, 250) g

NEEDLES: U.S. sizes 1.5 and 2.5 (2.5 and 3 mm): 16 and 32 in (40 and 80 cm) circulars

NOTIONS: 5 (5, 6, 6, 7, 7) buttons, ⅝ in (15 mm) in diameter

GAUGE: 27 sts on larger size needle = 4 in (10 cm).
Adjust needle size to obtain correct gauge if necessary.

The cardigan begins at the lower edge and is worked back and forth.

With smaller size circular, CO 241 (266, 286, 311, 321, 346) sts.
Knit 2 ridges (1 ridge = 2 knit rows). Change to larger size circular and knit 1 row.
Next Row: P3, *p2, yo*, p2tog, p1; rep *-* until 3 sts rem, p3.
Next Row: K3, *k2tog, yo, k1, yo, sl 1, k1, psso; * rep *-* until 3 sts rem, k3.
Purl 1 row.
Next Row: K1, *k2tog, yo, k3*; rep *-* until 5 sts rem, k2tog, yo, k3.
Purl 1 row, knit 1 row, purl 1 row.
Next Row: K1, *k3, k2tog, yo*; rep *-* until 5 sts rem, k5.
Work 5 (5, 5, 7, 7, 9) rows in stockinette.

Change to smaller size circular.
Next Row: K1 (0, 0, 1, 1, 0), *k2tog*; rep *-* to end of row = 121 (133, 143, 156, 161, 173) sts rem.

Change to larger size circular.
Purl 1 row, placing markers:
P19 (19, 19, 25, 25, 25), pm, p83 (95, 105, 106, 111, 123), pm, p19 (19, 19, 25, 25, 25).
The outermost st at each side is a stockinette edge st and always knit on RS and purl on WS. Work rem sts on each front piece following the chart and work back in stockinette.
Continue as est until piece measures 5¼ (6, 7, 8, 8¾, 9½) in [13 (15, 18, 20, 22, 24) cm].

On next row (RS), divide sts for body and sleeves as follows:
Work in pattern as est, k4 (6, 7, 4, 5, 8), BO 15 (16, 19, 20, 20, 21), k45 (51, 53, 58, 61, 65), BO 15 (16, 19, 20, 20, 21), k4 (6, 7, 4, 5, 8), work in pattern to end of row.

LEFT FRONT
Row 1 (WS): Purl.
Next Row: K1, k2tog, work to end of row as est.
Work these 2 rows a total of 3 (4, 4, 3, 4, 4) times = 20 (21, 22, 26, 26, 29) sts rem.
Work back and forth in pattern as est until front measures 2¾ (2¾, 3¼, 3¼, 3½, 3½) in [7 (7, 8, 8, 9, 9) cm] from underarm.
Next Row (WS): Work first 11 (11, 12, 14, 14, 15) sts and then slip them onto a holder. The rem 9 (10, 10, 12, 12, 14) sts will be worked separately for the shoulder.
P9 (10, 10, 12, 12, 14).
Next Row: Work in stockinette and pattern as est until 4 sts rem, k1, k2tog, k1.
Next Row: Purl across.

Work these 2 rows a total of 3 (3, 4, 4, 4, 4) times. Continue in pattern (with outermost st at each side in stockinette edge sts) for ¾ (¾, ¾, ¾, 1¼, 1¼) in [2 (2, 2, 2, 3, 3) cm].

Next Row (RS): BO knitwise.

RIGHT FRONT

Row 1 (WS): Purl.

Next Row: Work until 3 sts rem, sl 1, k1, psso, k1.

Work these 2 rows a total of 3 (4, 4, 3, 4, 4) times = 20 (21, 22, 26, 26, 29) sts rem.

Work back and forth in pattern as est until front measures 2¾ (2¾, 3¼, 3¼, 3½, 3½) in [7 (7, 8, 8, 9, 9) cm] from underarm.

Next Row (WS): Purl last 11 (11, 12, 14, 14, 15) sts and then slip them onto a holder. Cut yarn and work the rem 9 (10, 10, 12, 12, 14) sts separately for shoulder.

Next Row: K1, k2tog, k1, work in stockinette and pattern to end of row.

Next Row: Purl across.

Work these 2 rows a total of 3 (3, 4, 4, 4, 4) times. Continue in pattern (with outermost st at each side in stockinette edge sts) for ¾ (¾, ¾, ¾, 1¼, 1¼) in [2 (2, 2, 2, 3, 3) cm].

Next Row (RS): BO knitwise.

BACK

Row 1 (WS): Purl.

Next Row: K1, k2tog, knit until 3 sts rem, sl 1, k1, psso, k1.

Work these 2 rows a total of 3 (4, 4, 4, 4, 4) times = 39 (43, 45, 50, 53, 57) sts rem.

Continue back and forth in stockinette without any decreases until back measures 3½ (3½, 4, 4, 4¼, 4¼) in [9 (9, 10, 10, 11, 11) cm] from underarms.

On next WS row, purl the first 30 (33, 35, 38, 41, 43) sts and place those sts on a holder; purl last 9 (10, 10, 12, 12, 14) sts for right shoulder.

Next Row: Knit until 3 sts rem, k2tog, k1.

Purl next row.

Work these 2 rows a total of 3 (3, 4, 4, 4, 4) times.

Next Row (RS): BO all sts knitwise.

Work the last 9 (10, 10, 12, 12, 14) sts from holder for left shoulder (from RS) and leave rem sts on holder.

K1, k2tog, knit to end of row.

Next Row: Purl across.

Work these 2 rows a total of 3 (3, 4, 4, 4, 4) times.

Next Row (RS): BO all sts knitwise.

Join shoulders.

RIBBED NECKBAND

With smaller size needle, k11 (11, 12, 14, 14, 15) sts from holder, pick up and knit 14 (16, 22, 22, 22, 22) sts along shoulder edge, k21 (23, 25, 24, 29, 29) sts from holder, pick up and knit 14 (16, 22, 22, 22, 22) sts along shoulder edge, k11 (11, 12, 14, 14, 15) sts from holder = 71 (77, 93, 96, 101, 103) sts.

Work 5 (5, 7, 7, 7, 7) rows in k1, p1 ribbing. BO in ribbing on next row.

FRONT BANDS

Work bands with smaller size needle. Pick up and knit 3 sts for every 4 rows/sts along sweater front/neck edges, except for ruffle.

Working buttonholes on Row 2 as described below, knit 4 rows. BO knitwise on next row.

On 2nd row, with (k2tog, yo) for each buttonhole, make 5 (5, 6, 6, 7, 7) buttonholes evenly spaced on right front, above ruffle (see photos).

SLEEVES

With larger size circular, beginning at center of underarm, pick up and knit 65 (65, 85, 85, 89, 89) sts around armhole, pm for beginning of rnd.

Knit 1 rnd.

Shape sleeve with German short rows (see video at klompelompe.no/en/).

Work back and forth as follows:

0–2 AND 3 MONTHS:

K50; turn and p35; turn.
K36; turn and p37; turn.
K38; turn and p39; turn.
K40; turn and p41; turn.
K42, k2tog; turn and p44, p2tog; turn.
K46, k2tog; turn and p48, p2tog; turn.
K50, k2tog; turn and p52, p2tog; turn.
K54, k2tog; turn and p56, p2tog; turn.
Knit to end of rnd.

You should now be at beginning of rnd = 57 sts.

Work and turn as follows:

Knit until 4 sts rem; turn and purl until 4 sts rem; turn.

Knit until 2 sts before previous turn. Work 3 times on each side. Knit to end of rnd.

6–9 MONTHS AND 1 YEAR:

K67; turn and p51; turn.

K52; turn and p53; turn.
K54; turn and p55; turn.
K56; turn and p57; turn.
K58, k2tog; turn and p60, p2tog; turn.
K62, k2tog; turn and p64, p2tog; turn.
K66, k2tog; turn and p68, p2tog; turn.
K70, k2tog; turn and p72, p2tog; turn. K75.
You should now be at beginning of rnd = 77 sts.

Work and turn as follows:

Knit until 6 sts rem; turn and purl until 6 sts rem; turn.

Turn 2 sts before previous turn a total of 3 times on each side. Knit to end of rnd.

2 AND 4 YEARS:
K71; turn and p55; turn.
K56; turn and p57; turn.
K58; turn and p59; turn.
K60; turn and p61; turn.
K62, k2tog; turn and p64, p2tog; turn.
K66, k2tog; turn and p68, p2tog; turn.
K70, k2tog; turn and p72, p2tog; turn.
K74, k2tog; turn and p76, p2tog; turn. K79.
You should now be at beginning of rnd = 81 sts.

Work and turn as follows:

Knit until 6 sts rem; turn and purl until 6 sts rem; turn.

Turn 2 sts before previous turn a total of 3 times on each side. Knit to end of rnd.

ALL SIZES (WORK IN THE ROUND FROM THIS POINT ON):
Knit 3 rnds.

Next Rnd: K15 (18, 14, 14, 16, 16), *k2tog, k1*; rep *-* a total of 9 (7, 16, 16, 16, 16) times, k15 (18, 15, 15, 17, 17) = 48 (50, 61, 61, 65, 65) sts rem.

Continue around in stockinette. After ⅝ in (1.5 cm), decrease as follows: K1, k2tog, knit until 3 sts rem, sl 1, k1, psso, k1.

Decrease the same way, every ¾ (¾, ¾, ¾, 1¼, 1¼) in 2 (2, 2, 2, 3, 3) cm] until 36 (38, 45, 45, 49, 49) sts rem. Continue around in stockinette without further decreasing until sleeve measures 4¾ (5½, 6¾, 7½, 9½, 10¾) in [12 (14, 17, 19, 24, 27) cm,. Knit 1 rnd decreasing 0 (0, 1, 1, 1, 1) st.

Change to smaller size needle. Work 2 garter ridges (1 ridge = purl 1 rnd, knit 1 rnd). BO purlwise on next rnd.

Make second sleeve the same way.

WINGS

Use larger size needle.

Note: After each turn, slip first st and tighten yarn a bit.

Pick up and knit sts in a stripe from the lower edge of pattern section around to lower edge of stockinette section of back. On left wing, begin picking up on the front and on right wing, begin picking up on back. The sts should be picked up on the last row of the pattern section (see photo). Pick up and knit 1 st in each st on yoke (see photo).

Knit 2 rows.

K16, M1, *k6, M1*; rep *-* until 16 sts rem, knit to end of row. Knit 3 rows.

SIZES 0–2 AND 3 MONTHS:

K10, M1, *k7, M1*; rep *-* until 6 sts rem; turn and knit until 6 sts rem; turn.
Knit until 8 sts before previous turn; turn.
Knit until 8 sts before previous turn; turn.
Knit to end of row.
BO knitwise on next row.

SIZES 6–9 MONTHS AND 1, 2, AND 4 YEARS:

K10, M1, *k7, M1*; rep *-* until 10 sts rem; knit to end of row. Knit 1 row.
Knit until 8 sts rem; turn and knit until 8 sts rem; turn.
Knit until 5 sts before previous turn; turn.
Knit until 5 sts before previous turn; turn.
Knit until 5 sts before previous turn; turn.
Knit to end of row.
Knit 1 row.
BO knitwise on next row..

ALL SIZES:

Sew ends of wings securely to sweater.

FINISHING

Weave in all ends neatly on WS. Sew on buttons spaced as for buttonholes.

Block sweater by dampening it and laying it flat on a towel, patted out to finished measurements, until completely dry.

Anne Ruffled Cardigan

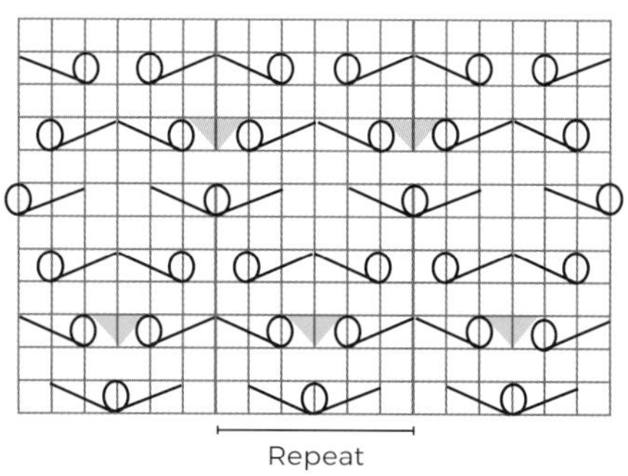

= knit on RS, purl on WS
= 1 yo between 2 sts
= k2tog
= sl 1, k1, psso
= kf&b
= k1 on RS, p1 on WS

Baby Go-Bag Cap

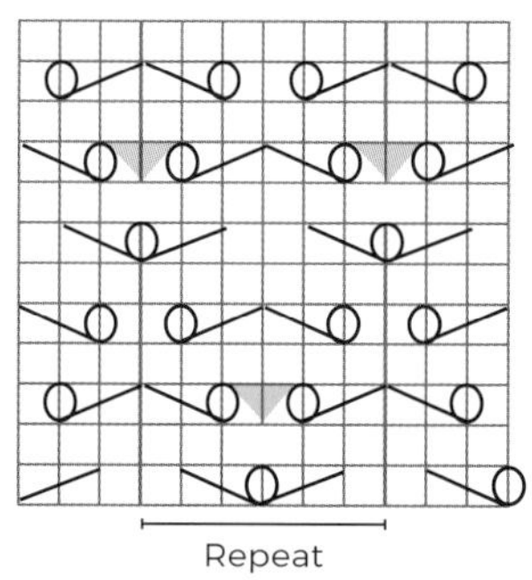

Baby Go-Bag Cap

A simple cap with a delicate structure, for any time a bit of warmth is called for. It's perfect for packing into the baby supply bag.

SKILL LEVEL: 2

SIZES: preemie (0–1, 1–3, 3–6, 9–12 months, 1–2 years)

YARN: Sandnes Garn Klompelompe Tynn Merinoull [CYCA #1 – fingering, 100% fine Merino wool, 191 yd (175 m) / 50 g]

YARN COLORS AND AMOUNTS
Color 3355 or 2650: 50 (50, 50, 50, 50, 50) g

NEEDLES: U.S. sizes 1.5 and 2.5 (2.5 and 3 mm): 16 and 32 in (40 and 80 cm) circulars

GAUGE: 27 sts on larger size needle = 4 in (10 cm). Adjust needle size to obtain correct gauge if necessary.

With smaller size circular, CO 72 (78, 90, 96, 102, 108) sts. JoIn, being careful not to twist cast-on row; pm for beginning of rnd.

Work around in k1, p1 ribbing for 1¼ in (3 cm).

Change to larger size needle and knit 1 rnd.

Begin pattern following chart on page 54.

After competing charted rows, knit in stockinette until cap measures 3½ (4, 4¼, 4¾, 5¼, 5½) in [9 (10, 11, 12, 13, 14) cm].

Knit 1 rnd adjusting stitch count to space increases evenly across. 72 (72, 88, 96, 96, 104) sts.

Decrease Rnd 1: *K6, k2tog*; rep *-* around.
Knit 3 rnds.
Decrease Rnd 2: *K5, k2tog*; rep *-* around.
Knit 3 rnds.
Decrease Rnd 3: *K4, k2tog*; rep *-* around.
Knit 3 rnds.
Decrease Rnd 4: *K2, k2tog*; rep *-* around until 1 (1, 3, 0, 0, 1) sts rem. K1 (1, 3, 0, 0, 1).
Knit 2 rnds.
Decrease Rnd 5: *K1, k2tog*; rep *-* around until 1 (1, 0, 0, 0, 1) sts rem. K1 (1, 0, 0, 0, 1).
Knit 1 rnd.
Decrease Rnd 6: *K2tog*; rep *-* around until 1 (1, 0, 0, 0, 1) sts rem. K1 (1, 0, 0, 0, 1).
Knit 1 rnd.

Decrease Rnd 7: *K1, k2tog*; rep *-* around until 0 (0, 2, 0, 0, 2) sts rem. K0 (0, 2, 0, 0, 2).
Knit around for 4 in (10 cm).
Cut yarn. Draw end through rem sts; tighten

FINISHING

Weave in all ends neatly on WS.

Block by laying cap between two damp towels until completely dry.

Anne Blanket

SKILL LEVEL: 2

FINISHED MEASUREMENTS: 27½ x 32¼ in (70 x 82 cm)

YARN: Sandnes Garn Klompelompe Tynn Merinoull) [CYCA #1 – fingering, 100% fine Merino wool, 191 yd (175 m) / 50 g]

YARN COLORS AND AMOUNTS
Color 3355 or 2650: 350 g

NEEDLES: U.S. size 2.5 (3 mm): 32 in (80 cm) circular

GAUGE: 27 sts on gauge-size needle = 4 in (10 cm).

Adjust needle size to obtain correct gauge if necessary.

With gauge-size circular, CO 188 sts.

Work the entire blanket following the chart.

When blanket is approx. 31½ in (80 cm) long and you are on last chart row, BO on last row.

Now make an I-cord bind-off edging to go around the blanket:

CO 3 sts. Slip those sts onto left needle.

*K2, k2tog tbl. Slip the 3 sts back to left needle *; rep *-* until 3 sts rem. Pick up and knit (3 sts for every 4 sts) along sides; 1 st in each st of cast-on row) all around blanket edge (work one side at a time). Continue I-cord BO until 3 sts rem at end. BO last 3 sts as usual.

FINISHING

Weave in all ends neatly on WS.

Block blanket by laying it flat on a damp towel, patted out to finished measurements, until completely dry.

Anne Bonnet and Anne Blanket

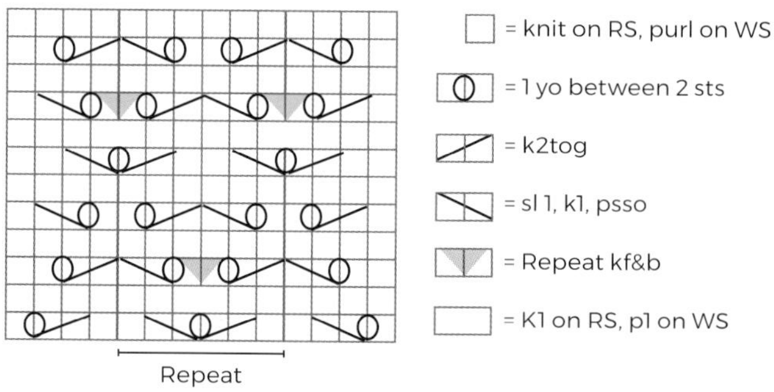

Anne Bonnet

A simple and delicate bonnet adorned with the same fine lace pattern as on the rest of the layette set.

SKILL LEVEL: 2

SIZES: preemie (0–3, 3–6, 6–12 months, 1–2 years)

YARN: Sandnes Garn Klompelompe Tynn Merinoull [CYCA #1 – fingering, 100% fine Merino wool, 191 yd (175 m) / 50 g]

YARN COLORS AND AMOUNTS
Color 1013: 50 (50, 50, 50, 50) g

NEEDLES: U.S. sizes 1.5 and 2.5 (2.5 and 3 mm): sets of 5 dpns and 16 in (40 cm) circulars; optional: 32 in (80 cm) circular for magic loop

GAUGE: 27 sts on larger size needle = 4 in (10 cm).
Adjust needle size to obtain correct gauge if necessary.

BONNET CONSTRUCTION
The bonnet is worked back and forth on a circular needle.

With smaller size circular, CO 77 (83, 91, 95, 103) sts.
Work 4 rows k1, p1 ribbing.

Change to larger size circular and purl 1 row on WS, adjusting stitch count to 80 (86, 92, 98, 104) sts (space increases evenly across).
Work lace pattern following chart.
After completing charted rows, continue back and forth in stockinette until bonnet measures 3¼ (4, 4¼, 4¾, 5¼) in [8 (10, 11, 12, 13) cm].
Now join sts to work in the round. On first rnd, decrease 8 (6, 2, 8, 4) sts evenly spaced around = 72 (80, 90, 90, 100) sts rem.
Knit 3 rnds.

WORK ON ALL SIZES EXCEPT PREEMIE :
Next Rnd: *K8, k2tog* rep *-* around.
Knit 2 rnds.

ALL SIZES:
Next Rnd: *K7, k2tog*; rep *-* around.
Knit 2 rnds.
Next Rnd: *K6, k2tog*; rep *-* around.
Knit 1 rnd.
Next Rnd: *K5, k2tog*; rep *-* around.
Knit 1 rnd.
Next Rnd: *K4, k2tog*; rep *-* around.
Knit 1 rnd.
Next Rnd: *K3, k2tog*; rep *-* around.
Knit 1 rnd.
Next Rnd: *K2, k2tog*; rep *-* around.
Knit 1 rnd.
Next Rnd: *K1, k2tog*; rep *-* around.
Next Rnd: *K2tog*; rep *-* around.
Cut yarn and draw end through rem sts; tighten.

NECKBAND
With smaller size needle, pick up and knit 2 sts for every 3 sts around neck edge.
Leave sts on a spare circular. CO 4 sts on smaller size needle and knit an I-cord 8 in (20 cm) long. Cut yarn and draw end through rem sts; tighten.

Work an I-cord bind-off along neck sts until 4 sts rem (see video at klompelompe.no/en/).
End with an 8 in (20 cm) I-cord. Cut yarn and draw end through rem sts; tighten.

FINISHING
Weave in all ends neatly on WS.
Block by laying cap between two damp towels until completely dry.

Anne Baby Socks

Delicate and sweet baby socks with a fine lace pattern. The cords help keep the socks on baby's feet.

SKILL LEVEL: 2

SIZES: 0–1 (3, 6, 9–12, 18–24 months, 2–3 years)

YARN: Sandnes Garn Klompelompe Tynn Merinoull [CYCA #1 – fingering, 100% fine Merino wool, 191 yd (175 m) / 50 g]
+ Sandnes Garn Alpakka Følgetråd [CYCA #0 – lace, 100% alpaca, 437 yd (400 m) / 50 g]

YARN COLORS AND AMOUNTS
Merinoull, Color 2650: 50 (50, 50, 50, 50, 50) g
Følgetråd, Color 2321: 50 (50, 50, 50, 50, 50) g

NEEDLES: U.S. size 4 (3.5 mm): 32 in (80 cm) circular

GAUGE: 22 sts on gauge-size needle with 1 strand of each yarn held together = 4 in (10 cm).

Adjust needle size to obtain correct gauge if necessary.

SOCK CONSTRUCTION
The socks begin at the top.

We recommend knitting with a long magic loop circular (see video at klompelompe.no/en/). If you prefer, you can knit both socks at the same time on the circular.

Holding 1 strand of each yarn together, CO 30 (30, 36, 36, 42, 48) sts. Join to work in the round. Work 2 garter ridges (1 ridge = purl 1 rnd, knit 1 rnd).

Now work following chart. After working chart pattern 2 (2, 2, 3, 3, 4) times, make an eyelet rnd:

K3 (3, 2, 2, 1, 0) *k2, yo, k2tog*; rep *-* around until 3 (3, 2, 2, 1, 0) sts rem, k3 (3, 2, 2, 1, 0).

Knit 2 rnds.

Knit 1 rnd decreasing 0 (0, 2, 2, 4, 6) sts evenly spaced around.

HEEL (Work heel with German short rows. See video at klompelompe.no/en/)

K9 (11, 12, 14, 15, 16); turn and p18 (22, 24, 28, 30, 32); turn. Knit until 1 st before previous turn; turn and purl until 1 st before previous turn.

Continue turning the same way until you've turned 6 (7, 8, 10, 11, 12) times on each side.

Knit 1 rnd.

K7 (8, 8, 9, 9, 10); turn and p14 (16, 16, 18, 18, 20); turn. Knit until 1 st before previous turn; turn and purl until 1 st before previous turn. Continue turning the same way until you've turned 4 (5, 5, 6, 7, 7) times on each side.

Knit around for 1¼ (1⅜, 1½, 2, 2½, 3¼) in [3 (3.5, 4, 5, 6, 8) cm].

Decrease as follows:

SIZE 2–3 YEARS:
K8, k2tog, k1, k2tog tbl, k8; rep *-* to end of rnd. Knit 1 rnd.

SIZES 18–24 MONTHS AND 2–3 YEARS:
K7, k2tog, k1, k2tog tbl, k7; rep *-* to end of rnd.

SIZES 6, 9–12, 18–24 MONTHS AND 2–3 YEARS:
K6, k2tog, k1, k2tog tbl, k6; rep *-* to end of rnd.

ALL SIZES:
K5, k2tog, k1, k2tog tbl, k5; rep *-* to end of rnd.
Knit 1 rnd.

K4, k2tog, k1, k2tog tbl, k4; rep *-* to end of rnd.
K3, k2tog, k1, k2tog tbl, k3; rep *-* to end of rnd.
K2, k2tog, k1, k2tog tbl, k2; rep *-* to end of rnd.
K1, k2tog, k1, k2tog tbl, k1; rep *-* to end of rnd.

Cut yarn and draw end through rem sts; tighten.

Make second sock the same way.

FINISHING
Weave in all ends neatly on WS.
Block by laying socks between two damp towels until completely dry.

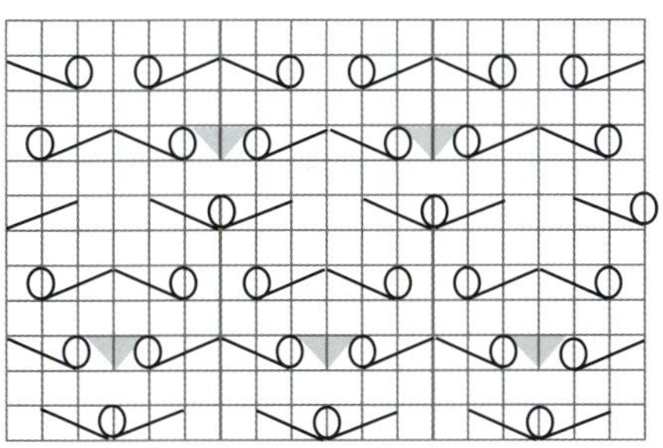

Repeat

= knit on RS, purl on WS
= 1 yo between 2 sts
= k2tog
= sl 1, k1, psso
= Repeat kf&b
= K1 on RS, p1 on WS

Oline Rompers

Sweet rompers knitted with fine yarn and featuring many special details as well as shoulder ties.

SKILL LEVEL: 2

SIZES: preemie (0–1, 2–3, 6–9, 12, 18 months)

FINISHED MEASUREMENTS
Chest: Approx. 14¼ (15, 15½, 16¼, 17¼, 18½) in [36 (38, 39, 41, 44, 47) cm]
Length: Approx. 11¾ (13, 14½, 15¾, 17¼, 19¼) in [30, 33, 37, 40, 44, 49) cm]

YARN: Sandnes Garn Klompelompe Tynn Merinoull [CYCA #1 – fingering, 100% fine Merino wool, 191 yd (175 m) / 50 g]

YARN COLORS AND AMOUNTS
Color 4344: 100 (100, 100, 100, 150, 150) g

NEEDLES: U.S. sizes 1.5 and 2.5 (2.5 and 3 mm): 16 and 32 in (40 and 80 cm) circular s

NOTIONS: 4 snaps for leg closings

GAUGE: 27 sts on gauge-size needle = 4 in (10 cm).
Adjust needle size to obtain correct gauge if necessary.

The rompers begin with the straps on the back.

With smaller size circular, CO 4 sts. Knit an I-cord 4¼ (4¼, 4½, 4¾, 5¼, 5½) in [11 (11, 11.5, 12, 13, 14) cm] long (see video at klompelompe.no/en/).
Pick up 34 (34, 36, 38, 42, 46) sts along I-cord and begin working back and forth in stockinette.

Note: Take all measurements down center of piece.

Work in stockinette until piece measures 2⅜ (2½, 2¾, 3¼, 3½, 4) in [6 (6.5, 7, 8, 9, 10) cm].
Increase Row: K2, M1, knit until 2 sts rem on back, M1, k2.
Purl 1 row.
Rep Increase Row.
Next Row: P2, M1p, purl until 2 sts rem, M1p, p2 = 40 (40, 42, 44, 48, 52) sts.

FRONT
With smaller size circular, CO 4 sts. Knit an I-cord 5¼ (5¼, 5½, 5¾, 6⅛, 6½) in [13.5 (13.5, 14, 14.5, 15.5, 16.5) cm] long (see video at klompelompe.no/en/).
Pick up 40 (40, 42, 44, 48, 52) sts along I-cord (see photo on page 15) and begin working back and forth in stockinette.

Note: Take all measurements down center of piece.

Work in stockinette until piece measures 1⅜ (1½, 2, 2½, 2¾, 3¼) in [3.5 (4, 5, 6, 7, 8) cm].
Increase Row: K2, M1, knit until 2 sts rem on back, M1, k2.
Purl 1 row.
Rep Increase Row.
Next Row: P2, M1p, purl until 2 sts rem, M1p, p2 = 46 (46, 48, 52, 54, 58) sts.

Now join the pieces to work in the round as follows:
Knit across front sts, CO 6 (8, 8, 8, 9, 9), k40 (40, 42, 44, 48, 52) sts of back, CO 6 (8, 8, 8, 9, 9) = a total of 98 (102, 106, 112, 120, 128) sts. Cut yarn and begin rnd at center back from now on.
Knit 2 rnds.

Change to larger size circular.
Next Rnd: *K3, M1*; rep *-* until 2 (0, 4, 4, 0, 2) sts rem, k2 (0, 4, 4, 0, 2) = 130 (136, 140, 148, 160, 170) sts.

Note: Now take measurements from underarm cast-on rows.

Knit around in stockinette until body measures 5½ (6, 6¼, 6¾, 7½, 9) in [14 (15, 16, 17, 19, 23) cm] from underarms.

Cut yarn and begin again at center back.

Raise back with German short rows (see video at klompelompe.no/en/).

K20 (20, 21, 23, 26, 29); turn and p39 (40, 42, 45, 52, 57); turn.

K35 (36, 38, 41, 48, 51); turn and p31 (32, 34, 37, 44, 47); turn.

Knit to end of rnd.

Knit 2 rnds.

Divide for legs:

K14 (14, 15, 15, 17, 17), knit next 40 (43, 43, 47, 49, 54) onto spare needle, k23 (23, 25, 29, 29) (front), k40 (43, 43, 47, 49, 54) onto spare needle, k13 (13, 14, 14, 16, 16) (back).

Cut yarn. Knit the front first.

FRONT

The first row is on RS. K1, k2tog, knit until 3 sts rem, sl 1, k1, psso, k1.

Purl 1 row.

Rep these 2 rows until 13 sts rem (all sizes).

Work 8 (12, 12, 12, 14, 14) rows in stockinette and BO on last row.

Fold last 4 rows under and sew down on WS.

BACK

Work as for front, decreasing down to 13 sts (all sizes). Work 7 (11, 11, 11, 13, 13) rows in stockinette. BO knitwise on next row.

Fold last 4 rows under and sew down on WS.

With smaller size circular, pick up and knit sts on back up to held sts. Work *k1, k2tog*; rep *-* on all held sts, pick up and knit sts of front. Cut yarn and begin again on RS.

BO with I-cord bind-off.

Sew snaps on underside of front and outside of back.

Pick up and knit sts along top of bib, down under armhole, and up back. Set piece aside.

CO 4 sts with smaller size needle. Make an I-cord 4 (4, 5¼, 6¼, 6¼, 6¼) in [10 (10, 13, 16, 16, 16) cm] long, knit sts on holder and *at the same time* BO with I-cord bind-off. Repeat until 4 sts rem, make another I-cord 4 (4, 5¼, 6¼, 6¼, 6¼) in [10 (10, 13, 16, 16, 16) cm] long. Edge the opposite side the same way.

RUFFLES

Make ruffles under the I-cord (see photo on page 15) on the bib and around the leg openings. With larger size needle, pick up each backmost st all along I-cord.

Purl 1 row.

Next Row: *K1, M1*; rep *-* to end of row.

Work 3 rows in stockinette.

Next Row (RS): BO purlwise.

RUFFLE ON TOP OF BIB

With larger size needle, pick up the same sts as at beginning.

Begin on RS. Work 1 row of twisted knit (knit in back loop of each st).

Purl 1 row.

Next Row: *K2, M1*. Rep *-* until 2 sts rem, k2.

Purl 1 row.

Knit 1 row.

Next Row (WS): BO knitwise.

FINISHING

Weave in all ends neatly on WS.

Block by laying rompers flat, patted out to finished measurements between two damp towels until completely dry.

Striped Summer Onesie

The sweetest summer outfit, knitted in a wool/cotton yarn with toffee stripes.

SKILL LEVEL: 2

SIZES: 3 (6–9 months, 1, 2, 3, 4 years)

FINISHED MEASUREMENTS
Chest: Approx. 15 (17¼, 19¼, 21½, 21½, 22¾) in [38 (44, 49, 54.5, 54.5, 58) cm]
Length: Approx. 15½ (17, 19¼, 19¾, 22½, 24¾) in [39, 43, 49, 50, 57, 63) cm]

YARN: Sandnes Garn Duo [CYCA #3 – DK/light worsted 55% Merino wool/45% cotton, 126 yd (115 m) / 50 g]

YARN COLORS AND AMOUNTS
Color A, 1015: 100 (100, 150, 150, 200, 200) g
Color B, 2564: 50 (50, 50, 50, 50, 50) g

NEEDLES: U.S. sizes 2.5 and 4 (3 and 3.5 mm): 16 and 24 in (40 and 60 cm) circulars; sets of 5 dpn for sleeves if you prefer instead of magic loop.

NOTE: 6 (6, 6, 6, 6, 6) buttons, ⅝ in (15 mm) in diameter

GAUGE: 22 sts on larger size needle = 4 in (10 cm).
Adjust needle size to obtain correct gauge if necessary.

The onesie is worked from the bottom up, beginning with the legs.

With smaller size circular and color A, CO 42 (48, 54, 60, 60, 64) sts. Working back and forth, knit 2 ridges (1 ridge = knit 2 rows). Change to larger size needle and work in stockinette until piece measures ⅝ (1, 1¾, 2¼, 2½, 3) in [1.5 (2.5, 4.5, 5.5, 6.5, 7.5) cm].

Next Row (RS): K19 (22, 25, 28, 28, 30), M1, k4, M1, k19 (22, 25, 28, 28, 30).

Purl 1 row.

Next Row (RS): K1, M1, knit until 1 st rem, M1, k1. Purl 1 row. Set piece aside and make another the same way

CO 3 sts, knit across sts of one leg, CO 6 sts, knit across sts of other leg, CO 3 sts. Join and begin knitting in the round. The rnd begins at center back. Pm on each side of the 6 sts at center front and center back = 104 (116, 128, 140, 140, 148) sts total.

Knit 1 rnd.

Next Rnd: K3, *sl 1, k1, psso, knit until 2 sts rem before next marker, k2tog*, k6, rep *-*, k3.

Decrease as above on every 3rd rnd a total of 4 times = 88 (100, 112, 124, 124, 132) sts rem. **Note:** Change to color B after you've decreased a total of 3 times.

Continue in stripes.

STRIPE SEQUENCE

Work 6 rnds color B, 15 (18, 21, 23, 19, 21) rnds color A.

Tip: For jogless stripes after a color change: Change color, knit 1 rnd. On next rnd, slip first st.

Once you've knitted 2 rnds with color A after the first stripe, raise back section with German short rows (see video at klompelompe.no/en/):

K22 (25, 28, 31, 31, 33); turn and p44 (50, 56, 62, 62, 66); turn. K22 (25, 28, 31, 31, 33).

Rep the short rows when you've knitted 2 rnds with color A after the next stripe.

When you've knitted 3 rnds with color A after the 3rd (3rd, 3rd, 3rd, 4th, 4th) stripe, work next rnd as follows:

K18 (21, 24, 27, 27, 29), k2tog, k4, k2tog, k36 (42, 48, 54, 54, 58), k2tog, k4, k2tog, k18 (21, 24, 27, 27, 29).

SIZES 3, 6-9 MONTHS AND 1, 2 YEARS:
Knit 3 rnds.

Next Rnd: K17 (20, 23, 26, -, -), k2tog, k4, k2tog, k34 (40, 46, 52, -, -), k2tog, k4, k2tog, k17 (20, 23, 26, -, -).

All Sizes = 80 (92, 104, 116, 120, 128) sts. Continue in stripes until piece measures approx. 9¾ (11, 12¼, 13, 14½, 16¼) in [25 (28, 31, 33, 37, 41) cm] up center front (from crotch). You should now have knitted 4 rnds with color B on the 4th (4th, 4th, 4th, 5th, 5th) stripe.

Next Rnd (with color B): K17 (20, 23, 26, 27, 29), BO 6 sts, k34 (40, 46, 52, 54, 58), BO 6 sts, k17 (20, 23, 26, 27, 29).

Set aside body while you knit the sleeves.

SLEEVES

Knit sleeves with dpn or magic loop, as you prefer (see video of technique at klompelompe.no/en/).

With smaller size needles and color A, CO 34 (38, 42, 46, 46, 48) sts. Join to knit in the round.

Work 2 ridges (1 ridge = purl 1 rnd, knit 1 rnd). Change to larger size needle.

Knit 1 (2, 3, 4, 5, 5) rnds. Change to color B and knit 4 rnds.

Next Rnd: BO 3 sts, k28 (32, 36, 40, 40, 42), BO 3 sts.

Set first sleeve aside and make a second sleeve the same way.

Arrange sleeve and body sts on same larger size circular, matching underarms = 124 (144, 164, 184, 188, 200) sts total. Pm at each intersection of body and sleeve.

Knit 1 rnd. Change to color A and knit 1 rnd. Continue with color A to end of onesie yoke.

On next rnd, begin raglan shaping as follows: Knit until 3 sts before raglan marker, k2tog, k2, sl 1, k1, psso*; work *-* a total of 4 times, knit to end of rnd.

Decrease for raglan shaping on *every other rnd* until you've decreased a total of 5 (7, 9, 11, 11, 12) times and 84 (88, 92, 96, 100, 104) sts rem.

Next Rnd (no decreases): Knit around and *at the same time* place the center front 6 (8, 10, 12, 12, 14) sts onto a holder (same size spare needle recommended). Now you'll make the back neck opening and work the right and left shoulders separately.

LEFT SHOULDER

Knit, including raglan decreases, until 2 sts before held sts, sl 1, k1, psso. Purl 1 row.

Work *-* a total of 3 times.

Next Row: Knit, including raglan decreases, until 3 sts rem, sl 2 (1 at a time), k1, psso.

Pick up and knit 5 sts down to held sts, knit sts on holder. Leave sts on holder and work right shoulder separately.

Begin on right side of sts on needle and work back and forth from now on.

RIGHT SHOULDER

K2tog, knit to end of row, including raglan decreases. Purl 1 row.

Work *-* a total of 3 times.

Next Row: K3tog, knit to end of row, including raglan decreases. Cut yarn.

Pick up and knit 5 sts from row on st holder up to right shoulder. Cut yarn.

Change to smaller size needle and begin at center back at right shoulder.

Knit 3 rows. BO knitwise on next row.

BUTTON BAND AT BACK NECK

With smaller size needle and color A, pick up and knit sts along back neck opening. Knit 3 rows. BO knitwise on next row. *At the same time*, on left side, make 1 buttonhole on Row 1 with k2tog, yo.

BUTTON BAND ON CROTCH

With smaller size needle and color A, pick up and knit 3 sts for every 4 sts/rows on back of crotch. Knit 4 rows. BO knitwise on next row.

Make front crotch band the same way, but, on Row 2, make 5 buttonholes evenly spaced across (1 buttonhole = k2tog, yo).

FINISHING

Weave in all ends neatly on WS.

Sew buttons on crotch and neck bands.

Block by laying onesie flat, patted out to finished measurements between two damp towels until completely dry.

Johanna's Rompers

Sweet and summery rompers knitted with a fine lace pattern and squishy ruffles.

SKILL LEVEL: 2

SIZES: 3 (6, 9–12 months, 2 years)

FINISHED MEASUREMENTS
Chest: Approx. 21¾ (22¾, 27½, 27½) in [55.5 (58, 70, 70) cm]
Length: Approx. 14½ (15½, 17, 18½) in [37 (39, 43, 47) cm]

YARN: Sandnes Garn Mandarin Naturell [CYCA #3 – DK/light worsted, 100% cotton, 142 yd (130 m) / 50 g]

YARN COLORS AND AMOUNTS
Color 1012: 150 (150, 150, 200) g

NEEDLES: U.S. size 6 (4 mm): 24 or 32 in (60 or 80 cm) circular

NOTIONS: 4 snaps for leg closings; 1 button for back neck opening; crochet hook U.S. G-6 (4 mm) for making button loop

GAUGE: 19 sts on gauge-size needle = 4 in (10 cm).
Adjust needle size to obtain correct gauge if necessary.

The rompers begin with the straps.

With gauge-size circular, CO 4 sts. Knit an I-cord 12¾ (13½, 14¼, 15) in [32 (34, 36, 38) cm] long (see video at klompelompe.no/en/). Cut yarn, draw end through rem sts and tighten.

Pick up 26 (26, 32, 32) sts centered on I-cord for front of rompers. Purl 1 row.
Now knit the outermost 3 sts on each side (knit on both RS and WS) as edge sts throughout and work lace pattern on center 20 (20, 26, 26) sts.
Pm on each side of lace panel. Now increase on each RS row as follows: K4, M1, work in stockinette and pattern until 4 sts rem, M1, k4.

Increase the same way on every other row a total of 12 (12, 15, 15) times = 50 (50, 62, 62) sts.
Work 1 row on WS.
Slip sts to a holder and begin working back.

RIGHT BACK
Pick up 14 (14, 16, 16) sts on end of I-cord (= right back). Purl 1 row.
Work outermost 3 sts at each side in garter ridges for edge sts and button band (knit on both RS and WS) and work stockinette on rem sts.
Increase at armhole edges, on every RS row as follows:
Knit until 4 sts rem, M1, k4.

Increase the same way a total of 12 (12, 15, 15) times.

Work 1 row on WS.
Slip sts to a holder and work left back.

LEFT BACK
Pick up 14 (14, 16, 16) sts on other end of I-cord (= left back). Purl 1 row.
Work outermost 3 sts at each side in garter ridges for edge sts and button band (knit on both RS and WS) and work stockinette on rem sts.

Increase at armhole edges, on every RS row as follows:
K4, M1, knit to end of row.

Increase the same way a total of 12 (12, 15, 15) times.

Work 1 row on WS.
Cut yarn. Arrange all the pieces on one needle.
Beginning at center back, work in the round from this point on.

Knit sts of right back, CO 2 (4, 5, 5) sts, work in stockinette and pattern as est across front, CO 2 (4, 5, 5) sts, knit left back = 106 (110, 134, 134) sts total.

Continue in stockinette and pattern, except for sts at and below underarms which continue in garter ridges.

Work as est until there are 3 garter ridges below underarms.

Now knit around in stockinette on all sts except for pattern sts until you have completed all chart rows.

NEXT RND:
Knit 1 rnd, increasing 32 (36, 24, 32) sts evenly spaced around = 138 (146, 158, 166) sts total.

From this point on, take measurements down from the shoulders.

Knit around in stockinette until piece measures 12¾ (13½, 15, 16½) in [32 (34, 38, 42) cm].

Raise back with German short rows (see video at klompelompe.no/en/) :

K10; turn and purl 20; turn.

K25; turn and p30; turn.

K35; turn and p40; turn.

K20 (you should now be back at beginning of rnd). Knit 2 rnds.

Cut yarn and slip the last 10 (10, 14, 16) sts to left needle. Work the next 20 (20, 28, 32) sts (back) back and forth (place rem sts on a holder).

Work 2 rows in stockinette.

Decrease as follows on next row: K2tog, knit until 2 sts rem, sl 1, k1, psso.

Purl across WS.

Decrease the same way on all RS rows until 8 (8, 12, 14) sts rem. Work 5 rows in stockinette. BO purlwise on next row.

Place each set of 51 (55, 53, 53) sts on each side of the holder, on a separate holder and then work the 16 (16, 24, 28) sts for the front separately.

Shape as for back until 8 (8, 12, 14) sts rem. Work 9 rows in stockinette. BO purlwise on next row.

Join the back and front pieces with Kitchener st.

LEG EDGINGS

Change to smaller size needle. Starting at beginning of rnd on the crotch, pick up and knit 16 (16, 18, 18) sts, knit held sts and then pick up and knit 16 (16, 18, 18) sts to end of rnd = 83 (87, 89, 89) sts total.

Next Rnd: K17 (17, 19, 19), *k2tog*; rep *-* 25 (27, 26, 26) times, k16 (16, 18, 18).

Knit 5 (5, 7, 7) rnds. Purl 1 rnd, knit 5 (5, 7, 7) rnds. BO knitwise on next rnd.

Fold edging and sew down on WS.

RUFFLE

With smaller size circular, pick up purl sts at bottom edge of pattern panel. Pick up sts on diagonal of pattern panel and angle up over to the 6th (6th, 10th, 10th) ridge. Also pick up the 3 ridge sts on each side.

Begin on RS.

Knit garter ridges on the outermost 3 sts on each side.

Knit 1 row, purl 1 row.

Next Row: K3 (edging), *k1, M1*; rep *-* until 3 sts rem, k3.

Work in stockinette for 8 (10, 10, 10) rows. Knit 2 rows. BO knitwise on next row.

Sew ends of ruffle to rompers.

FINISHING

Make a ch-4 button loop on one side of back opening. Sew button on opposite side.

Weave in all ends neatly on WS.

Block by laying rompers flat, patted out to finished measurements, between two damp towels until completely dry.

Sizes 3 and 6 months

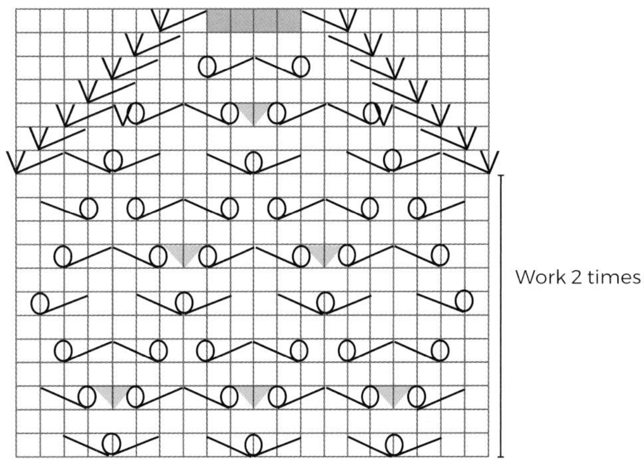

- = knit on RS, purl on WS
- = 1 yo between 2 sts
- = k2tog on RS, p2tog tbl on WS
- = sl 1, k1, psso on RS, p2tog on WS
- = kf&b
- = M1L on RS, M1p on WS
- = purl on RS, knit on WS
- = M1L

Sizes 9–12 months and 2 years

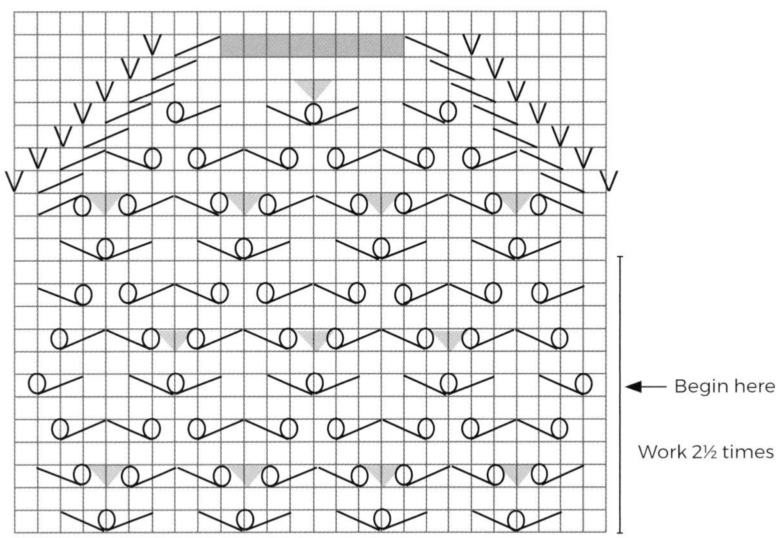

Favorite Child Layette Set

Favorite Child Cardigan

We like good, classic, and simple garments that are durable, garments that can be worn by both boys and girls, and which can be handed down from older siblings.

SKILL LEVEL: 2

SIZES: preemie (0–1, 3, 6–9 months, 1, 2, 3 years)

FINISHED MEASUREMENTS
Chest: Approx. 17¾ (18¾, 19¼, 21¾, 24, 25¼, 27¼) in [45 (47.5, 49, 55, 61, 64, 69) cm]
Length: Approx. 8½ (8⅞, 9½, 10¾, 11¾, 13, 14¼) in [21.5 (22.5, 24, 27, 30, 33, 36) cm]

YARN: Sandnes Garn Klompelompe Tynn Merinoull [CYCA #1 – fingering, 100% fine Merino wool, 191 yd (175 m) / 50 g]
+ Sandnes Garn Alpakka Følgetråd [CYCA #0 – lace, 100% alpaca, 437 yd (400 m) / 50 g]

YARN COLORS AND AMOUNTS
Merinoull, Color 1013: 100 (100, 100, 100, 150, 150, 200) g
Følgetråd, Color 1015: 50 (50, 50, 50, 50, 100, 100) g

NEEDLES: U.S. sizes 1.5 and 2.5 (2.5 and 3 mm): 16 and 32 in (40 and 80 cm) circulars

NOTIONS: 6 (7, 7, 8, 8, 9, 10) buttons, ⅝ in (15 mm) in diameter

GAUGE: 24 sts on larger size needle with 1 strand of each yarn held together = 4 in (10 cm).
Adjust needle size to obtain correct gauge if necessary.

The cardigan begins at the top and is worked back and forth on a circular needle.

With smaller size circular and 1 strand of each yarn held together, CO 69 (71, 71, 77, 83, 83, 87) sts. Work 8 rows in k1, p1 ribbing, and on Row 4 (WS), make a buttonhole: Work in ribbing until 5 sts rem, BO 2 sts, work 3 sts ribbing. On next row, CO 2 sts over gap.

Change to larger size circular.
The outermost 5 sts on each side are now worked in garter stitch ridges (knit on both RS and WS) with the rest of the sts in stockinette.
Row 1: K14 (15, 15, 16, 17, 17, 18), M1, k1 (raglan st), M1, k7, M1, k1 (raglan st), M1, k23 (23, 23, 27, 31, 31, 33), M1, k1 (raglan st), M1, k7, M1, k1 (raglan st), M1, k14 (15, 15, 16, 17, 17, 18) = 8 sts increased.

Raise back with German short rows (see video at klompelompe.no/en/).

Next Row: K5, purl until 14 sts rem; turn. Knit including raglan increases until 14 sts rem; turn and purl until 12 sts rem; turn. Knit including raglan increases until 12 sts rem; turn and purl until 10 sts rem; turn. Knit including raglan increases until 10 sts rem; turn and purl until 5 sts rem; k5.

Continue as est, with raglan increases on every RS row.

Knit 1 row.

STRIPE SEQUENCE
Knit 1 row on WS.
Work 7 rows in stockinette.

Work Stripe Sequence throughout unless otherwise specified.

BUTTONHOLES
After working for 1⅜ (1¼, 1¼, 1¼, 1⅜ 1⅜, 1⅜) in [3.5 (3, 3, 3, 3.5, 3.5, 3.5) cm], on a RS row, work: K2, BO 2

Beige cardigan: colors 2650 and 2321

sts, knit to end of row. On next row, CO 2 sts over gap. Make a total of 6 (7, 7, 8, 8, 9, 10) buttonholes.

After you've increased a total of 13 (14, 15, 17, 19, 21, 23) times in the raglan yoke, work 3 rows without any increases = 173 (183, 191, 213, 235, 251, 271) sts.

Next row: Knit to raglan st, place raglan st, sleeve sts, and next raglan st on a holder, CO 5 sts, knit to raglan st, place raglan st, sleeve sts, and next raglan st on a holder, CO 5 sts, knit to end of row = 113 (119, 123, 137, 151, 159, 171) sts rem for body.

Continue Stripe Sequence and garter st edgings until body measures 7½ (8, 8¼, 9½, 10¾, 11¾, 13) in [19 (20, 21, 24, 27, 30, 33) cm] from shoulder. Change to smaller size needle and work 8 (8, 10, 10, 10, 10, 10) rows in k1, p1 ribbing, binding off in ribbing on last ribbing row. Note that the last buttonhole is centered on the ribbing.

SLEEVES

Beginning at center of the 5 underarm sts, pick up and knit 3 sts along underarm, 1 st in gap between underarm and armhole, knit the 35 (37, 39, 43, 47, 51, 55) held sleeve sts, pick up and knit 1 st in gap between armhole and underarm, and 2 sts along underarm = a total of 42 (44, 46, 50, 54, 58, 62) sts.

Work sleeve in Stripe Sequence. When it is ¾ in (2 cm) long, begin shaping: K1, k2tog, knit until 3 sts rem, k2tog, k1. Decrease the same way every ¾ in (2 cm) a total of 4 (5, 6, 7, 8, 9, 10) times = 34 (34, 34, 36, 38, 40, 42) sts rem. When sleeve measures 3½ (4¾, 5½, 6¾, 8, 9½, 10¾) in [9 (12, 14, 17, 20, 24, 27) cm], knit 1 rnd, decreasing evenly spaced around to 28 (28, 30, 32, 34, 36, 36) sts. Change to smaller size needle and work 7 (7, 9, 9, 9, 9, 9) rnds in k1, p1 ribbing. Change to larger size needle. BO in k1, p1 ribbing on next rnd.

Make second sleeve the same way.

FINISHING

Weave in all ends neatly on WS. Sew buttons on, spaced as for buttonholes.

Block by laying sweater flat, patted out to finished measurements, between two damp towels until completely dry.

Favorite Child Fine Pants

Based on a classic favorite among our designs, this pair of pants offers a new thin variation.

SKILL LEVEL: 2

SIZES: 0–1 (3, 6, 9, 12, 18 months)

FINISHED MEASUREMENTS
Chest: Approx. 19 (19, 21, 21, 22, 22) in [48 (48, 53, 53, 56, 56) cm]
Total Length (excluding straps): Approx. 12¼ (13¾, 14½, 16½, 18¼, 19¾) in [31 (35, 37, 42, 46, 50) cm]

YARN: Sandnes Garn Klompelompe Tynn Merinoull [CYCA #1 – fingering, 100% fine Merino wool, 191 yd (175 m) / 50 g]

YARN COLORS AND AMOUNTS
Merinoull, Color 2652, 2650, or 9871: 100 (100, 100, 150, 150, 200) g

NEEDLES: U.S. sizes 1.5 and 2.5 (2.5 and 3 mm): 16 and 32 in (40 and 80 cm) circulars

NOTIONS: 2 (2, 2, 2, 2, 2) buttons, ⅝ in (15 mm) in diameter, stitch markers

GAUGE: 27 sts on larger size needle = 4 in (10 cm).
Adjust needle size to obtain correct gauge if necessary.

With smaller size needle, CO 130 (130, 142, 142, 152, 152) sts. Join, being careful not to twist cast-on row; pm for beginning of rnd.

Work 19 rnds in k1, p1 ribbing, and, on the 8th rnd, make 2 buttonholes on the front:

Rib 52 (52, 57, 57, 60, 60), k2tog, yo, rib 22 (22, 24, 24, 28, 28), yo, sl 1, k1, psso, rib 52 (52, 57, 57, 60, 60).

Change to larger size needle and knit 1 rnd.

Now, raise the back of the pants with German short rows (see video at klompelompe.no/en/ for how to avoid holes when turning).

K10; turn and p20; turn.
K25; turn and p30.
K35; turn and p40; turn. Knit to end of rnd.

Continue in Stripe Sequence: Knit 7 rnds, purl 1 rnd.

When piece measures 7 (8¾, 9, 10¼, 11, 11½) in [18 (22, 23, 26, 28, 29) cm], pm on each side of the center 8 sts on both front and back.

Increase 1 st with M1 on each side of the 8 marked sts *on every other rnd* = 4 sts increased per rnd.

After you've worked 4 increase rnds, on next rnd, BO the center 8 sts on front and back.

Now work each leg separately = 65 (65, 71, 71, 76, 76) sts per leg. Work in stripe pattern until leg measures 4 (4¼, 4¾, 5½, 6¼, 7½) in [10 (11, 12, 14, 16, 19) cm] and *at the same time* after ⅜ in (1 cm), decrease as follows: K1, k2tog, knit until 3 sts rem, sl 1, k1, psso, k1.

Decrease the same way every ¾ in (2 cm) until 55 (55, 59, 59, 64, 64) sts rem.

Knit 1 rnd, adjusting stitch count to 40 (40, 42, 42, 44, 44) sts (spacing decreases evenly around). Change to smaller size needle.

Work 20 rnds in k1, p1 ribbing, binding off in ribbing on last rnd.

Make second leg the same way.

STRAPS
With smaller size needle, pick up and knit 19 sts along center back and work 12 rows back and forth in k1, p1 ribbing. On next row, BO the center st and work each side separately until strap measures 7 (7, 8, 8¾, 8¾, 9½) in [18 (18, 20, 22, 22, 24) cm] from row where you picked up sts. BO in ribbing.

FINISHING
Sew a button on each strap end. Weave in all ends neatly on WS. Block by laying pants flat, patted out to finished measurements, on a damp towel until completely dry or gently steam iron under a damp pressing cloth.

Brown: color 2652
Beige: color 2650
Green: color 9871

Favorite Child Fine Cap

A simple cap that goes perfectly with the Favorite Child pants.

SKILL LEVEL: 2

SIZES: preemie (0–1, 1–3, 3–6, 9–12 months, 1–2 years)

YARN: Sandnes Garn Klompelompe Tynn Merinoull [CYCA #1 – fingering, 100% fine Merino wool, 191 yd (175 m) / 50 g]

YARN COLORS AND AMOUNTS
Merinoull, Color 2650: 50 (50, 50, 50, 50, 50) g

NEEDLES: U.S. sizes 1.5 and 2.5 (2.5 and 3 mm): 16 and 32 in (40 and 80 cm) circulars

GAUGE: 27 sts on larger size needle = 4 in (10 cm).
Adjust needle size to obtain correct gauge if necessary.

With smaller size circular, CO 72 (78, 90, 96, 102, 108) sts. Join, being careful not to twist cast-on row; pm for beginning of rnd.

Work around in k1, p1 ribbing for 1¼ in (3 cm).

Change to larger size needle.

Continue in Stripe Sequence: Knit 7 rnds, purl 1 rnd.

Tip: For jogless rnds between stripes: Slip 1st st of 1st knit rnd (after a purl rnd) to right needle without knitting it.

Continue in Stripe Sequence until cap measures 3½ (4, 4¼, 4¾, 5¼, 5½) in [9 (10, 11, 12, 13, 14) cm].

Knit 1 rnd, adjusting stitch count to 72 (72, 88, 96, 96, 104) sts, decreasing evenly spaced around.

Decrease Rnd 1: *K6, k2tog*; rep *-* around.
Knit 3 rnds.
Decrease Rnd 2: *K5, k2tog*; rep *-* around.
Knit 3 rnds.
Decrease Rnd 3: *K4, k2tog*; rep *-* around.
Knit 3 rnds.
Decrease Rnd 4: *K2, k2tog*; rep *-* until 0 (0, 3, 0, 0, 1) st rem. KO (0, 3, 0, 0, 1).
Knit 2 rnds.
Decrease Rnd 5: *K1, k2tog*; rep *-* until 0 (0, 0, 0, 0, 1) st rem. KO (0, 0, 0, 0, 1).
Knit 1 rnd.
Decrease Rnd 6: *K2tog*; rep *-* until 0 (0, 0, 0, 0, 1) st rem. KO (0, 0, 0, 0, 1).
Knit 1 rnd.
Decrease Rnd 7: *K1, k2tog*; rep *-* until 0 (0, 2, 0, 0, 2) sts rem. KO (0, 2, 0, 0, 2).

Knit around in stockinette for 4 in (10 cm).

Cut yarn and draw end through rem sts; tighten.

FINISHING

Weave in all ends neatly on WS.

Block by laying cap between two damp towels until completely dry.

Favorite Child Playsuit

A perfect play garment with a stripe pattern you'll recognize from all the other Favorite Child outfits.

SKILL LEVEL: 2

SIZES: preemie (0–1, 1–3, 6, 9, 12, 18 months, 2 years)

FINISHED MEASUREMENTS

Chest: Approx. 16¾ (18½, 19¾, 21½, 23¼, 24¼, 26¼, 27¼) in [42.5 (47, 50, 54.5, 59, 61.5, 66.5, 69) cm]
Total Length (excluding straps): Approx. 15½ (17, 19¼, 22, 22¼, 24½, 26½, 28¼) in [39 (43, 49, 56, 59, 62, 67, 72) cm]

YARN: Sandnes Garn Klompelompe Tynn Merinoull [CYCA #1 – fingering, 100% fine Merino wool, 191 yd (175 m) / 50 g]

YARN COLORS AND AMOUNTS

Merinoull, Color 9871: 150 (150, 200, 200, 250, 250, 300, 300) g

NEEDLES: U.S. sizes 1.5 and 2.5 (2.5 and 3 mm): 16 and 32 in (40 and 80 cm) circulars

NOTIONS: 8 (8, 8, 10, 10, 10, 12, 12) buttons, ⅝ in (15 mm) in diameter; crochet hook U.S. C-2 (2.5 mm) for chain loop buttonhole

GAUGE: 27 sts on larger size needle = 4 in (10 cm).

Adjust needle size to obtain correct gauge if necessary.

The playsuit begins at the I-cord neck (see video at klompelompe.no/en/).

With smaller size needle, CO 4 sts. Knit an I-cord 9 (9½, 9⅝, 10, 10½, 10¾, 11½, 11¾) in 23 (24, 24.5, 25.5,

26.5, 27.5, 29, 30) cm] long. Change to larger size circular.

Pick up 71 (74, 76, 79, 83, 86, 92, 95) sts along I-cord. Knit 1 row, purl 1 row.

Next Row: K12 (13, 13, 14, 15, 16, 17, 18), M1, k1 (raglan st), M1, k9 (sleeve sts), M1, k1 (raglan st), M1, k25 (26, 28, 29, 31, 32, 36, 37), M1, k1 (raglan st), M1, k9 (sleeve sts), M1, k1 (raglan st), M1, k12 (13, 13, 14, 15, 16, 17, 18) = 8 sts increased.

Raise back neck with German short rows (see video at klompelompe.no/en/).

Knit, including raglan increases, until 6 sts in on front; turn and purl to end of row.

Knit, including raglan increases, until 9 sts in on front; turn and purl to end of row.

Knit 1 row, including raglan increases.

Purl until 6 sts in on front; turn and knit including raglan increases to end of row.

Knit until 9 sts in on front; turn and knit including raglan increases to end of row.

Purl 1 row.

Tip For jogless rnds between stripes: Slip 1st st of 1st knit rnd (after purl rnd) to right needle without knitting it.

Purl 1 row on RS when piece measures 1 in (2.5 cm). Rep the purl row every 1 in (2.5 cm) throughout). Increase as est on every other row until you've increased a total of 8 (8, 9, 9, 10, 10, 11, 11) times. Join to work in the round from this point on.

Continue increasing on every other rnd until you've increased a total of 13 (15, 17, 19, 21, 22, 24, 25) times = 175 (194, 212, 231, 251, 262, 284, 295) sts.

Knit 1 rnd.

Next Rnd: Knit to and including raglan st, place sleeve sts on a holder, CO 5 sts over gap, knit to and including raglan st, place sleeve sts on a holder, CO 5 sts over gap, knit to end of rnd = 115 (126, 136, 147, 159, 166, 180, 187) sts,

Continue in stockinette.

After 1¼ in (3 cm), M1 on each side of the 5 underarm sts at each side.

Increase the same way after 1¼ (1¼, 1¼, 1½, 1½, 2, 2, 2) in [3 (3, 3, 4, 4, 5, 5, 5) cm] a total of 3 (3, 3, 3, 4, 4, 4, 5) times = 127 (138, 148, 159, 175, 182, 196, 207) sts.

Measure down center back. Continue as est until piece measures 9¾ (10¾, 11¾, 13½, 14, 14½, 15¾, 16½) in [25 (27, 30, 34, 35.5, 37, 40, 42) cm].

Decrease 1 (0, 0, 1, 1, 0, 0, 1) st on next rnd.

Lengthen back with German short rows (see video at klompelompe.no/en/).

K20; turn and p40. K43; turn and p46. K49; turn and p52; turn.

SIZES 9, 12, 18 MONTHS AND 2 YEARS:
K55; turn and p58; turn.

SIZES 18 MONTHS AND 2 YEARS:
K61; turn and p64; turn.

ALL SIZES:
Knit to end of rnd.

Pm on each side of the center 8 sts at both front and back.

Next Rnd: M1 on each side of the marked 8 sts on front and back.

Increase the same way on every 3rd rnd a total of 5 times.

Next Rnd: BO the center 8 sts on front and back. Work legs separately, back and forth = 65 (71, 76, 81, 89, 93, 100, 105) sts for each leg.

Purl 1 row.

Next Row: K1, k2tog, knit until 3 sts rem, sl 1, k1, psso, k1.

Decrease the same way every 4th row a total of 8 (8, 9, 9, 10, 10, 11, 11) times = 49 (55, 58, 63, 69, 73, 78, 83) sts rem.

Continue back and forth in stockinette until leg measures 4¼ (5¼, 6¼, 7½, 8, 8¾, 9½, 10¾) in [11 (13, 16, 19, 20.5, 22, 24, 27) cm] and next row will be on WS.

Purl 1 row adjusting stitch count to 32 (34, 36, 36, 38, 38, 40, 40) sts by decreasing evenly spaced across.

Change to smaller size needle and BO with I-cord bind-off (see video at klompelompe.no/en/).

BUTTON BAND

(**Note:** In this case, pick up and knit stitches instead of picking up only.)

With smaller size needle, pick up and knit 3 sts for every 4 sts. When picking up over the bound-off sts of crotch, pick up and knit 1 st in every st.

Knit 7 rows (= 3.5 ridges). BO knitwise on next row.

Buttonhole: K2tog. On following row, CO 1 st over each gap.

On front, make 7 (7, 7, 9, 9, 9, 11, 11) buttonholes evenly spaced on 2nd row of garter-st band.

SLEEVES

With larger size needle and beginning in center of the 5 underarm sts, pick up and knit 3 sts, pick up and knit 1 st in gap between underarm and armhole, knit held sleeve sts, pick up and knit 1 st in gap between armhole and underarm, pick up and knit 2 sts along underarm. Pm for beginning of rnd. Continue in Stripe Sequence on sleeves as for body.

Work around on sleeve until it measures 4 (4¾, 5½, 6¼, 6¾, 7, 8, 9) in [10 (12, 14, 16, 17, 18, 20, 23) cm].

Knit 1 rnd, adjusting stitch count to 34 (36, 38, 40, 40, 42, 42, 44) sts.

Change to smaller size needle and BO with I-cord bind-off (see video at klompelompe.no/en/).

Make second sleeve the same way.

BUTTONHOLE ON BACK NECK

With crochet hook, attach yarn with 1 sl st on one side of back neck and ch 4. Attach ch with 1 sl st, making sure loop is long enough for button to go through.

FINISHING

Weave in all ends neatly on WS.

Sew buttons on front band and back neck opening.

Block by laying playsuit flat, patted out to finished measurements, on a damp towel until completely dry.

Favorite Child Bonnet

This bonnet with a classic stripe pattern adorably suits both girls and boys.

SKILL LEVEL: 2

SIZES: preemie (0–3, 3–6, 6–12 months, 1–2 years)

YARN: Sandnes Garn Klompelompe Tynn Merinoull [CYCA #1 – fingering, 100% fine Merino wool, 191 yd (175 m) / 50 g]

YARN COLORS AND AMOUNTS
Merinoull, Color 9871: 50 (50, 50, 50, 50) g

NEEDLES: U.S. sizes 1.5 and 2.5 (2.5 and 3 mm): 16 and 32 in (40 and 80 cm) circulars

GAUGE: 27 sts on larger size needle = 4 in (10 cm).
Adjust needle size to obtain correct gauge if necessary.

The bonnet is worked back and forth on a circular needle.

With smaller size circular, CO 77 (83, 93, 93, 103) sts.

Work back and forth in k1, p1 ribbing for 4 rows. CO 3 sts.
BO with I-cord bind-off (see technique video at klompelompe.no/en/).

With larger size needle, pick up each st at back of I-cord = 77 (83, 93, 93, 103) sts.
Work in stockinette for 1 in (2.5 cm) and then begin Stripe pattern with first purl row on RS after stockinette).

Continue as est (the purl row is repeated every 1 in (2.5 cm until bonnet measures 3¼ (4, 4¼, 4¾, 5¼) in [8 (10, 11, 12, 13) cm]. Join to knit in the round. On first rnd, decrease 5 (3, 3, 3, 3) sts evenly spaced around. From 3rd rnd, continue in stockinette only.

ALL SIZES EXCEPT PREEMIE:
Next Rnd: *K8, k2tog*; rep *-* around.
Knit 2 rnds.
Next Rnd: *K7, k2tog*; rep *-* around.
Knit 2 rnds.
Next Rnd: *K6, k2tog*; rep *-* around.
Knit 1 rnd.
Next Rnd: *K5, k2tog*; rep *-* around.
Knit 1 rnd.
Next Rnd: *K4, k2tog*; rep *-* around.
Knit 1 rnd.
Next Rnd: *K3, k2tog*; rep *-* around.
Knit 1 rnd.
Next Rnd: *K2, k2tog*; rep *-* around.
Knit 1 rnd.
Next Rnd: *K1, k2tog*; rep *-* around.
Next Rnd: *K2tog*; rep *-* around.
Cut yarn and draw end through rem sts; tighten.

NECKBAND
With smaller size needle, pick up and knit 1 st in every other st along neck. Place sts on another same size circular.
With smaller size needle, CO 4 sts and knit an I-cord 8 in (20 cm) long. BO the held neck sts with I-cord bind-off (see technique video at klompelompe.no/en/) until 4 sts rem. End with another 8 in (20 cm) I-cord.

FINISHING
Weave in all ends neatly on WS.
Block by laying bonnet flat between two damp towels until completely dry.

Olav Cardigan

We like good, traditional garments. A classic cardigan has always been a part of our children's wardrobes. This time, we decided to use a different construction rather than the traditional round yoke of our standard Klompelompe cardigan. We think the result is especially beautiful.

SKILL LEVEL: 3

SIZES: 0–1 (3, 6, 12, 18, 24 months)

FINISHED MEASUREMENTS
Chest: Approx. 20 (21¼, 22½, 24¾, 25¾, 27) in [51 (54, 57, 63, 65.5, 68.5) cm]
Length: Approx. 10¾ (11¼, 12¼, 13½, 14¼, 14¾) in [27.5 (28.5, 31, 34, 36.5, 37.5) cm]

YARN: Sandnes Garn Klompelompe Tynn Merinoull [CYCA #1-- fingering, 100% fine Merino wool, 191 yd (175 m) / 50 g]

YARN COLORS AND AMOUNTS
Color A, 3355: 100 (100, 150, 150, 200, 200) g
Color B, 2650: 50 (50, 50, 50, 50, 50) g

NEEDLES: U.S. sizes 1.5 and 2.5 (2.5 and 3 mm): 16 and 32 in (40 and 80 cm) circulars

NOTIONS: 7 (7, 8, 8, 9, 9) buttons, ⅝ in (15 mm) in diameter

GAUGE: 27 sts on larger size needle = 4 in (10 cm).
Adjust needle size to obtain correct gauge if necessary.

The cardigan begins at the lower edge and is first worked back and forth on a circular needle.

With smaller size circular and color A, CO 137 (145, 153, 169, 177, 185) sts. Work back and forth in k1, p1 ribbing for 1¼ (1¼, 1¼, 1⅜, 1⅜, 1⅜) in [3 (3, 3, 3.5, 3.5, 3.5) cm].

Change to larger size needle.

Knit 1 row and CO 9 sts at end of row for the steek. Do not include steek sts in stitch counts or work them in pattern. Join to knit in the round.

Work following chart A.

Next, work following chart B. When body measures 6 (6¼, 7, 8, 9, 9) in [15 (16, 18, 20, 23, 23) cm} and next rnd is one without lice, BO 8 sts at each side for underarms: K29 (31, 33, 37, 39, 41), BO 8 sts, k63 (67, 71, 79, 83, 87), BO 8 sts, k29 (31, 33, 37, 39, 41).

Next Rnd: Work in pattern and CO 8 sts at each side (over bound-off sts) = armhole steek sts. Pm on each side of each 8-st steek.

Continue, working 0 (0, 2, 4, 4, 6) rnds of chart B except over new steek sts.

Work following chart C.

On last rnd of chart, BO steek sts at center front and place the first 10 (10, 11, 11, 12, 12) and last 10 (10, 11, 11, 12, 12) sts of rnd on holders.

Next Row (WS): Work back and forth following chart D.

Next Row: K2tog, work as est until 2 sts rem, sl 1, k1, psso. Decrease the same way on every 4th row a total of 3 times.

Next Row (with color A): K16 (18, 19, 23, 24, 26), BO steek sts, k16 (18, 19, 23, 24, 26), place next 31 (31, 33, 33, 35, 35) sts on a holder, k16 (18, 19, 23, 24, 26), BO steek sts, k16 (18, 19, 23, 24, 26).

turn; turn; knit to end of row. Change to color B and purl 1 row. BO knitwise on next row.

Seam shoulders.

NECKBAND RIBBING

With smaller size circular, knit the held 10 (10, 11, 11, 12, 12) sts, pick up and knit 3 sts for every 4 sts. Knit the held 31 (31, 33, 33, 35, 35) sts, pick up and knit the held 10 (10, 11, 11, 12, 12) sts.

Work back and forth in k1, p1 ribbing for ¾ (¾, 1, 1, 1¼, 1¼) in [2 (2, 2.5, 2.5, 3, 3) cm]. BO in ribbing.

ARMHOLE STEEKS

Machine-stitch two fine lines on each side of the center steek sts. Carefully cut steek open up center.

SLEEVES

With larger size needle and color A, pick up and knit 64 (64, 66, 68, 68, 70) sts around armhole. Join and pm for beginning of rnd.

Work following chart B.

When sleeve measures ⅝ in (1.5 cm), decrease as follows: K1, k2tog, knit until 3 sts rem, sl 1, k1, psso, k1.

Decrease the same way every ⅝ (⅝, ⅝, ⅝, ¾, ¾) in [1.5 (1.5, 1.5, 1.5, 2, 2) cm] a total of 8 (9, 10, 12, 10, 10) times.

When sleeve measures 3¾ (4, 4½, 6, 6¾, 7½) in [9.5 (10.5, 11.5, 15, 17.5, 19) cm], work chart A.

Knit 1 rnd with color A adjusting stitch count to 38 (38, 38, 40, 42, 48) sts, decreasing evenly spaced around.

Change to smaller size needle and work around in k1, p1 ribbing for 1¼ (1¼, 1¼, 1⅜, 1⅜, 1⅜) in [3 (3, 3, 3.5, 3.5, 3.5) cm]. BO in ribbing.

FRONT STEEK FINISHING

Machine-stitch two fine lines on each side of the center front steek st. Carefully cut steek open up center st.

With color A and smaller size needle, pick up and knit approx. 3 sts for every 4 rows for button band.

Work 8 rows in k1, p1 ribbing and BO (not too tightly). For the boy's version, make buttonholes on left side and, for the girl's, on the right side. Make 7 (7, 8, 8, 9, 9) buttonholes evenly spaced down band. Make buttonholes on 3rd row of ribbing with k2tog, yo.

RIGHT FRONT

Next Row (WS): Change to color B. Purl 1 row. Change to color A. Knit until 2 sts rem; turn and purl to end of row; turn. Knit until 3 sts before previous turn; turn; purl to end of row. Change to color B and knit 1 row. BO purlwise on next row.

RIGHT BACK

Next Row (RS): Change to color B and knit 1 row. Change to color A. Purl until 2 sts rem; turn and knit to end of row; turn. Purl until 3 sts before previous turn; turn and knit to end of row. Change to color B and purl 1 row. BO knitwise on next row.

LEFT BACK

Next Row (WS): Change to color B and purl 1 row. Change to color A. Knit until 2 sts rem; turn and purl to end of row; turn. Knit until 3 sts before previous turn; turn and purl to end of row. Change to color B and knit 1 row. BO purlwise on next row.

LEFT FRONT

Next Row (RS): Change to color B. Knit 1 row. Change to color A. Purl until 2 sts rem; turn and knit to end of row; turn. Purl until 3 sts before previous

Fold each steek cut edge to WS and sew down with small stitches. If it is difficult to make a fine edge, you can knit a facing to sew over the steek cut edge. Pick up and knit sts (as for front bands). Work a stockinette band long enough to cover steek edges. BO and sew down on WS. It will look best if you sew down using the main color of the cardigan so it won't show.

FINISHING

Weave in all ends neatly on WS. Sew buttons on, spaced as for buttonholes.

Block by laying sweater flat, patted out to finished measurements, on a damp towel until completely dry or carefully steam press under a damp pressing cloth.

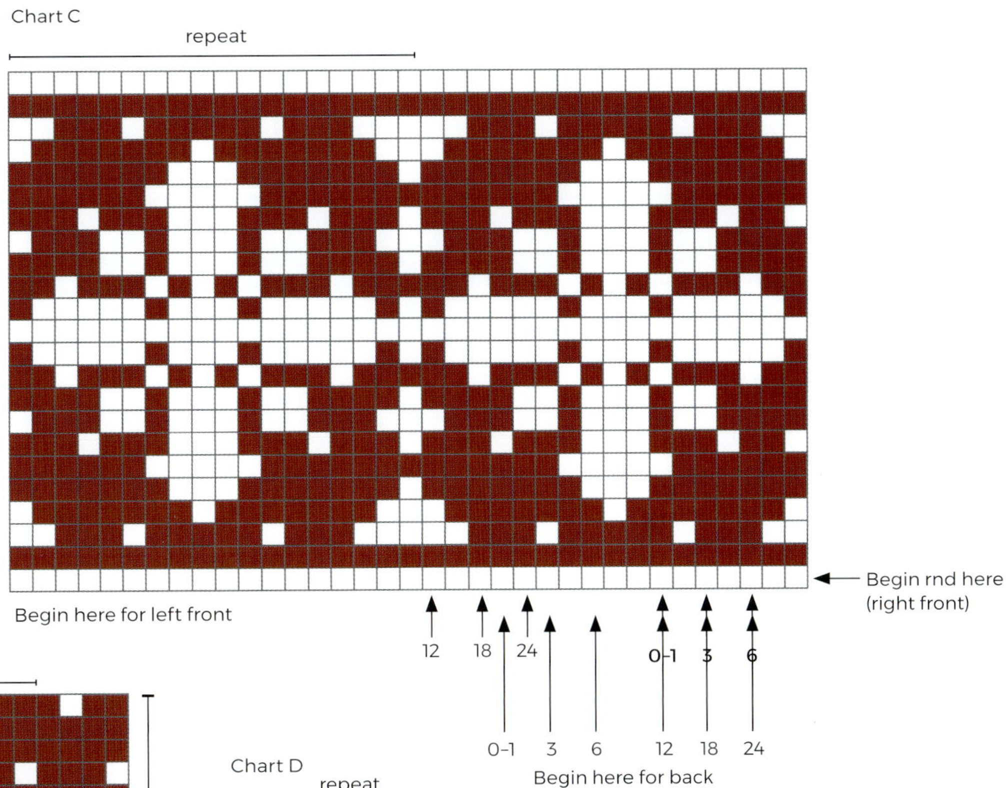

■ = color A

□ = color B

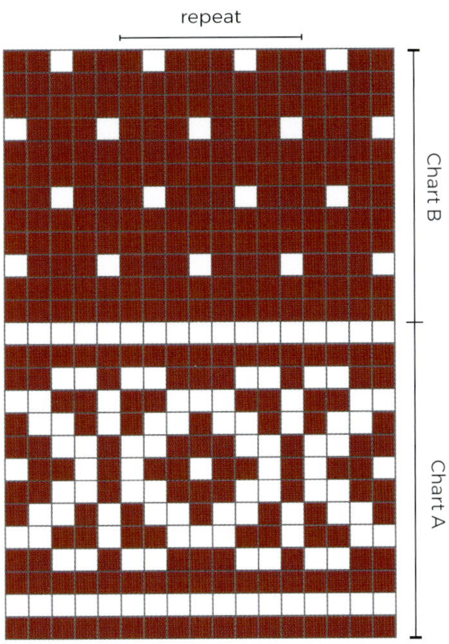

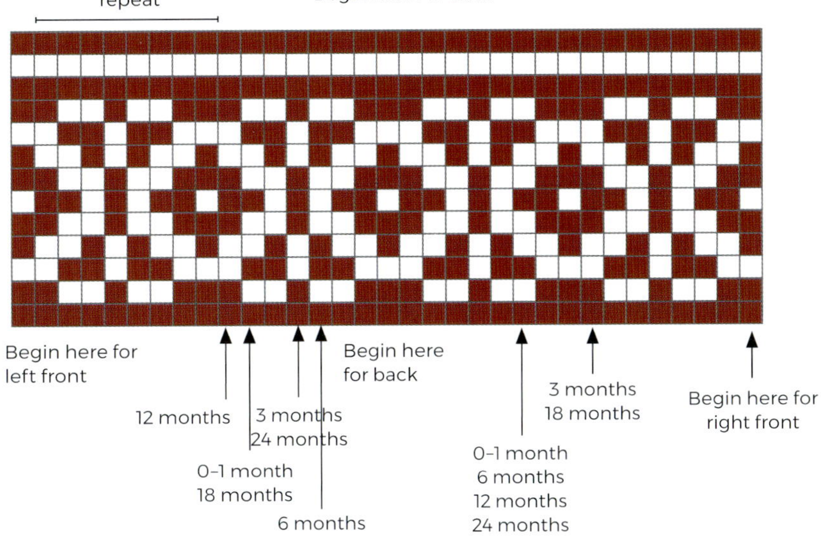

Olav Pants

Complete the set with a fine-looking pair of pants featuring the same pattern as the cardigan.

SKILL LEVEL: 2

SIZES: 0–1 (3–6, 9–12, 18–24 months)

FINISHED MEASUREMENTS
Top of pants: Approx. 15¾ (17½, 18¾, 19¾) in [40 (44.5, 47.5, 50) cm]
Total Length: Approx. 9½ (12⅞, 15, 17⅛) in [24.5 (32.5, 38, 43.5) cm]

YARN: Sandnes Garn Klompelompe Tynn Merinoull [CYCA #1 – fingering, 100% fine Merino wool, 191 yd (175 m) / 50 g]

YARN COLORS AND AMOUNTS
Color A, 3355: 50 (100, 100, 100) g
Color B, 2650: 50 (50, 50, 50) g

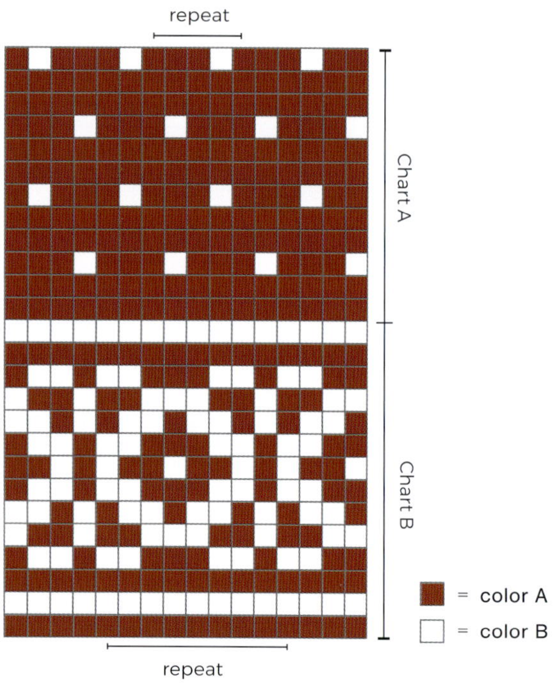

NEEDLES: U.S. sizes 1.5 and 2.5 (2.5 and 3 mm): 16 and 32 in (40 and 80 cm) circulars

GAUGE: 27 sts on larger size needle = 4 in (10 cm). Adjust needle size to obtain correct gauge if necessary.

The pants begin at the waist and are knitted in the round on a circular needle.

With smaller size circular and color A, CO 100 (114, 122, 130) sts. Join, being careful not to twist cast-on row; pm for beginning of rnd. Work 14 rnds in k1, p1 ribbing.

Change to larger size needle and knit 1 rnd.

Next Rnd: Knit, increasing 8 (6, 6, 6) sts evenly spaced around = 108 (120, 128, 136) sts,
Knit 1 rnd.

Raise back with German short rows (see video at klompelompe.no/en/):

K20; turn and p40; turn.
K43; turn and p46; turn.
K49; turn and p52; turn.

SIZES 9–12 AND 18–24 MONTHS:
K55; turn and p58; turn. K61; turn and p64; turn.

ALL SIZES: Knit to end of rnd.

Now work following chart A until pants measure 4¾ (5½ (6¼, 7) in [12 (14, 16, 18) cm] down center front.

Pm on each side of the center 6 sts at both front and back.

Continue following chart A, on both the sts between markers and rem sts around.

Increase 1 st on each side of the 6 marked sts at front and back.

Inecrease on every 3rd rnd a total of 5 times (adding new sts into lice pattern when possible).

Next Rnd: BO the 6 center sts at front and back. Work each leg separately = 58 (64, 68, 72) sts for each leg. Pm for beginning of rnd at center of inner leg.

LEGS

Work around one leg following chart A until it measures 3 (5¼, 6½, 7¾) in [7.5 (13.5, 16.5, 19.5) cm]. *At the same time*, decrease every 1 in (2.5 cm) as follows: K1, k2tog, knit until 3 sts rem, sl 1, k1, psso, k1. Note that the pattern gradually disappears. Decrease a total of 3 (4, 5, 4) times.

Knit 1 rnd with color A, decreasing 4 (0, 2, 0) sts evenly spaced around = 48 (56, 56, 64) sts rem.

Work chart B pattern.

Knit 1 rnd with color A.

Knit 1 rnd, decreasing evenly spaced around to 36 (40, 44, 44) sts. Change to smaller size needle.

Work around in k1, p1 ribbing for 1¼ (1¼, 1⅜, 1⅜) in [3 (3, 3.5, 3.5) cm]. BO in ribbing.

Make second leg the same way.

FINISHING

Weave in all ends neatly on WS.

Block by laying pants flat, patted out to finished measurements, on a damp towel until completely dry.

Olav Carriage Blanket

A double-sided blanket with reversed colors on the back. Thick, snug, and decorative.

SKILL LEVEL: 3

FINISHED MEASUREMENTS
Approx. 23¾ x 27½ in (60 x 70 cm)

YARN: Sandnes Garn Klompelompe Merinoull (Merino wool) [CYCA #3 - DK, 100% Merino wool, 114 yd (104 m) / 50 g]

YARN COLORS AND AMOUNTS
Color A, 3355: 300 g
Color B, 2650: 300 g

NEEDLES: U.S. size 4 (3.5 mm): 32 in (80 cm) circular

GAUGE: 22 sts on gauge-size needle = 4 in (10 cm).
Adjust needle size to obtain correct gauge if necessary.

The blanket is knitted in the round on a circular needle (first half of sts = front; second half of sts = back).

With color A, CO 290 sts. Join, being careful not to twist cast-on row; pm for beginning of rnd.

Divide work into two with a marker at each side: Pm, 145 sts (front), pm, 145 sts (back). **Note:** End the front and back with an edge st.

The front is worked with color A as the main color while the back has color B as the main color. Don't forget to reverse the chart colors when you are working on the back!

Work following chart A and then chart B. After completing chart B, work following chart C until blanket is approx. 27½ in (70 cm) long. BO.

FINISHING
Seam bottom and top of blanket. Weave in all ends neatly on WS. Block.

Chart A

Chart C

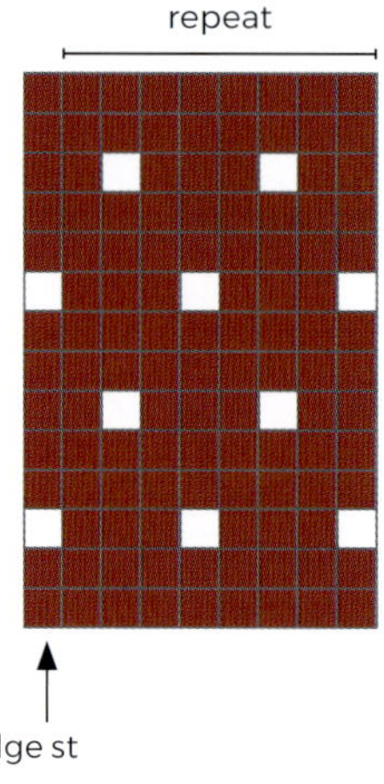

Chart B

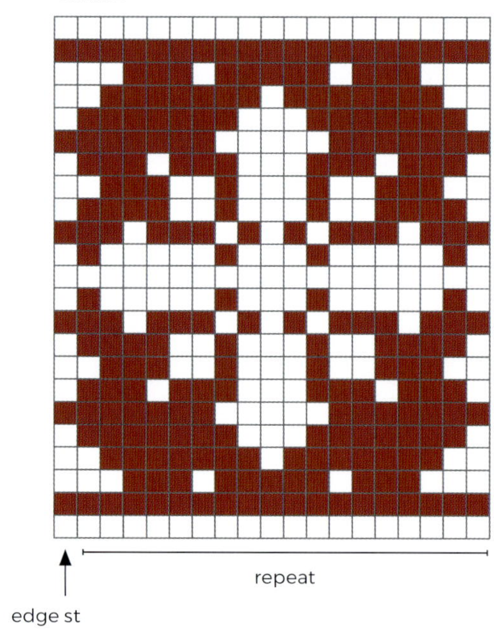

■ = color A
□ = color B

Olav Mittens

These mittens fit well and beautifully accent the other items in the set.

SKILL LEVEL: 2

SIZES: 0–1 (3, 6 months, 1–2, 3–4 years)

MATERIALS
Yarn: Sandnes Garn Klompelompe Tynn Merinoull [CYCA #1 – fingering, 100% fine Merino wool, 191 yd (175 m) / 50 g]

YARN COLORS AND AMOUNTS
Color A, 2650: 50 (50, 50, 50, 50) g
Color B, 6061: small amount for each size

NEEDLES: U.S. sizes 1.5 and 2.5 (2.5 and 3 mm): 32 in (80 cm) circulars

GAUGE: 27 sts on larger-size needle = 4 in (10 cm).
Adjust needle size to obtain correct gauge if necessary.

The mittens are knitted in the round with round beginning at the side. Divide sts in half on a magic loop circular (see video of technique at klompelompe.no/en/).

With larger size circular and color A, CO 32 (32, 40, 40, 48) sts. Join, being careful not to twist cast-on row; pm for beginning of rnd.
Knit 1 rnd.
Knit following chart A.

Knit 0 (0, 2, 4, 6) rnds.

Change to smaller size needle and work in k1, p1 ribbing for ¾ (1, 1¼, 1¼, 1¼) in [2 (2.5, 3, 3, 3) cm].

Change to larger size needle.
Knit following chart B.

SIZES 1–2 AND 3–4 YEARS:
When mitten measures ⅝ (¾) in [1.5 (2) cm] above ribbing, mark placement for thumbhole as follows:

LEFT MITTEN: Knit across front, knit until 7 (8) sts rem on palm, knit next 6 (7) sts with smooth, contrast color waste yarn, place the 6 (7) sts back onto left needle and knit with working yarn. Knit to end of rnd.

RIGHT MITTEN: Knit across front, k1 on palm, knit next 6 (7) sts with smooth, contrast color waste yarn, place the 6 (7) sts back onto left needle and knit with working yarn. Knit to end of rnd.

Continue in pattern as est. Pm at each side with same number of sts each for front and palm.

ALL SIZES:
When mitten measures 2⅜ (2½, 3¼, 4, 4¼) in [6 (6.5, 8, 10, 11) cm] above ribbing, shape top as follows:
K1, k2tog, knit until 3 sts before marker, sl 1, k1, psso, k1; rep *-* around on every rnd until 8 sts total rem.

Cut yarn and draw end through rem sts; tighten.

THUMB
Insert needle through the 6 (7) sts below waste yarn and another needle into the 6 (7) sts above waste yarn; carefully remove waste yarn. With color A, knit around, and *at the same time* pick up and knit 1 st at each side. Continue around with color A until thumb measures 1⅜ (1¾) in [3.5 (4.5) cm]. K2tog around.

Cut yarn and draw end through rem sts; tighten.

FINISHING
Weave in all ends neatly on WS.
Block by laying mittens flat between two damp towels until completely dry.

Chart A

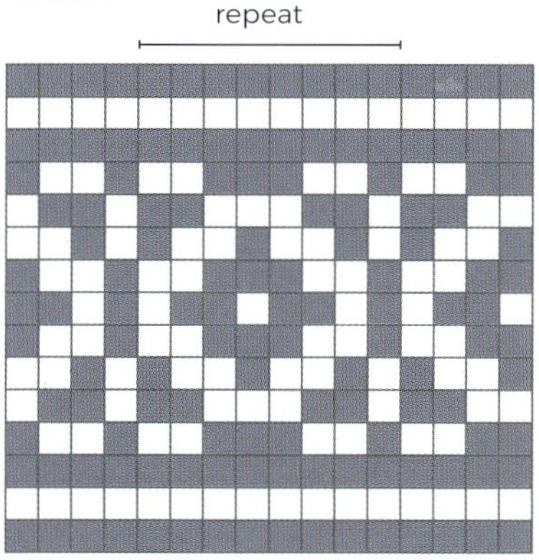

Chart B

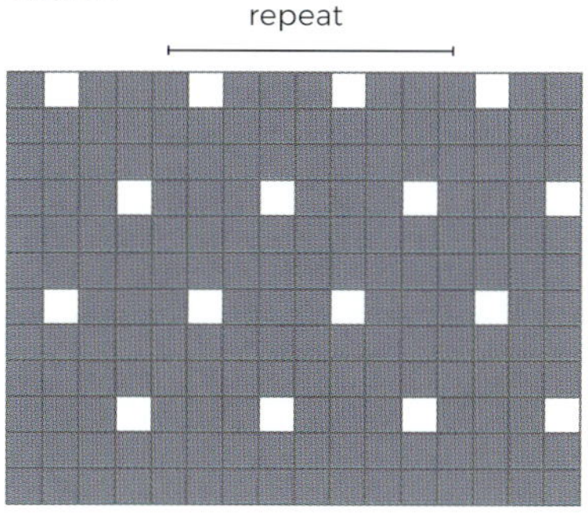

■ = color A

□ = color B

Layette Set for the Littlest Ones

Chunky Onesie for the Littlest Ones

When the youngest of our children was born, we made a Littlest One Cardigan. We were very happy with this pattern, and a chunky onesie version had been on the ideas list for a long time.

SKILL LEVEL: 2

SIZES: 0–1 (3, 6–9, 12, 18 months, 2 years)

FINISHED MEASUREMENTS
Chest: Approx. 14½ (15¼, 16¼, 16¾, 18, 18¾) in [37 (38.5, 41.5, 42.5, 45.5, 47.5) cm]
Length: Approx. 18¼ (20½, 23¾, 26, 28, 30) in [46 (52, 60, 66, 71, 76) cm]

YARN: Sandnes Garn Kos [CYCA #5 – bulky, 62% alpaca, 29% polyamide, 9% wool, 164 yd (150 m) / 50 g]

YARN COLORS AND AMOUNTS
Color 2611: 150 (150, 200, 200, 250, 250) g

NEEDLES: U.S. sizes 4 and 8 (3.5 and 5 mm): 24 and 32 in (60 and 80 cm) circulars; cable needle

NOTIONS: 6 (6, 7, 8, 8, 9) buttons, ⅝ in (15 mm) in diameter

GAUGE: 16 sts on larger size needle = 4 in (10 cm).
Adjust needle size to obtain correct gauge if necessary.

The onesie is worked from the top down, primarily back and forth on a circular needle.

With larger size circular, CO 41 (41, 45, 45, 49, 49) sts. Change to smaller size needle and work 10 (10, 10, 10, 12, 12) rows in k1, p1 ribbing. Change to larger size needle and knit 1 row. *At the same time*, join every other st with corresponding cast-on st with k2tog. If you think this is too difficult, you can fold the edge down later and sew it down.

Purl 1 row, increasing 8 sts evenly spaced around. Pm without knitting row: 4 (4, 5, 5, 6, 6) sts, pm, 11 sts (pattern sts), pm, 1 st, pm, 1 st (raglan st on back), pm, 15 (15, 17, 17, 19, 19) sts (back), pm, 1 st (raglan st on back), pm, 1 st, pm, 11 sts (pattern sts), pm, 4 (4, 5, 5, 6, 6) sts.

Begin pattern following the chart over the 11 pattern sts and make the raglan increases. Increase with M1 on each side of the 11 pattern sts and on each side of the raglan sts on back = 8 sts increased per row.

Continue, working the pattern over the 11 pattern sts in each of the two front raglan sections. Make raglan increases on every other row on RS.

The rest of each row is worked in stockinette (knit on RS and purl on WS).

The 2nd time you increase, work short rows to raise back neck as follows: Knit, including raglan increases, until 1 st before 2nd pattern section; turn and purl until 1 st before second pattern section; turn. Knit, including raglan increases, to end of row.

Continue raglan increases until you've increased a total of 11 (12, 13, 14, 15, 16) times on front = 141 (149, 161, 169, 181, 189) sts.

NEXT ROW:
Work to and including center pattern st, place next pattern sts and sleeve sts on a holder. CO 5 sts for underarm, knit raglan st, back, and next raglan st, place sleeve sts and the first 5 pattern sts on a holder, CO 5 sts for underarm, knit rem sts = 93 (97, 105, 109, 117, 121) sts rem for body.

Work back and forth, continuing pattern sts as est. The st which was previously the center st of pattern is now purled for remainder of work.

Continue back and forth as est until piece measures 10¼ (11½, 13, 14¼, 15½, 16¼) in [26 (29, 33, 36, 39, 41) cm].

CO 3 sts. Now join to work in the round.

Lengthen back as follows:

Pm on center back st—it will be the center st for the turns.

Knit to center back of onesie.

Knit until 8 sts before pattern section; turn and purl until 8 sts before pattern section; turn. Knit until 5 sts before previous turn; turn and purl until 5 sts before previous turn; turn.

Knit until 3 sts before previous turn; turn and purl until 3 sts before previous turn; turn. Knit to end of rnd.

Pm on each side of the center 5 sts at both front and back.

Now increase 1 st on each side of the 5 marked sts on front and back on every 3rd rnd a total of 4 (4, 4, 5, 5, 6) times.

Knit 1 rnd and *at the same time* BO the center 5 sts on front and back = 51 (53, 57, 61, 65, 69) sts rem for each leg.

LEGS

Pm at crotch. Knit around in stockinette, continuing the pattern as est.

After 1½ in (4 cm), decrease as follows: K1, k2tog, knit until 3 sts before marker, sl 1, k1, psso, k1.

Decrease the same way every 1½ in (4 cm) a total of 2 (3, 4, 4, 5, 5) times. Continue working around until leg measures 4¾ (6, 7½, 8¼, 9, 9¾) in [12 (15, 19, 21, 23, 25) cm].

Knit 1 rnd, adjusting stitch count to 30 (30, 32, 34, 36, 38) sts.

Change to smaller size needle and work 19 (19, 23, 23, 25, 25) rnds in k1, p1 ribbing. BO in ribbing.

Make second leg the same way.

SLEEVES

With larger size needle, beginning at center of the 5 underarm sts, pick up and knit 3 sts, pick up and knit 1 st in gap between underarm and armhole, knit the 29 (31, 33, 35, 37, 39) held sleeve sts (continuing pattern in pattern section as est), pick up and knit 1 st in gap between armhole and underarm, pick up and knit 2 sts along underarm.

The st that comes into the pattern section at the body, is now purled down the sleeve. The first st is a marked st and purled down the sleeve.

After 1½ in (4 cm), decrease as follows: P1, k2tog, knit until 2 sts rem, sl 1, k1 psso.

Decrease the same way every 1½ in (4 cm) a total of 2 (3, 4, 4, 5, 5) times. Continue as est until

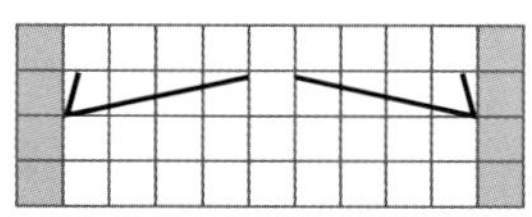

← Begin here

= Place 3 sts on a cable needle and hold in back of work, k1, k3 from cable needle.

= Place 1 st on a cable needle and hold in front of work, k3, k1 from cable needle.

= knit on RS, purl on WS

= purl on RS, knit on WS

sleeve measures 4¾ (5½, 6¼, 7½, 8¼, 9½) in [12 (14, 16, 19, 21, 24) cm]. When the decreases come to the pattern section, decrease on the other side of the pattern.

Knit 1 rnd, adjusting stitch count to 24 (24, 26, 26, 28, 30) sts.

Change to smaller size needle and work 20 (20, 24, 24, 26, 26) rnds in k1, p1 ribbing. BO in ribbing.

Make second sleeve the same way.

FRONT BANDS

Right Front and Neck Band: With smaller size needle, pick up and knit 3 sts for every 4 rows along front edge. Also pick up and knit sts along neck ribbing. Work 6 rows in k1, p1 ribbing. BO in ribbing on last row.

Left front band: Pick up and knit same number of sts and work same number of rows of ribbing as on right front edge. On 2nd row of band, make 6 (6, 7, 8, 8, 9) buttonholes evenly spaced down band. Buttonhole = K2tog, yo.

FINISHING

Weave in all ends neatly on WS. Sew buttons on, spaced as for buttonholes.Block by laying onesie flat, patted out to finished measurements, on a damp towel until completely dry.

Cozy Pixie Cap

Soft, sweet, and super-easy cap.

SKILL LEVEL: 1

SIZES: preemie (1–3, 3–6, 6–9 months, 1–2, 3–4 years)

YARN: Sandnes Garn Kos [CYCA #5 – bulky, 62% alpaca, 29% polyamide, 9% wool, 164 yd (150 m) / 50 g]

YARN COLORS AND AMOUNTS

Color 2543 or 2611: 50 (50, 50, 50, 50, 50) g

NEEDLES: U.S. sizes 6 and 11 (4 and 8 mm): 16 in (40 cm) circulars

GAUGE: 11.5 sts on larger size needle with 2 strands of yarn held together = 4 in (10 cm). Adjust needle size to obtain correct gauge if necessary.

With larger size circular and 2 strands of yarn held together, working a bit tightly, CO 36 (38, 40, 44, 44, 46) sts.

Work back and forth in stockinette st until piece measures 4 (4¼, 4¾, 5¼, 5½, 6) in [10 (11, 12, 13, 14, 15) cm].

Shape cap with German short rows (see video at klompelompe.no/en/) as follows:

Next Row (WS): Purl until 4 sts rem; turn and knit until 4 sts rem; turn.

Purl until 4 sts before previous turn; turn and knit until 4 sts before previous turn; turn.

SIZES 6–9 MONTHS, 1–2, AND 3–4 YEARS: Purl until 4 sts before previous turn; turn and knit until 4 sts before previous turn; turn.

ALL SIZES: Purl to end of row.

Fold cap with RS facing RS. Using a third needle, work 3-needle BO: Insert needle knitwise into 2 sts—the first st on each needle—and knit them together. *K2tog with next pair of sts, pass first worked st on right needle over second;* rep * to * until all sts have been bound off.

With smaller size needle, RS facing, and 1 strand of yarn, pick up and knit 1 st in each st along neck edge. Purl 1 row on WS. BO knitwise on next row.

On each side of cap front edge: Pick up and knit 4 sts at end of neck edge. Make an I-cord (see video at klompelompe.no/en/) to length you prefer.

FINISHING

Weave in all ends neatly on WS.

Block by laying cap between two damp towels until completely dry.

Onesie for the Littlest Ones

We quite like the pattern used in our Littlest Ones series, and we were excited to design this cute onesie with a fine cable and raglan pattern. We think it is super sweet and perfect for wearing while resting in the baby carriage, or under a rain suit at nursery school.

SKILL LEVEL: 2

SIZES: 0–1 (3, 6–9, 12, 18, 24 months)

FINISHED MEASUREMENTS
Chest: Approx. 17¾ (18¼, 20½, 22, 23¼, 25) in [45 (46.5, 52, 56, 59, 63.5) cm]
Length: Approx. 17¼ (20, 23¼, 25½, 27½, 29¼) in [44 (51, 59, 65, 70, 74) cm]

YARN: Sandnes Garn Klompelompe Tynn Merinoull [CYCA #1 – fingering, 100% fine Merino wool, 191 yd (175 m) / 50 g]

YARN COLORS AND AMOUNTS
Color 2650: 150 (150, 200, 200, 250, 300) g

NEEDLES: U.S. sizes 1.5 and 2.5 (2.5 and 3 mm): 24 and 32 in (60 and 80 cm) circulars; cable needle

NOTIONS: 5 (6, 6, 8, 8, 9) buttons, ⅝ in (15 mm) in diameter

GAUGE: 27 sts on larger size needles = 4 in (10 cm).
Adjust needle size to obtain correct gauge if necessary.

The onesie is primarily worked back and forth on a circular needle, from the top down.

With smaller size circular, CO 77 (77, 83, 89, 89, 93) sts. Work a total of 9 rows in k1, p1 ribbing (the first row = WS). On the 5th row, make buttonhole: rib 2 sts, k2tog, yo, rib to end of row.
Change to larger size needle.

Now begin charted pattern and raglan shaping. Before you begin knitting, read all through the next sections. Increases are made with M1 (see video at klompelompe.no/en/).

Begin pattern on Row 1 and increase for raglan as follows:

K5 (= garter st edge sts), k5 (5, 7, 8, 8, 8) (= left front), M1, 11 charted pattern sts (= marked sts, raglan), M1, k6 (6, 6, 7, 7, 7) (= left sleeve), M1, k1 (= marked st, raglan), M1, k21 (21, 23, 25, 25, 29) (= back), M1, k1 (= marked st, raglan), M1, k6 (6, 6, 7, 7, 7) (= right sleeve), M1, 11 charted pattern sts (= marked sts, raglan), M1, k5 (5, 7, 8, 8, 8) (= right front), k5 (= garter st edge sts) = 8 sts increased on row.

Continue, working charted pattern on the 11 pattern sts on each of the two raglan front sections. Increase for raglan shaping on every other row (= on all RS rows).

The rest of the sts are worked in stockinette (knit on RS and purl on WS) except for the edge sts which are knitted in garter st throughout.

When you've worked approx. 1¾ in (4.5 cm) from previous buttonhole, make another buttonhole: K1, k2tog, yo, k2. Make a total of 5 (6, 6, 8, 8, 9) buttonholes.

Work raglan increases a total of 16 (17, 19, 21, 23, 25) times.

Next Row (RS): Work to and including center st of pattern, place sleeve sts on a holder (including the last 5 pattern sts), CO 4 sts for underarm, work across back and the 2 raglan sts on back, place sleeve sts on a holder (including the first 5 pattern sts), CO 4 sts for underarm, work to end of row = 127 (131, 145, 157, 165, 177) sts rem for body.

Continue in stockinette with the 5-st garter front edges until onesie measures 10¾ (11¾, 13½, 14½, 15¾, 16½) in [27 (30, 34, 37, 40, 42) cm].

Overlap buttonhole band over button band and knit the sts together, joining 1 front st with 1 back st with k2tog. Now begin knitting in the round.

Knit 1 rnd.

Lengthen back with German short rows (see video at klompelompe.no/en/).

Pm on center back st so it will be the center st for the turns.

Knit to center back of onesie.

SIZES 0–1, 3, 6–9 MONTHS:
K25; turn and p50; turn. K55; turn and p60; turn. Knit to end of rnd,

SIZES 12, 18, 24 MONTHS:
K30; turn and p60; turn. K65; turn and p70; turn. Knit to end of rnd,

ALL SIZES:
Pm on each side of the center 5 sts on both front and back.

Increase 1 st on each side of the 5 marked sts. Increase on every 4th rnd a total of 4 (4, 4, 5, 5, 6) times.

Knit 1 rnd and *at the same time* BO the 5 marked sts at front and back = 64 (66, 73, 81, 85, 93) sts rem for each leg.

LEGS
Pm for beginning of round at center of inner leg. Knit around in stockinette.

After ¾ in (2 cm), decrease as follows:

K1, k2tog, knit until 3 sts before marker, sl 1, k1, psso, k1.

Decrease the same way every ¾ in (2 cm) a total of 5 (5, 6, 6, 7, 8) times. Continue around until leg measures 4¾ (6, 7½, 8¼, 9, 9¾) in [12 (15, 19, 21, 23, 25) cm]

Knit 1 rnd, adjusting stitch count to 40 (42, 44, 46, 48, 48) sts.

Change to smaller size needle and work around in k1, p1 ribbing for 1¼ (1½, 1½, 2, 2, 2) in [3 (4, 4, 5, 5, 5) cm. BO in ribbing. Make second leg the same way.

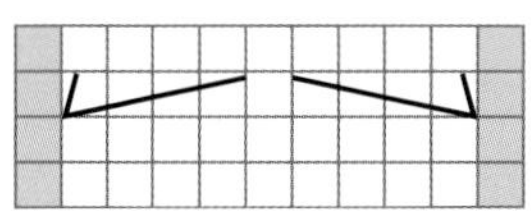

← Begin here

 = Place 3 sts on cable needle and hold in back of work. K1, k3 from cable needle.

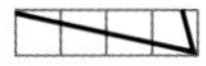 = Place 1 st on cable needle and hold in front of work. K3, k1 from cable needle.

☐ = knit on RS, purl on WS

■ = purl on RS, knit on WS

SLEEVES

With larger size needle, beginning at center of underarm, pick up and knit 2 sts along underarm, 1 st in gap between underarm and armhole, knit the held 43 (45, 49, 54, 58, 62) sleeve sts, pick up and knit 1 st in gap between armhole and underarm, and 2 sts along underarm = 49 (51, 55, 60, 64, 68) sts total. PM for beginning of rnd at center of underarm.

Knit around for ¾ in (2 cm) and then decrease 1 st before (sl 1, k1, psso) and 1 st after (k2tog) marker. Decrease the same way every ¾ in (2 cm) until 39 (39, 41, 42, 42, 42) sts rem. Continue without further decreasing until sleeve measures 4¾ (5½, 6¼, 7½, 8¼, 9½) in [12 (14, 16, 19, 21, 24) cm]. On smallest four sizes, decrease 1 st on last rnd. Change to smaller size needle.

Finish with 7 (7, 9, 9, 11, 11) rnds in k1, p1 ribbing. BO in ribbing on next rnd.

Make second sleeve the same way.

FINISHING

Weave in all ends neatly on WS. Sew buttons on, spaced as for buttonholes.

Block by laying onesie flat, patted out to finished measurements, on a damp towel until completely dry.

Texture-Fiesta Baby Sweater

A fun project you won't want to put down. Striking texture panels and fun techniques make this a great knitting experience.

SKILL LEVEL: 2

SIZES: 3 (6–9, 12, 24, 36 months)

FINISHED MEASUREMENTS
Chest: Approx. 21¾ (23¼, 25¼, 25¼, 27½) in [55 (59, 64, 64, 70) cm]
Length: Approx. 9½ (10¼, 11, 12¼, 12¾) in [24 (26, 28, 31, 32) cm]

YARN: Sandnes Garn Klompelompe Merinoull [CYCA #3 – DK/light worsted, 100% Merino wool, 114 yd (104 m) / 50 g]

YARN COLORS AND AMOUNTS
Color 2650: 150 (200, 200, 250, 300) g

NEEDLES: U.S. sizes 2.5 and 4 (3 and 3.5 mm): 16 and 24 in; or 32 in for magic loop (40 and 60 cm; 80 cm for magic loop) circulars; optional: cable needle

NOTIONS: 6 (6, 6, 8, 8, 9) buttons, ⅝ in (15 mm) in diameter

GAUGE: 22 sts on larger size needles = 4 in (10 cm).
Adjust needle size to obtain correct gauge if necessary.

The sweater begins at lower edge of front and is initially worked back and forth.

With smaller size circular, CO 70 (74, 78, 78, 86) sts. Work 8 rows in k2, p2 ribbing. Place sts on a holder and begin back.

With smaller size circular, CO 70 (74, 78, 78, 86) sts. Work 12 rows in k2, p2 ribbing.

Arrange front and back sts on same needle. Change to larger size needle and join to knit in the round; pm for beginning of rnd. Knit 1 rnd, adjusting stitch count to 121 (130, 140, 140, 154) sts.

Knit 1 rnd. The rnd now begins 2 sts before the side opening.

Begin with **Pattern A:**
Rnd 1: *P5 (4, 4, 4, 5), k1, p5*; rep *-* around.
Rnd 2: Knit around.
Rnd 3: *P5 (4, 4, 4, 5), k1, p5*; rep *-* around.
Rnd 4: # K2 (1, 1, 1, 2), *insert needle in at side of knit st 4 rnds below (2 ridges down). Pick up and knit a long st and slip it onto the left needle. K1 and pass the long st over*, k5; rep *-*, k2 #; rep #-# around.

Work Rnds 3–4 a total of 2 (3, 4, 4, 5) times.

Purl 2 rnds.
Decrease I st on 2nd rnd of smallest size.

Pattern B (Kjekka Pattern):
Rnd 1: *K1, p1*; rep *-* around.
Rnd 2: *K1, p1*; rep *-* around.
Rnd 3: Knit around.
Rnd 4: Purl around.

Work pattern B a total of 1 (2, 2, 2, 2) times.

Purl 1 rnd, adjusting stitch count to 120 (136, 144, 144, 152) sts.

Pattern C (Albert Pattern):
(See video for right cross (RC) and left cross (LC) at klompelompe.no/en/ and read explanations below.)

Note: On sizes 3 and 6–9 months, work only through Rnd 10.

EXPLANATION OF RC:
Option 1: Skip 1st st, but leave st on needle. Knit 2nd st on needle in front of 1st st. Purl 1st st.
Option 2: Place 1st st on cable needle and hold in back of work. Knit 2nd st (in front of st on cable needle). Purl st on cable needle.

EXPLANATION OF LC:
Option 1: Skip 1st st, but leave st on needle. Purl 2nd st on needle behind 1st st. Knit 1st st.
Option 2: Place 1st st on cable needle and hold in front of work. Purl 2nd st (in back of st on cable needle). Knit st on cable needle.

Rnd 1: *P3, k2, p3*; rep *-* around.
Rnd 2: *P3, sl 2, p3*; rep *-* around.
Rnd 3: *P3, k2, p3*; rep *-* around.
Rnd 4: *P3, sl 2, p3*; rep *-* around.
Rnd 5: *P2, RC, LC, p2*; rep *-* around.
Rnd 6: *P2, sl 1, p2, sl 1, p2*; rep *-* around.
Rnd 7: *P1, RC, p2, LC, p1*; rep *-* around.
Rnd 8: *P1, sl 1, p4, sl 1, p1*; rep *-* around.
Rnd 9: *RC, p4, LC*; rep *-* around.
Rnd 10: *Sl 1, p6, sl 1*; rep *-* around.
Rnd 11: *K1, p6, k1*; rep *-* around.
Rnd 12: *Sl 1, p6, sl 1*; rep *-* around.
Rnd 13: *K1, p6, k1*; rep *-* around.
Rnd 14: *Sl 1, p6, sl 1*; rep *-* around.
Rnd 15: *LC, p4, RC*; rep *-* around.
Rnd 16: *P1, sl 1, p4, sl 1, p1*; rep *-* around.
Rnd 17: *P1, LC, p2, RC, p1*; rep *-* around.
Rnd 18: *P2, sl 1, p2, sl 1, p2*; rep *-* around.
Rnd 19: *P2, LC, RC, p2*; rep *-* around.
Rnd 20: *P3, sl 2, p3*; rep *-* around.

Work the pattern a total of 0.5 (0.5, 1, 1, 1) time,
Purl 2 rnds.

Knit 2 rnds.

BOBBLE:
Work into same st: K1, yo, k1, yo, k1. Place the 5 sts back on left needle, k5, place 3 sts back on left needle, k3tog, slip the last 2 sts over = 1 st rem.

Next Rnd: *K3, bobble*; rep *-* around.
Knit 2 rnds.
Purl 2 rnds.
Knit 2 rnds.

STITCH NOTE: 1lk = long knit (also called a "dip stitch"): see *lang rett* video at klompelompe.no/en/. **K1lk =** Knit 1 in the space between the k2tog and k2tog tbl 2 rnds/rows below, lengthening new st to reach sts on needle as you place it on right needle. Work next k1lk into same hole.

Pattern D (Lillemor Pattern): See video on long knit stitch at klompelompe.no/en/.
Rnd 1: *K4, k2tog, k2tog tbl*; rep *-* around.
Rnd 2: Knit around.
Rnd 3: *K4, 1lk, k2, 1 lk*; rep *-* around.
Rnd 4: Knit around.
Rnd 5: *K2tog, k2tog tbl, k4*; rep *-* around.
Rnd 6: Knit around.
Rnd 7: *1lk, k2, 1lk, k4*; rep *-* around.
Rnd 8: Knit around.

1 repeat = 8 rnds / 2 lines of "flowers."

After working 0.5 (0.5, 0.5, 1, 1) rep of pattern D, and when next rnd is either Rnd 4 or 8, BO to shape underarms as follows:

BO 4 sts, k56 (64, 68, 68, 72), BO 4 sts, k56 (64, 68, 68, 72). Cut yarn. Work front yoke, beginning on RS.

FRONT

K2tog, k2, work pattern D until 4 sts rem, k2, sl 1, k1, psso.

Purl 1 row (including pattern as est).

Next Row: K2tog, k1, work in pattern until 3 sts rem, k1, sl 1, k1, psso.

Purl 1 row.

Continue in stockinette on 2 outermost sts at each side and pattern on rem sts. Work 4 rows in pattern.

Purl 1 row on RS.

Knit 1 row.

Pattern E (Pilot Pattern):

Row 1: P1, *k2, p2*; rep *-* until 3 sts rem, k2, p1.

Row 2: K1, *p2, k2*; rep *-* until 3 sts rem, k2, p1.

Row 3: Knit.

Row 4: Knit.

Work Rows 1–4 a total of 1 (1, 1, 2, 2) times.

On first row of next pattern, adjust stitch count to 51 (61, 63, 63, 68) sts.

P0 (0, 1, 1, 1), work following Littlest Ones pattern chart until 1 (1, 2, 2, 1) sts rem, p1 (1, 2, 2, 1).

The purl sts at each side continue as purl sts throughout.

On 5th row of charted pattern, divide front for neck:

Work 19 (23, 24, 24, 26) sts in pattern, place next 13 (15, 15, 15, 16) sts on a holder, work 19 (23, 24, 24, 26) sts in pattern.

RIGHT FRONT

Work 1 row in pattern on WS.

Next Row: K2tog, work pattern to end of row.

Work 1 row in pattern.

Next Row: K2tog, work pattern to end of row.

Continue in pattern, following chart.

The 5th (5th, 5th, 5th, 5th) time you cross the cables, work short rows as follows:

Work in pattern until 2 sts rem; turn and work to end of row.

Work in pattern until 3 sts before previous turn; turn and work to end of row.

Work in pattern until 4 sts before previous turn; turn and work to end of row.

Work 1 row in pattern and then purl 1 row, binding off at the same time.

LEFT FRONT

Work 1 row in pattern on WS.

Next Row: Work pattern until 2 sts rem, sl 1, k1, psso.

Work 1 row in pattern.

Next Row: Work pattern until 2 sts rem, sl 1, k1, psso.

Continue in pattern, following chart.

The 5th (5th, 5th, 5th, 5th) time you cross the cables, work short rows as follows:

Work in pattern to end of row. Purl until 2 sts rem; turn, work in pattern to end of row.

Work in pattern until 3 sts before previous turn; turn and work in pattern to end of row.

Work in pattern until 4 sts before previous turn; turn and work in pattern to end of row.

Work 1 row in pattern. BO purlwise on next row.

BACK

The first row is on RS.

K2tog, k2, work pattern D until 4 sts rem, k2, sl 1, k1, psso.

Purl 1 row (including pattern as est).

Littlest Ones Pattern Chart

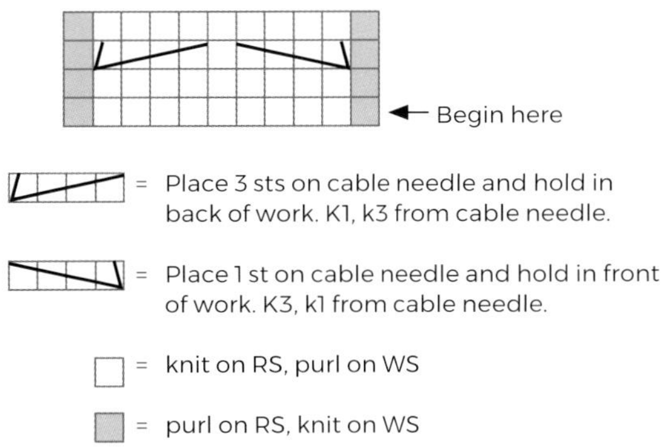

Next Row: K2tog, k1, work in pattern until 3 sts rem, k1, sl 1, k1, psso.

Purl 1 row.

Continue in stockinette on 2 outermost sts at each side and pattern on rem sts. Work 4 rows in pattern.

Purl 1 row on RS.

Knit 1 row.

Pattern E (Pilot Pattern):

Work Pilot Pattern Rows 1–4 a total of 1 (1, 1, 2, 2) times.

On first row of next pattern, adjust stitch count to 51 (61, 63, 63, 68) sts.

Work following Littlest Ones chart, keeping outermost sts st each side as purl sts The purl sts at each side continue as purl sts throughout.

The 5th (5th, 5th, 5th, 5th) time you cross the cables, divide back for shoulders (work the first 18 (22, 23, 23, 25) sts and place rem sts on a holder.

Work 18 (22, 23, 23, 25) sts in pattern; turn and p2tog. Work in pattern until 2 sts rem; turn and work to end of row; turn.

Work in pattern until 3 sts before previous turn; turn and work to end of row.

Work in pattern until 4 sts before previous turn; turn and work to end of row.

Work 1 row in pattern on WS, binding off at the same time.

LEFT SHOULDER

Leave the center 15 (17, 17, 17, 18) sts on holder and work rem 18 (22, 23, 23, 25) sts separately.

RIGHT SIDE:

K2tog, work in pattern until 2 sts rem; turn and work to end of row.

Work in pattern until 3 sts before previous turn; turn and work to end of row.

Work in pattern until 4 sts before previous turn; turn and work to end of row.

Work 1 row in pattern.

Next Row (WS): BO in pattern.

NECKBAND

With smaller size needle, beginning on the held 15 (17, 17, 17, 18) sts on back, k8 (8, 8, 8, 9), pick up and knit 20 (20, 20, 22, 21) sts, knit the 13 (15, 15, 15, 16) held front sts, pick up and knit 20 (20, 20, 22, 21) sts, k7 (9, 9, 9, 9). Join to work in the round.

Work 7 rnds in k2, p2 ribbing.

Work 6 rnds in k1, p1 ribbing. BO in ribbing on next rnd.

Fold edge to WS and sew down securely. Seam shoulders.

SLEEVES

With larger size needle, pick up and knit 54 (54, 54, 60, 60) sts around armhole. Pm for beginning of rnd at center of underarm.

Work Pattern B (Kjekka Pattern) a total of 1 (2, 2, 2, 2) times.

Next Rnd: P1, k2tog, purl until 3 sts rem, p2tog, p1.

Pattern C (Albert Pattern):

SIZE 12 MONTHS: Work only a half pattern.

Begin and end with p2 (2, 2, 1, 1).

ALL SIZES EXCEPT 3, 6–9, AND 12 MONTHS:

At the center of the pattern, p2tog, work in pattern until 2 sts rem, p2tog.

Work pattern a total of 0.5 (0.5, 1, 1, 1) times.

Purl 1 rnd.

Next Row: P1, p2tog, purl until 3 sts rem, p2tog, p1 = 50 (50, 50, 54, 54 sts rem.

Knit 2 rnds.

Next Row: *K3, bobble*; rep *-* until 2 sts rem, k2.

Knit 2 rnds.

Purl 1 rnd.

Next Rnd: P1, p2tog, purl until 3 sts rem, p2tog, p1.

Knit 1 rnd.

Pattern D (Lillemor Pattern):

After a complete pattern (2 lines of “flowers), decrease as follows:

K1, k2tog, k1, work in pattern until 4 sts rem, k1, k2tog, k1.

Keep first 3 and last 3 sts as knit sts.

Decrease as above after every complete pattern.

Continue in pattern until sleeve measures 5¼ (6, 7, 8¾, 9½) in [13 (15, 18, 22, 24) cm].

Knit 1 rnd, adjusting stitch count to 36 (40, 40, 44, 44) sts. Change to smaller size needle and work 23 rnds in k2, p 2 ribbing. BO in ribbing.

FINISHING

Weave in all ends neatly on WS.

Block by dampening sweater and laying it flat, patted out to finished measurements, on towel until completely dry.

Texture-Fiesta Baby Blanket

A nice large blanket, full of beautiful textures.

SKILL LEVEL: 2

FINISHED MEASUREMENTS
Approx. 41 x 47¼ in (104 x 120 cm)

YARN: Sandnes Garn Klompelompe Merinoull [CYCA #3 – DK/light worsted, 100% Merino wool, 114 yd (104 m) / 50 g]

YARN COLORS AND AMOUNTS
Color 9871: 700 g

NEEDLES: U.S. size 6 (4 mm): 32 in (80 cm) circular; optional cable needle

GAUGE: 20 sts on gauge-size needle = 4 in (10 cm).
Adjust needle size to obtain correct gauge if necessary.

With gauge-size circular, CO 207 sts.
Work 20 rows in seed st:
Row 1: (K1, p1) across.
Row 2 and all following rows: Work purl over knit and knit over purl.
For remainder of blanket, keep the 10 sts at each side in seed st and work rem 187 sts between edges in pattern.

Pattern A: See video at klompelompe.no/en/.
Row 1 (WS): *K5, p1, k5*; rep *-* in pattern section.
Row 2: Knit across pattern section.
Row 3: *K5, p1, k5*; rep *-* in pattern section.
Row 4: # K2, *insert needle at side of the knit st 4 rows (= 2 ridges) below st on needle, bring yarn through and make a long knit st and place it on right needle. K1 and slip long st over*, k5; rep *-*, k2 #. Rep #-# across pattern area.

Rep Rows 3–4 a total of 7 times.

Knit 1 row on WS.

Kjekka Pattern:
Row 1 (RS): *K1, p1*; rep *-* across pattern section.
Row 2: *K1, p1*; rep *-* across pattern section.
Row 3: Knit across pattern section.
Row 4: Knit across pattern section.

Work pattern 3 times.

Knit 1 row on WS, decreasing 1 st in pattern section.

Pattern C (Albert Pattern):
Note: If you are slipping 1 st in pattern when you are on WS, the yarn must lie on WS of work.
See video for right cross (RC) and left cross (LCF) at klompelompe.no/en/ and read explanations below.
Begin on RS (pattern is repeated to specified length).

EXPLANATION OF RC:
Option 1: Skip 1st st, but leave st on needle. Knit 2nd st on needle in front of 1st st. Purl 1st st.
Option 2: Place 1st st on cable needle and hold in back of work. Knit 2nd st (in front of st on cable needle). Purl st on cable needle.

EXPLANATION OF LC:
Option 1: Skip 1st st, but leave st on needle. Purl 2nd st on needle behind 1st st. Knit 1st st.
Option 2: Place 1st st on cable needle and hold in front of work. Purl 2nd st (in back of st on cable needle). Knit st on cable needle.

Row 1: P1, *p3, k2, p3*; rep *-* until 1 st rem, p1.
Row 2: K1, *k3, sl 2, k3*; rep *-* until 1 st rem, k1.
Row 3: P1, *p3, k2, p3*; rep *-* until 1 st rem, p1.
Row 4: K1, *k3, sl 2, k3*; rep *-* until 1 st rem, k1.
Row 5: P1, *p2, RC, LC, p2*; rep *-* until 1 st rem, p1.
Row 6: K1, *k2, sl 1, k2, sl 1, k2*; rep *-* until 1 st rem, k1.
Row 7: P1, *p1, RC, p2, LC, p1*; rep *-* until 1 st rem, p1.
Row 8: K1, *k1, sl 1, k4, sl 1, k1*; rep *-* until 1 st rem, k1.
Row 9: P1, *RC, p4, LC*; rep *-* until 1 st rem, p1.

Row 10: K1, *sl 1, k6, sl 1*; rep *-* until 1 st rem, k1.
Row 11: P1, *k1, p6, k1*; rep *-* until 1 st rem, p1.
Row 12: K1, *sl 1, k6, sl 1*; rep *-* until 1 st rem, k1.
Row 13: P1, *k1, p6, k1*; rep *-* until 1 st rem, p1.
Row 14: K1, *sl 1, k6, sl 1*; rep *-* until 1 st rem, k1.
Row 15: P1, *LC, p4, RC*; rep *-* until 1 st rem, p1.
Rnd 16: K1, *k1, sl 1, k4, sl 1, k1*; rep *-* until 1 st rem, k1.
Row 17: P1, *p1, LC, p2, RC, p1*; rep *-* until 1 st rem, p1.
Row 18: K1, *k2, sl 1, k2, sl 1, k2*; rep *-* until 1 st rem, k1.
Row 19: P1, *P2, LC, RC, p2*; rep *-* until 1 st rem, p1.
Row 20: K1, *k3, sl 2, k3*; rep *-* until 1 st rem, k1.

Work the Albert pattern a total of 2 times.

Purl 1 row on RS, knit 1 row on WS.
Work 2 rows in stockinette.

BOBBLE: Work into same st: K1, yo, k1, yo, k1. Place the 5 sts back on left needle, k5, place 3 sts back on left needle, k3tog, slip the last 2 sts over = 1 st rem.

Next Row: K1, *k3, bobble*; rep *-* until 1 st rem in pattern section, k1.

Work 2 rows in stockinette.
Knit 1 row on WS. Purl 1 row on RS.
Purl 1 row on WS.

STITCH NOTES: lk = long knit (also called a "dip stitch"); see video on long knit stitch at klompelompe.no/en/. **K1lk** = Knit 1 in the space between the k2tog and k2tog tbl 2 rnds/rows below, lengthening new st to reach sts on needle as you place it on right needle. Work next k1lk into same hole.

Pattern D (Lillemor Pattern): See video on long knit stitch at klompelompe.no/en/.
Row 1: K1, *k4, k2tog, k2tog tbl*; rep *-* until 1 st rem in pattern section, k1.
Row 2: Purl across pattern section.
Row 3: K1, *k4, 1lk, k2, 1 lk*; rep *-* until 1 st rem in pattern section, k1.
Row 4: Purl across pattern section.
Row 5: K1, *k2tog, k2tog tbl, k4*; rep *-* until 1 st rem in pattern section, k1.
Row 6: Purl across pattern section.
Row 7: K1, *1lk, k2, 1lk, k4*; rep *-* until 1 st rem in pattern section, k1.
Row 8: Purl across pattern section.

Work Pattern D a total of 5 times.

Purl 1 row on RS, knit 1 row on WS.

Pattern E (Pilot Pattern):
Row 1: P1, *k2, p2*; rep *-* until 1 st rem in pattern section, p1.
Row 2: K1, *p2, k2*; rep *-* until 1 st rem in pattern section, k1.
Row 3: Knit across pattern section.
Row 4: Knit across pattern section.

Work Rows 1–4 a total of 2 times.

Purl 1 row on RS, knit 1 row on WS, increasing 1 st in pattern section.

Work following Littlest One charted pattern. Work charted rows a total of 8 times.

Purl 1 row on RS, knit 1 row on WS, decreasing 1 st in pattern section.

Pattern E (Pilot Pattern):
Row 1: P1, *k2, p2*; rep *-* until 1 st rem in pattern section, p1.
Row 2: K1, *p2, k2*; rep *-* until 1 st rem in pattern section, k1.
Row 3: Knit across pattern section.
Row 4: Knit across pattern section.

Work Rows 1–4 a total of 2 times.

Purl 1 row on RW, knit 1 row on WS.

Pattern D (Lillemor Pattern):
Row 1: K1, *k4, k2tog, k2tog tbl*; rep *-* until 1 st rem in pattern section, k1.
Row 2: Purl across pattern section.
Row 3: K1, *k4, 1lk, k2, 1 lk*; rep *-* until 1 st rem in pattern section, k1.
Row 4: Purl across pattern section.
Row 5: K1, *k2tog, k2tog tbl, k4*; rep *-* until 1 st rem in pattern section, k1.
Row 6: Purl across pattern section.
Row 7: K1, *1lk, k2, 1lk, k4*; rep *-* until 1 st rem in pattern section, k1.
Row 8: Purl across pattern section.

Work Pattern D a total of 5 times.

Purl 1 row on RS, knit 1 row on WS.
Work 2 rows in stockinette.

Next Row: K1, *k3, bobble*; rep *-* until 1 st rem in pattern section, k1.

Work 2 rows in stockinette.
Knit 1 row on WS. Purl 1 row on RS.
Purl 1 row on WS.

Work Albert Pattern 2 times.

Knit 1 row on WS.

Kjekka Pattern:
Row 1 (RS): *K1, p1*; rep *-* across pattern section.
Row 2: *K1, p1*; rep *-* across pattern section.
Row 3: Knit across pattern section.
Row 4: Knit across pattern section.

Work Kjekka pattern a total of 3 times, and increase 1 st on last row.

Pattern A:
Row 1 (WS): *K5, p1, k5*; rep *-* in pattern section.
Row 2: Knit across pattern section.
Row 3: *K5, p1, k5*; rep *-* in pattern section.
Row 4: # K2, *insert needle at side of the knit st 4 rows (= 2 ridges) below st on needle, bring yarn through and make a long knit st and place it on right needle. K1 and slip long st over*, k5; rep *-*, k2 #. Rep #-# across pattern area.

Rep Rows 3–4 a total of 7 times.

Work 19 rows seed stitch.
BO in seed st.

FINISHING
Weave in all ends neatly on WS.
Dampen blanket and lay it flat on a damp towel, patted out to finished measurements, until completely dry.

Littlest Ones Pattern Chart

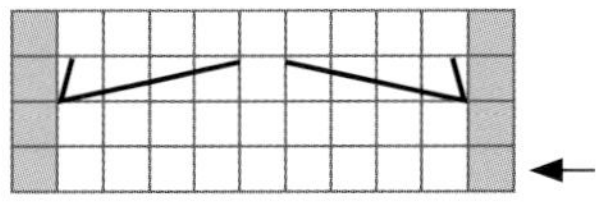

Begin here

 = Place 3 sts on cable needle and hold in back of work. K1, k3 from cable needle.

 = Place 1 st on cable needle and hold in front of work. K3, k1 from cable needle.

 = knit on RS, purl on WS

 = purl on RS, knit on WSn

Littlest Ones Pixie Cap

We used the Littlest Ones pattern for our sweet pixie cap, which fits comfortably and looks adorable.

SKILL LEVEL: 2

SIZES: preemie (1–3, 3–6, 6–9 months, 1–2, 3–4 years)

YARN: Sandnes Garn Klompelompe Merinoull [CYCA #3 – DK/light worsted, 100% Merino wool, 114 yd (104 m) / 50 g]

YARN COLORS AND AMOUNTS
Color 4344: 50 (50, 50, 100, 100, 100) g

NEEDLES: U.S. sizes 2.5 and 4 (3 and 3.5 mm): 16 and 32 in (40 and 80 cm) circulars; cable needle

GAUGE: 22 sts on larger size needle = 4 in (10 cm).
Adjust needle size to obtain correct gauge if necessary.

With smaller size circular, CO 65 (71, 77, 83, 83, 89) sts. Work 4 rows back and forth in k1, p1 ribbing.
Change to larger size needle. Work 1 row in pattern increasing 6 (6, 4, 5, 5, 2) sts evenly spaced across = 71 (77, 81, 88, 88, 91) sts.

Now work following charted pattern.

When cap measures 4¾ (5¼, 5½, 6, 6¼, 6¾) in [12 (13, 14, 15, 16, 17) cm], lengthen it with German short rows (see video at klompelompe.no/en/).

Work in pattern until 11 sts rem; turn and work in pattern until 11 sts rem; turn. Work in pattern until 5 sts before previous turn; turn and work in pattern until 5 sts before previous turn; turn.

SIZES 6–9 MONTHS, 1–2, AND 3–4 YEARS: Work in pattern until 5 sts before previous turn; turn and work in pattern until 5 sts before previous turn; turn.

Pattern for Littlest Ones Pixie Cap and Chunky Snuggly Travel Bag

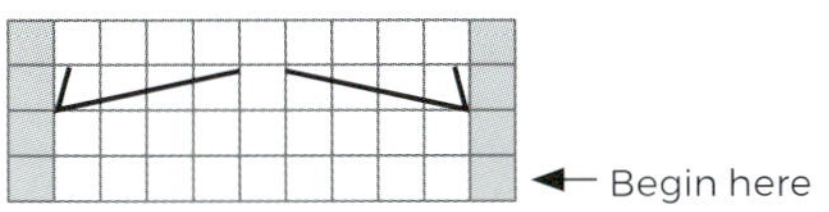

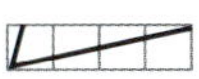 = Place 3 sts on cable needle and hold in back of work. K1, k3 from cable needle.

 = Place 1 st on cable needle and hold in front of work. K3, k1 from cable needle.

 = knit on RS

 = purl on WS

ALL SIZES: Work in pattern to end of row.

Fold cap with RS facing RS. Using a third needle, work 3-needle BO: Insert needle knitwise into 2 sts—the first st on each needle—and knit them together. *K2tog with next pair of sts, pass first worked st on right needle over second*; rep * to * until all sts have been bound off.

With smaller size needle, pick up and knit 37 (39, 43, 45, 47, 49) sts along neck for neckband. Work 4 (4, 4, 6, 6, 6) rows in k1, p1 ribbing. BO in ribbing on last row, but, leave the outermost 4 sts at each side for the I-cords.

I-CORDS

With each set of 4 sts, knit an I-cord (see video at klompelompe.no/en/) approx. 6¾ (6¾, 7, 7, 8, 8) in [17 (17, 18, 18, 20, 20) cm] long.

FINISHING

Weave in all ends neatly on WS.

Block by laying cap between two damp towels until completely dry.

Chunky Snuggly Travel Bag

A smart choice for your baby to wear while in the car seat on cold days.

SKILL LEVEL: 2

SIZES: 0–6 (9–18 months)

FINISHED MEASUREMENTS
Chest: Approx. 22½ (25¼) in [57 (64) cm]
Length: Approx 24¾ (28¼) in [63 (72) cm]

YARN: Sandnes Garn Kos [CYCA #5 – bulky, 62% alpaca, 29% polyamide, 9% wool, 164 yd (150 m) / 50 g]

YARN COLORS AND AMOUNTS
Color 4032 or 1012: 200 (200) g

NEEDLES: U.S. sizes 4 and 8 (3.5 mm and 5): 24 and 32 in (60 and 80 cm) circulars; cable needle

NOTIONS: 7 (8) buttons, ⅝ in (15 mm) in diameter

GAUGE: 16 sts on larger size needle = 4 in (10 cm). Adjust needle size to obtain correct gauge if necessary.

The bag is worked from the top down, primarily back and forth on a circular needle.

With larger size circular, CO 41 (45) sts. Change to smaller size needle and work 10 (12) rows in k1, p1 ribbing. Change to larger size needle. Knit 1 row and *at the same time* join every other st with corresponding cast-on st with k2tog. If you think this is too difficult, later on, you can fold the edge down and sew it down. Purl 1 row and *at the same time* increase 8 sts evenly spaced across.

Pm without knitting row: 4 (5) sts, pm, 11 sts (pattern sts), pm, k1, pm, k1 (raglan st, back), pm, 15 (17) sts (back), pm, k1 (raglan st, back), pm, k1, 11 sts (pattern sts), pm, 4 (5) sts.

Begin working pattern following chart on page 113 over the pattern sts and raglan increases. The increases are made with M1. Increase on each side of the 11 pattern sts and on each side of the back raglan sts = 8 sts increases per row.

Continue in pattern over the 11 pattern st sections on each side of the two raglan panels on the front. Increase for the raglan shaping on every other row (= on every RS row). The rest of the sts are worked in stockinette (= knit on RS and purl on WS).

The 2nd time you increase, lengthen back neck with German short rows (see video at klompelompe.no/en/):

Work, including raglan increases until 1 st before 2nd pattern section; turn and purl until 1 st before 2nd pattern section; turn. Knit, including raglan increases, to end of row.

Continue with raglan increases every time you are on a RS row until you've increased a total of 13 (15) times on the front = 149 (169) sts.

Next Row:
Work to and including center pattern st, place next pattern st and sleeve sts on a holder, CO 5 sts for underarm, knit raglan st, back, and next raglan st, place sleeve sts and first 5 pattern sts on a holder, CO 5 sts for underarm, work rem sts = 91 (103) sts rem.

Work back and forth, still including the pattern sts. The st which was previously the center st in the pattern will now be purled throughout.

Continue until piece measures 13 (15½) in [33 (39) cm].

CO 3 sts and begin knitting in the round.

Knit 4 in (10 cm) in stockinette and pattern as est. On next rnd, BO 9 sts each at center front and back. CO 9 sts over gap on following rnd.

Continue around in stockinette and pattern for 8 (9) in [20 (23) cm].

BO on next rnd. Seam bottom opening.

SLEEVES
With larger size needle, beginning at center of underarm, pick up and knit 3 sts along underarm, 1 st in gap between underarm and armhole, knit the 33 (37) held sleeve sts (including pattern sts in pattern section), pick up and knit 1 st in gap between armhole and underarm, and 2 sts along underarm; pm for beginning of rnd = 40 (44) sts for sleeve.

The st that was next to the pattern section at the body is now purled down the sleeve.

The first st is a marked st (at center of underarm) and purled throughout.

Work as est until sleeve measures 1½ in (3.5 cm), and then begin sleeve shaping as follows: P1, k2tog, work as est until 2 sts rem, sl 1, k1, psso.

Decrease the same way every 1½ in (4 cm) a total of 4 (5) times. Continue without further shaping until sleeve measures 6¼ (8¼) in [16 (21) cm]. When decreases hit the pattern section, decrease on the other side of the pattern.

Knit 1 rnd, adjusting stitch count to 26 (26) sts.

Change to smaller size needle and work 23 rnds in k1, p1 ribbing. BO in ribbing on next rnd.

Make second sleeve the same way.

FRONT BANDS
With smaller size needle, pick up and knit 3 sts for every 4 rows/sts. Also pick up and knit sts in neck ribbing. Work 6 rows k1, p1 ribbing.

Note: On left side, make 7 (8) buttonholes evenly spaced on 2nd row: k2tog, yo for each buttonhole.

BO in ribbing.

FINISHING
Weave in all ends neatly on WS. Sew buttons on, spaced as for buttonholes.

Dampen bag and lay it flat on a damp towel, patted out to finished measurements, until completely dry.

Striped Layette Set

Little Brother Striped Cardigan

A simple, useful jacket, perfect for any brother's *or* sister's layette set.

SKILL LEVEL: 2

SIZES: 0–1 (3, 6–12, 18–24 months)

FINISHED MEASUREMENTS
Chest: Approx. 16½ (19, 21¼, 23¾) in [42 (48, 54, 60) cm]
Total Length: Approx. 9 (11¼, 13, 15¾) in [23 (28.5, 33, 40) cm]

YARN: Sandnes Garn Klompelompe Tynn Merinoull [CYCA #1 – fingering, 100% fine Merino wool, 191 yd (175 m) / 50 g]

YARN COLORS AND AMOUNTS
Color A, 2560: 100 (100, 150, 150) g
Color B, 9871: 50 (50, 50, 50) g

NEEDLES: U.S. sizes 1.5 and 2.5 (2.5 and 3 mm): 16 and 32 in (40 and 80 cm) circulars

NOTIONS: 8 (8, 8, 9) buttons, ⅝ in (15 mm) in diameter

GAUGE: 27 sts on larger size needle = 4 in (10 cm). Adjust needle size to obtain correct gauge if necessary.

The sweater is worked back and forth on a circular needle, from the bottom up.

With larger size circular and color A, CO 116 (145, 157, 171) sts. Work 3 rows back and forth in stockinette.

Next Row (WS): Purl until 5 sts rem, BO 2 sts, k3. On next row, CO 2 sts over gap (= first buttonhole on facing).

Work 8 rows in stockinette.

Next Row (RS): Make another buttonhole: K3, BO 2 sts, knit to end of row.

On next row, CO 2 sts over gap (= first buttonhole on front band).

Work a total of 18 rows in stockinette.

Next Row: Knit 1 row and a*t the same time* join every other st with k2tog to a corresponding st on cast-on row. At end of row, CO 6 sts (facing).

Purl 1 row and CO 6 sts at end of row.

Work 2 rows in stockinette.

Make a total of 8 (8, 8, 9) buttonholes, spaced about 1¼ (1⅜, 1½, 2) in [3 (3.5, 4, 5) cm] apart, working each buttonhole as follows:

(**RS**): K2, BO 2 sts, k5, BO 2 sts, knit to end of row. On next row, CO 2 sts each gap.

Change to color B and work 4 rows in stockinette.
Change to color A and work 6 rows in stockinette.
Change to color B and work 4 rows in stockinette.
Change to color A and work 6 rows in stockinette.
Change to color B and work 4 rows in stockinette.
Change to color A and continue in stockinette.

When piece measures 5½ (7, 8¼, 10¼) in [14 (18, 21, 26) cm], BO as follows:

K13 (edge sts), pm, k48 (62, 69, 76), BO 4 sts, knit until 17 sts rem, BO 4 sts, k13 (edge sts).

SLEEVES

With smaller size needle and color A, CO 40 (40, 42, 42) sts. Join to work in the round pm for beginning of rnd. Knit 8 rnds.

Change to larger size needle and knit 8 rnds. Fold piece in half and knit 1 rnd, joining every other st with k2tog to a corresponding st on cast-on row. If you think this is too difficult, you can later fold the facing in and sew it down.

Knit 1 rnd.

Change to color B and knit 4 rnds.

When you have ⅜ in (1 cm) in stockinette, begin increasing to shape sleeve.

P1, M1, knit to end of rnd, M1. Increase the same way about every ¾ in (2 cm) until there are 46 (52, 60, 62) sts.

Change to color A and knit 6 rnds.
Change to color B and knit 4 rnds.
Change to color A and knit 6 rnds.
Change to color B and knit 4 rnds.
Change to color A and knit around until sleeve measures 5½ (6¼, 8, 9¾) in 14 (16, 20, 25) cm. BO 4 sts at center of underarm.

Make a second sleeve the same way.

Arrange sleeves on larger size needle with body, matching underarms = 204 (245, 273, 291) sts total.

The first row is on WS. Pm at each intersection of sleeve and body = 4 stitch markers.

On every RS row: decrease as follows:

K12, sl 1, k1, psso, knit as est until 4 sts before marker.

K2tog, k4, sl 1, k1, psso, knit until 4 sts before marker; rep *-* 2 more times, knit until 14 sts rem, k2tog, k12.

The button band will curve in for the rest of the work.

Repeat the decreases on every RS row.

Decrease a total of 12 (16, 19, 21) times = 108 (117, 121, 123) sts rem.

Next Row (RS): K12, sl 1, k1, psso, k3; turn and purl to end of row.

K12, sl 1, k, psso, k1; turn and purl to end of row.

K12, sl 1, k1, psso, knit to end of row decreasing as est.

Purl until 9 sts in on front (count from center of raglan); turn and knit with raglan decreases to end of row.

Purl to st before previous turn; turn and knit with raglan decreases to end of row.

Change to smaller size needle, BO first 6 sts, knit to end of row.

Next Row: BO first 6 sts, knit to end of row.

Knit 7 rows. BO knitwise on next row.

Note: The last buttonhole is on the 3rd row of garter st ridges.

FINISHING

Seam underarms. Weave in all ends neatly on WS. Sew buttons on, spaced as for buttonholes.

Block by laying sweater flat, patted out to finished measurements on a between damp towel until completely dry or gently steam press sweater under a damp pressing cloth.

Little Brother Striped Pants

Simple thin baby pants featuring fine details, such as the contrast color for the facing and pleats at the sides.

SKILL LEVEL: 2

SIZES: preemie (0–1, 3–6, 9–12, 18–24 months)

FINISHED MEASUREMENTS
Waist: Approx. 13¾ (14½, 16½, 17¾, 19) in [35 (37, 42, 45, 48) cm]
Total Length: Approx. 9¾ (11, 14¼, 16½, 18½) in [25 (28, 36, 42, 47) cm]

YARN: Sandnes Garn Klompelompe Tynn Merinoull [CYCA #1 – fingering, 100% fine Merino wool, 191 yd (175 m) / 50 g]

YARN COLORS AND AMOUNTS
Color A, 9871: 100 (100, 100, 100, 150) g
Color B, 2650: 50 (50, 50, 50, 50) g

NEEDLES: U.S. sizes 1.5 and 2.5 (2.5 and 3 mm): 16 and 32 in (40 and 80 cm) circulars

GAUGE: 27 sts on larger size needle = 4 in (10 cm).

Adjust needle size to obtain correct gauge if necessary.

The pants begin at the waist and are worked in the round on a circular needle.

With smaller size circular and color A, CO 94 (100, 114, 122, 130) sts. Join, being careful not to twist cast-on row; pm for beginning of rnd. Work 14 rnds in k1, p1 ribbing.

Change to larger size needle and knit 1 rnd.

Knit 1 rnd, adjusting stitch count to 108 (114, 128, 136, 144) sts by increasing 14 (14, 14, 14, 14) sts evenly spaced around.

Knit 1 rnd.

Raise back with German short rows (see video at klompelompe.no/en/) as follows:

K20; turn and p40; turn. K43; turn and p46; turn. K49; turn and p52; turn.

SIZES 9–12 AND 18–24 MONTHS:
K55; turn and p58; turn. K61; turn and p64; turn.

ALL SIZES: Knit around.

Continue knitting around until piece measures 4¼ (4¾, 5½, 6¼, 7) in [11 (12, 14, 16, 18) cm down center front.

Pm on each side of the center 6 sts on both front and back.

Increase 1 st on each side of the front and back marked 6 sts.

Increase the same way on every 3rd row a total of 5 times.

Next Rnd: BO the 6 center front and back sts = 58 (61, 68, 72, 76) sts for each leg.

LEGS: Knit around in stockinette until leg measures 1 in (2.5 cm) and then decrease as follows:

K1, k2tog, knit until 3 sts rem, sl 1, k1, psso, k1.

Decrease the same way every 1 in (2.5 cm) a total of 3 (4, 4, 5, 5) times .

Continue knitting around until leg measures 4 (4¾, 7, 8¼, 9½) in [10 (12, 18, 21, 24) cm].

Knit 1 rnd, adjusting stitch count to 36 (36, 40, 44, 44) sts. Change to smaller size needle.

Work 8 (8, 8, 10, 10) rnds in k1, p1 ribbing. Change to color B. Knit 1 rnd. Work 7 (7, 7, 9, 9) rnds in k1, p1 ribbing. BO in ribbing on next rnd. Fold edge in and loosely sew down on WS.

Make second leg the same way.

SIDE SEAM/LEG PLEAT: Fold pants and sew a seam inside the 3 outermost sts on each side.

FINISHING: Weave in all ends neatly on WS. Block by laying pants flat, patted out to finished measurements, on a damp towel until completely dry.

Striped Tennis Socks

Small and sweet, these baby socks are inspired by traditional tennis socks.

SKILL LEVEL: 2

SIZES: 0–1 (3, 6, 9–12, 18–24 months, 2–3 years)

YARN: Sandnes Garn Klompelompe Tynn Merinoull [CYCA #1 – fingering, 100% fine Merino wool, 191 yd (175 m) / 50 g]

YARN COLORS AND AMOUNTS
Color A, 9871: 50 (50, 50, 50, 50, 50) g
Color B, 1013: small amount

NEEDLES: U.S. sizes 1.5 and 2.5 (2.5 and 3 mm): 32 in (80 cm) circulars

GAUGE: 27 sts on larger size needle = 4 in (10 cm).
Adjust needle size to obtain correct gauge if necessary.

The socks are worked cuff down.
We recommend knitting with the magic loop method (see video at klompelompe.no/en/). If you prefer, you can knit both socks at the same time on the circular.

Note: Each time you change colors, begin the new color with knit 1 rnd instead of ribbing.

With larger size circular and color A, CO 36 (40, 40, 44, 48, 48) sts. Change to smaller size needle.
Join and work 7 (7, 7, 7, 9, 9) rnds in k2, p2 ribbing.
Change to color B and knit 1 rnd (for a straight line around).
Work 2 rnds in ribbing.
Change to color A and knit 1 rnd.

Work 1 rnd in ribbing.

Change to color B and knit 1 rnd.

Work 1 rnd in ribbing.

Change to color A and knit 1 rnd.

Work 8 (10, 12, 12, 14, 14) rnds in ribbing.

Change to larger size needle.

Knit 1 rnd.

Knit 1 rnd, decreasing 6 (10, 6, 10, 10, 6) sts evenly spaced around.

HEEL

Work heel with German short rows (see video at klompelompe.no/en/):

Knit until 6 (6, 8, 8, 10, 10) sts rem; turn. Purl until 6 (6, 8, 8, 10, 10) sts rem; turn.

Continue turning until 1 st before previous turn until there are 8 sts between turns.

Knit around.

Knit until 10 (10, 12, 12, 14, 16) sts rem; turn. Purl until 10 (10, 12, 12, 14, 16) sts rem; turn.

Continue turning until 1 st after previous turn until there are 4 (4, 6, 6, 8, 8) sts. Knit to end of rnd.

Knit 11 (13, 15, 19, 23, 27) rnds.

SHAPE TOE:

SIZE 2–3 YEARS:

K8, k2tog, k1, k2tog tbl, k8; rep *-*.

Knit 1 rnd.

SIZES 18–24 MONTHS AND 2–3 YEARS:

K7, k2tog, k1, k2tog tbl, k7; rep *-*.

SIZES 6, 9–12, 18–24 MONTHS AND 2–3 YEARS:

K6, k2tog, k1, k2tog tbl, k6; rep *-*.

ALL SIZES:

K5, k2tog, k1, k2tog tbl, k5; rep *-*.
K4, k2tog, k1, k2tog tbl, k4; rep *-*.
K3, k2tog, k1, k2tog tbl, k3; rep *-*.
K2, k2tog, k1, k2tog tbl, k2; rep *-*.
K1, k2tog, k1, k2tog tbl, k1; rep *-*.

Cut yarn and draw end through rem sts; tighten.

Make second sock the same way.

FINISHING

Weave in all ends neatly on WS.

Block by laying socks between two damp towels until completely dry.

Striped Hipster Cap

A simple cap with a distinct look. The doubled brim makes this cap especially good and warm for the ears.

SKILL LEVEL: 2

SIZES: 3 (6–9 months, 1–3, 3–6 years)

YARN: Sandnes Garn Klompelompe Merinoull [CYCA #3 – DK/light worsted, 100% Merino wool, 114 yd (104 m) / 50 g]
+ Sandnes Garn Klompelompe Tynn Merinoull [CYCA #1 – fingering, 100% fine Merino wool, 191 yd (175 m) / 50 g]

YARN COLORS AND AMOUNTS

Merinoull, Color A, 6061: 50 (50, 50, 50, 50) g
Merinoull, Color B, 1013: 50 (50, 50, 50, 50) g or small leftover amount
Tynn Merinoull, 1013: 50 (50, 50, 50, 50) g

NEEDLES: U.S. sizes 2.5 and 4 (35 and 3.5 mm): 16 and 32 in (40 and 80 cm) circulars

GAUGE: 27 sts on smaller size needle = 4 in (10 cm). 22 sts on larger size needle = 4 in (10 cm).

Adjust needle size to obtain correct gauge if necessary.

The cap is knitted in the round on a circular needle.

With smaller size circular and Klompelompe Tynn Merinoull, CO 90 (98, 98, 108) sts.

Join, being careful not to twist cast-on row; pm for beginning of rnd. Knit around until cap measures 5 (5¼, 5½, 6) in [12.5 (13, 14, 15) cm.] Fold cast-on edge in and join every other live st with corrresponding cast-on st on next rnd. If you think this is too difficult, you can sew down edge when finishing. Knit 4 rnds.

Turn cap inside out so the WS is now the RS.

Change to larger size needle and Klompelompe Merinoull, color A. Knit 1 rnd adjusting stitch count to 72 (80, 80, 88) sts by decreasing 18 (18, 18, 20) sts evenly spaced around.

Tip: For a smooth transition between color rounds, change color, knit 1 round. On next round, slip first stitch.

Knit around until cap measures 2¾ (3, 3⅛, 3¼) in [7 (7.5, 8, 8.5) cm] from rnd where you attached cast-on edge. Change to color B and knit around for 1¼ in (3 cm). Change to color A and knit around until cap measures 4 (4¼, 5¼, 6) in [10 (11, 13, 15) cm] from round where you turned work.

SHAPE CROWN:

Decrease Rnd 1: *K6, k2tog*; rep *-* around. Knit 4 rnds.

Decrease Rnd 2: *K5, k2tog*; rep *-* around. Knit 4 rnds.

Decrease Rnd 3: *K4, k2tog*; rep *-* around. Knit 3 rnds.

Decrease Rnd 4: *K3, k2tog*; rep *-* around. Knit 1 rnd.

Decrease Rnd 5: *K2, k2tog*; rep *-* around.
Knit 1 rnd.
Decrease Rnd 6: *K1, k2tog*; rep *-* around.
Knit 1 rnd.
Decrease Rnd 7: *K2tog*; rep *-* around.

Cut yarn and draw end through rem sts; tighten.

EARS
Make both ears alike; ears for all sizes are the same.

With smaller size circular and Klompelompe Tynn Merinoull, CO 24 (24, 24, 24) sts.

Join and knit 8 rounds.

Decrease Rnd 1: *K4, k2tog*; rep *-* around.
Knit 1 rnd.
Decrease Rnd 2: *K3, k2tog*; rep *-* around.
Knit 1 rnd.
Decrease Rnd 3: *K2, k2tog*; rep *-* around.
Knit 1 rnd.
Decrease Rnd 4: *K1, k2tog*; rep *-* around.
Decrease Rnd 5: *K2tog*; rep *-* around.

Cut yarn and draw end through rem sts; tighten.

Fold base of ear into a W and sew together. Sew ears to top of cap spaced about 2½ (2¾, 3⅛, 3½) in [6.5 (7, 8, 9) cm] apart and about ⅜ in (1 cm) from top of cap.

FINISHING
Weave in all ends neatly on WS.

Block by laying cap flat between two damp towels until completely dry.

Striped Mittens

Eye-catching and easy striped mittens with contrast color ties.

SKILL LEVEL: 2

SIZES: 1–3 (6 months, 1–2, 3–4 years)

YARN: Sandnes Garn Klompelompe Merinoull [CYCA #3 – DK/light worsted, 100% Merino wool, 114 yd (104 m) / 50 g]

YARN COLORS AND AMOUNTS
Color A, 2650: 50 (50, 50, 50, 100) g
Color B, 2652: small amount

NEEDLES: U.S. sizes 2.5 and 4 (3 and 3.5 mm): 32 in (80 cm) circulars

GAUGE: 22 sts on larger size needle = 4 in (10 cm).

Adjust needle size to obtain correct gauge if necessary.

The mittens are knitted in the round; rounds begin at the side. We recommend knitting with the magic loop method (see video at klompelompe.no/en/).

With smaller size circular and color A, CO 28 (32, 36, 38) sts. Join to knit in the round; pm for beginning of rnd.

Knit 8 rnds.

Next Rnd (casing):

Left-hand mitten: K24 (28, 32, 34), BO 4 sts.
Right-hand mitten: K12 (14, 16, 17), BO 4 sts, knit to end of rnd.

Both mittens: Knit 1 rnd, and a*t the same time* CO 4 sts over bound-off sts.
Knit 5 rnds.

Next Rnd: Fold edge and join live sts to cast-on sts: pick up a cast-on st directly below next live st and knit it together with live st. Make sure the sts

align vertically. If you think this is too difficult, you can sew the edge when finishing.

Changer to larger size needle.

Knit around in stockinette for ⅜ in (1 cm).

Change to color B and knit ¾ in (2 cm) in stockinette.

Change to color A and continue in stockinette.

SIZES 1–2 AND 3–4 YEARS:
When mitten is 2¾ (3¼) in [7 (8) cm] long, make thumb opening.

Left-Hand Mitten:
Knit front of mitten, k12 (12). With a smooth, contrast color waste yarn, k5 (6). Place the 5 (6) sts back on left needle and knit to end of rnd.

Right-Hand Mitten:
Knit front of mitten, k1 (1). With a smooth, contrast color waste yarn, k5 (6). Place the 5 (6) sts back on left needle and knit to end of rnd.

ALL SIZES:
When mitten measures 2¾ (4, 5½, 6) in [7 (10, 14, 15) cm], begin shaping top:

K1, k2tog, knit until 3 sts before side marker, sl 1, k1, psso, k1: rep *-* once more.

Decrease the same way on every rnd until 8 sts rem.

Cut yarn and draw end through rem sts; tighten.

THUMB
Insert a needle into the 5 (6) sts below waste yarn and another needle into the 5 (6) sts above waste yarn. Carefully remove waste yarn. With A, knit around, and a*t the same time* pick up and knit 1 st at each side = 12 (14) sts total.

Knit around until thumb measures 1⅜ (1¾) in [3.5 (4.5) cm]. K2tog around.

Cut yarn and draw end through rem sts; tighten.

I-CORD TIES
Knit an I-Cord about 11¾ in (30 cm) long for each mitten (see video at klompelompe.no/en/ or use a knitting mill).

FINISHING
Weave in all ends neatly on WS.

Block by laying mittens between two damp towels until completely dry.

Striped Blanket

The striped blanket sports an I-cord bind-off edging all around. Cozy!

SKILL LEVEL: 2

FINISHED MEASUREMENTS
Approx. 28¼ x 33½ in (72 x 85 cm)

YARN: Sandnes Garn Klompelompe Tynn Merinoull [CYCA #1 – fingering, 100% fine Merino wool, 191 yd (175 m) / 50 g]

YARN COLORS AND AMOUNTS
Color A, 2560: 250 g
Color B, 9871: 150 g

NEEDLES: U.S. size 6 (4 mm): 32 in (80 cm) circular

GAUGE: 20 sts on gauge-size needle = 4 in (10 cm).
Adjust needle size to obtain correct gauge if necessary.

With gauge-size circular and color A, CO 140 sts.

Work back and forth in stockinette until blanket measures 4¾ in (12 cm).

Change to color B. Work in stockinette for 2½ in (6 cm). Change to color A. Work in stockinette for 4¾ in (12 cm). Rep *-* a total of 4 times.

Change to color B and knit 1 row.

Now make an I-cord edging all around the blanket (see video at klompelompe.no/en/):

CO 3 sts with color B. Slip the 3 sts to left needle.

K2, k2tog tbl. Slip the 3 sts on right needle back to left needle.

Rep *-* until 3 sts rem. With color B, pick up 3 sts for every 4 rows along one side (work on one side at a time). On the short side, pick up 1 st in each st. Work I-cord edging as before, beginning with the 3 sts you had last. Continue until you have gone all the way around the blanket. Join last 3 sts at end of I-cord with first 3 using Kitchener st.

FINISHING
Weave in all ends neatly on WS.

Block by laying blanket flat, patted out to finished measurements, on a damp towel until completely dry.

Big Brother Striped Cardigan

Stripes never go out of style. This cardigan is knitted in Merino wool so it is good and warm, and also makes a perfect outer layer through the spring and summer months.

SKILL LEVEL: 2

SIZES: 0–1 (3, 6–12, 18–24 months)

FINISHED MEASUREMENTS
Chest: Approx. 18¼ (20, 22½, 24½) in [46 (51, 57, 62) cm]
Total Length: Approx. 8¾ (9½, 11½, 13¾) in [22 (24, 29, 35) cm]

YARN: Sandnes Garn Klompelompe Tynn Merinoull [CYCA #1 - fingering, 100% fine Merino wool, 191 yd (175 m) / 50 g]

YARN: Sandnes Garn Klompelompe Merinoull [CYCA #3 – DK/light worsted, 100% Merino wool, 114 yd (104 m) / 50 g]

YARN COLORS AND AMOUNTS
Tynn Merinoull, 9871: 50 (50, 50, 50) g
Merinoull, Color A, 9871: 100 (100, 150, 200) g
Merinoull, Color B: 50 (50, 50, 50) g

NEEDLES: U.S. sizes 1.5 and 4 (2.5 and 3.5 mm): 16 and 32 in (40 and 80 cm) circulars

NOTIONS: 6 (7, 8, 9) buttons, ⅝ in (15 mm) in diameter

GAUGE: 22 sts on larger size needle = 4 in (10 cm).
Adjust needle size to obtain correct gauge if necessary.

The sweater is worked back and forth on a circular needle, from the top down.

With smaller size circular and Tynn Merinoull, CO 79 (85, 85, 87) sts. Work 16 rows back and forth in k1, p1 ribbing. *At the same time*, on Rows 4 and 12, make buttonholes as follows:

Work in ribbing as est until 5 sts rem, BO 2 sts, rib 3 sts. On next row, CO 2 sts over gap.

Next Row: Work in ribbing as est, but, join every other st to a corresponding st on cast-on row with k2tog. Cut yarn. Change to larger size needle and color A. Place the outermost 6 sts at each side on a holder.

Purl 1 row (WS), adjusting stitch count to 65 (71, 71, 73) sts [= decrease 14 (14, 14, 14) sts evenly spaced across].

Next Row (RS): K9 (10, 10, 10), M1, k3 (raglan st), M1, k6 (7, 7, 8) (sleeve sts), M1, k3 (raglan sts), M1, k23 (25, 25, 25), M1, k3 (raglan sts), M1, k6 (7, 7, 8), (sleeve sts), M1, k3 (raglan sts), M1, knit until 5 sts rem; turn and purl until 5 sts rem; turn. Knit, including raglan increases until 3 sts before previous turn; turn and purl until 3 sts before previous turn; turn. Knit, including increases to end of row.

Oon every RS row, continue raglan increases at each side of marked 3 raglan sts until you've increased a total of 11 (13, 16, 19) times = 153 (175, 199, 225) sts. Purl 1 row.

On next row, divide for body and sleeves:

Knit to and including center raglan st, place next raglan st, sleeve sts, and first raglan st on next raglan panel onto a holder, CO 4 sts. Knit to and including center raglan st, place next raglan st, sleeve sts, and first raglan st on next raglan panel on a holder, CO 4 sts, knit to end of row = 101 (113, 125, 137) sts rem for body.

Work 9 rows in stockinette. On next row, increase 1 st on each side of the 4 cast-on sts at each underarm.

Continue in stockinette until sweater measures 5½ (6¼, 8¼, 10¾) in [14 (16, 21, 27) cm] down from shoulder.

Change to color B and work ¾ in (2 cm) in stockinette.

Change to color A and work ⅝ in (1.5 cm) in stockinette.
Change to color B and work ¾ in (2 cm) in stockinette.
Change to color A and work 1 in (2.5 cm) in stockinette.

Place sts on a holder.

RIGHT FRONT BUTTON BAND

With smaller size circular and Tynn Merinoull, color A, beginning on WS, work back and forth in k1, p1 ribbing on the 6 held sts:

*Work 1 row in ribbing.

Next Row: With yarn in front, slip 1 st from yoke to left needle. P2tog, joining slipped st and first st of button band, work in ribbing to end of row*; rep *-* until all the way down to the held sts, but skip every 3rd st. Place sts on a holder and begin left band.

LEFT FRONT BUTTONHOLE BAND

Place 4 (5, 6, 7) markers evenly spaced down from first buttonhole so you'll know where to make the rem buttonholes.

Begin on WS and *work in ribbing as est to end of row.

Next Row: Rib 5, p2tog, joining next st with outermost st on yoke.* Rep *-* until you come all the way down to sts on holder, skipping every 3rd st. Place sts on a holder.

Lower edge facing with Tynn Merinoull and smaller size needle:

Work left buttonhole band in ribbing. Knit sts on holder and a*t the same time* increase 22 (26, 30, 32) sts evenly spaced, work sts of right button band in ribbing as est. Work in stockinette and ribbing until facing measures 1¼ in (3 cm). Don't forget to make the back of the lowest buttonhole centered on the facing. BO. Fold facing to WS and sew down. Sew outer edge of facing together.

SLEEVES

Work sleeves with Merinoull and larger size circular. Pick up and knit 2 sts, beginning at center of underarm, pick up and knit 1 st in gap between

underarm and armhole, knit the 30 (35, 41, 48) held sleeve sts, 1 st in gap between armhole and underarm, and 2 sts along underarm = 36 (41, 47, 54) sts total.

The first st is a marked st and is always purled down the sleeve.

Work around in stockinette for 1 in (2.5 cm).

Begin sleeve shaping on next rnd: P1, k2tog, knit until 2 sts rem, sl 1, k1, psso.

Decrease the same way every ¾ in (2 cm) until 30 (31, 33, 34) sts rem.

When sleeve measures 1¾ (2½, 4, 6½) in [4.5 (6.5, 10.5, 16.5) cm] begin striping:

Change to color B and work ¾ in (2 cm) in stockinette.
Change to color A and work ⅝ in (1.5 cm) in stockinette.
Change to color B and work ¾ in (2 cm) in stockinette.
Change to color A and work ¾ in (2 cm) in stockinette.
Change to smaller size needle and Tynn Merinoull.
Knit 1 rnd, increasing 4 (4, 6, 6) sts evenly spaced around. Knit around for 1¼ in (3 cm). BO. Fold facing in and sew down.

FINISHING

Sew any holes at underarms. Sew buttons on, spaced as for buttonholes.

Block cardigan flat, patted out to finished measurements, on a damp towel until completely dry or gently steam press it under a damp pressing cloth.

Big Brother Striped Pants

Perfect basic pants that work equally well for baby or for big sister's or brother's nursery school wardrobe.

SKILL LEVEL: 2

SIZES: 0–1 (3, 6, 12, 18 months, 2, 3 years)

FINISHED MEASUREMENTS
Waist: Approx. 13½ (15, 17¼, 19¼, 20, 21½, 22¾) in [34.5 (38, 44, 49, 51, 54.5, 58) cm]
Total Length: Approx. 12 (13½, 15¼, 16¾, 18, 19, 21½) in [30.5 (34.5, 38.5, 42.5, 45.5, 48.5, 54.5) cm]

Yarn: Sandnes Garn Klompelompe Merinoull [CYCA #3 - DK/light worsted, 100% Merino wool, 114 yd (104 m) / 50 g]

YARN COLORS AND AMOUNTS
Color A, 9871: 100 (100, 150, 150, 200, 200, 200) g
Color B, 1013: 50 (50, 50, 50, 50, 50, 50) g

NEEDLES: U.S. sizes 2.5 and 4 (3 and 3.5 mm): 24 and 32 in (60 and 80 cm) circulars

NOTIONS: Waistband elastic, long enough to go around waist plus seam allowance

GAUGE: 22 sts on larger size needle = 4 in (10 cm).
Adjust needle size to obtain correct gauge if necessary.

The pants begin at the waist and are worked in the round on a circular needle.

With smaller size circular and color A, *loosely* CO 76 (84, 96, 108, 112, 120, 128) sts. If necessary, use a larger size needle for the cast-on so the cast-on edge wil be loose. Join, being careful not to twist cast-on row; pm for beginning of rnd.

Knit 10 (10, 15, 15, 15, 15, 15) rnds. Purl 1 rnd.
Work 10 (10, 15, 15, 15, 15) rnds in k1, p1 ribbing.

Change to larger size needle and knit 1 rnd.

Raise back with German short rows (see video at klompelompe.no/en/) as follows:
K10; turn and p20; turn. Knit until 4 sts past previous turn; turn and purl until 4 sts past previous turn. Continue the same way until you've turned 3 (3, 4, 4, 5, 5, 5) times on each side, knit to end of rnd.

Continue knitting around in stockinette until piece measures 3¼ (3½, 4, 4¼, 4¾, 5¼, 5½) in [8 (9, 10, 11, 12, 13, 14) cm below rnd where you changed to larger size needle. Pm at each side of the center 4 (4, 6, 10, 10, 10, 10) sts at front and back.

With M1, increase 1 st on each side of the front and back sts.

Increase the same way on every 3rd row a total of 5 times = 96 (104, 116, 128, 132, 140, 148) sts for each leg.

Next Rnd: Knit around *and at the same time* BO the 4 (4, 6, 10, 10, 10, 10) sts center front and back center sts = 44 (48, 52, 54, 56, 60, 64) sts rem for each leg.

LEGS

Knit around in stockinette, but, always purl the first st (= marked st).

Knit until leg measures 1¼ in (3 cm) and then decrease as follows:

P1 (marked st), k2tog, knit until 2 sts rem, sl 1, k1, psso.

Decrease the same way every 1 (¾, 1¼, 1¼, 1⅜, 1½, 2) 14, 1 in [2.5 (2, 3, 3, 3.5, 4, 5) cm] until 36 (36, 40, 44, 48, 48, 52) sts rem.

Continue knitting around in stockinette until leg measures 3½ (4¾, 6, 7, 8, 8¾, 10¾) in [9 (12, 15, 18, 20, 22, 27) cm].

Change to color B and knit 6 rnds.

Change to color A and knit around for 1 in (⅜ cm). Changer to smaller size circular and knit 1 in (2.5 cm).

Change to color B and knit 1 in (2.5 cm), binding off on last rnd.

Make second leg the same way.

FINISHING

Seam the 4 (4, 6, 10, 10, 10, 10) crotch sts of front and back with Kitchener st. Fold waistband edge in and sew down on WS, leaving small opening. Insert waistband elastic, seam short ends of elastic, and complete casing closure.

Fold in color B facing on each leg and sew down on WS.

Weave in all ends neatly on WS.

Block by laying pants flat, patted out to finished measurements, on a damp towel until completely dry.

Striped Hooded Onesie

A lovely, loose-fitting onesie. Perfect as an outer garment on days when it's not too cold, and for baby to wear in the car seat when out on a drive.

SKILL LEVEL: 3

SIZES: 0–2 (3, 6–9 months, 1, 2, 3 years)

FINISHED MEASUREMENTS
Chest: Approx. 20 (22½, 24, 25½, 26½, 27¾) in [51 (57, 61, 65, 67, 70.5) cm]
Total Length, excluding hood: Approx. 17 (19, 21, 23¾, 26¾, 29½) in [43 (48, 53, 60, 68, 75) cm]

YARN: Sandnes Garn Klompelompe Merinoull [CYCA #3 – DK/light worsted, 100% Merino wool, 114 yd (104 m) / 50 g]

YARN COLORS AND AMOUNTS
Color A, 3355: 200 (250, 250, 300, 350, 400) g
Color B, 2560: 50 (50, 50, 50, 100, 100) g

NEEDLES: U.S. sizes 2.5 and 4 (3 and 3.5 mm): 24 and 32 in (60 and 80 cm) circulars

NOTIONS: Zipper to fit front opening

GAUGE: 22 sts on larger size needle = 4 in (10 cm).
Adjust needle size to obtain correct gauge if necessary.

The onesie begins with the hood and is worked back and forth on a circular needle.

With larger size circular and color A, CO 16 (16, 16, 20, 20, 20) sts.

Working back and forth, purl 1 row. Knit 1 row increasing 3 sts evenly spaced across. Continue back and forth in stockinette until piece measures 2¾ (3¼, 4, 4¾, 5¼, 5½) in [7 (8, 10, 12, 13, 14) cm]. Leave sts needle.

Now shape hood by increasing with M1:

Pick up and knit 17 (19, 24, 26, 28, 30) sts along left side of stockinette, knit sts on needle, pick up and knit 17 (19, 24, 26, 28, 30) sts along right side of stockinette = 53 (57, 67, 75, 79, 83) sts.

Pm on each side of the center 19 (19, 19, 23, 23, 23) sts.

Continue back and forth in stockinette.

Increase 1 st with M1 on each side of the marked 19 (19, 19, 23, 23, 23) sts on every RS row, a total of 6 times = 65 (69, 79, 87, 91, 95) sts.

Next RS Row: Lengthen back of hood with German short rows (see video at klompelompe.no/en/) as follows:

Knit to 2nd marker; turn and purl to 1st marker; turn. Knit until 1 st rem; turn and purl until 1 st rem; turn and knit to end of row.

Purl 1 row.

Repeat the short row turns once more.

Continue across in stockinette until hood measures 3½ (4, 4, 4, 4, 4¼) in [9 (10, 10, 10, 10, 11) cm] from last increase row. decrease as follows on next RS row:

Knit until 2 sts before marker, k2tog, knit to next marker, sl 1, k1, psso, knit to end of row.

Decrease the same way on every RS row a total of 2 (2, 3, 6, 8, 8) times = 61 (65, 73, 75, 75, 79) sts rem.

Continue in stockinette until hood measures 5½ (6, 6¼, 7, 7½, 8) in [14 (15, 16, 18, 19, 20) cm] from increases.

Knit 1 row on RS, adjusting stitch count to 53 (57, 63, 67, 67, 71) sts.

Purl 1 row and cut yarn.

On next row, divide sts for raglan shaping:

CO 3 sts, k6 (7, 9, 10, 10, 11), M1, k1 (marked raglan st), M1, k8, M1, k1 (marked raglan st), M1, k21 (23, 25, 27, 27, 29), M1, k1 (marked raglan st), M1, k8, M1, k1 (marked raglan st), M1, k6 (7, 9, 10, 10, 11), CO 3 sts.

Take all subsequent length measurements from this point on, unless otherwise specified.

Continue working back and forth in stockinette, increasing on each side of each marked st on every RS row = 8 sts increased per increase row.

Increase a total of 15 (17, 18, 19, 20, 21) times = 179 (199, 213, 225, 233, 245) sts.

Next Row (RS): Knit to marked st, place next 40 (44, 46, 48, 50, 52) sleeve sts, including marked sts) on a holder, CO 7 sts for underarm, knit across back, place next 40 (44, 46, 48, 50, 52) sleeve sts, including marked sts) on a holder, CO 7 sts for underarm, knit to end of row = 113 (125, 135, 143, 147, 155) sts rem for body.

Continue working back and forth in stockinette until body measures 6¼ (7, 8, 9½, 11, 11¾) in [16 (18, 20, 24, 28, 30) cm].
Change to color B and work in stockinette for 1 in (2.5 cm)

Change to color A and work in stockinette for 2 in (5 cm)

Change to color B and work in stockinette for 1 in (2.5 cm)

Change to color A and continue in stockinette until body measures 9¾ (11, 11½, 13, 14½, 15½) in [25 (28, 29, 33, 37, 39) cm] and next row is on RS.
Knit 1 row and CO 1 st at end of row. Now join to knit in the round.

Knit around until body measures 9½ (11½, 12¼, 13¾, 15½, 16¼) in [24 (29, 31, 35, 39, 41) cm].. Pm on each side of the center 7 sts on both back and front. With M1, increase 1 st on each side of the 7 marked center sts of back and front. Increase the same way on every other rnd a total of 4 times.

Next Rnd: BO marked center sts = 58 (64, 69, 73, 75, 80) sts rem for each leg.

LEGS

Note: Before you knit legs, read through entire section since several steps occur at the same time.

Pm for beginning of rnd and continue around in stockinette.

When leg measures 2 in (5 cm) from previous color B stripe, change to color B and knit 1 in (2.5 cm). Change to color A and continue with A to end of stockinette on legs.

When leg measures ⅜ in (1 cm), decrease as follows: K1, k2tog, knit until 2 sts rem, sl 1, k1, psso.

Decrease the same way every ⅜ (⅜, ⅜, ⅜, ⅝, ⅝) in [1 (1, 1, 1, 1.5, 1.5) cm] a total of 9 (11, 13, 14, 15, 18) times.

Continue around until leg measures 4¼ (5½, 6¾, 8, 9½, 11½) in [11 (14, 17, 20, 24, 29) cm].

Knit 1 rnd and a*t the same time* adjust stitch count to 30 (30, 32, 34, 36, 38) sts.

Change to smaller size needle and knit around in stockinette for 1¼ in (3 cm). Change to color B and work in k1, p1 ribbing for 1¼ in (3 cm). BO in ribbing on next rnd.

Fold in ribbing and sew down on WS.

SLEEVES

With larger size circular and color A, beginning at center of underarm, pick up and knit 4 sts, knit the 40 (44, 46, 48, 50, 52) held sleeve sts, pick up and knit 3 sts along underarm.

If you think it is difficult to pick up and knit sts, you can cast on sts and later seam the underarms.

When you reach the same length from underarm as for first stripe on body, with color B, knit 1 stripe 2 in (2.5 cm) long.

Continue in stockinette until sleeve measures 5½ (6¼, 7, 8, 9½, 10¼) in [14 (16, 18, 20, 24, 26) cm]. *At the same time,* when sleeve measures ¾ in (2 cm), decrease as follows: K1, k2tog, knit until 2 sts rem, k2tog.

Decrease the same way every ⅝ (⅝, ⅝, ⅝, ¾, 1) in [1.5 (1.5, 1.5, 1.5, 2, 2.5) cm] until 31 (31, 33, 35, 37, 39) sts rem. On last rnd, decrease 1 st.

Change to smaller size needle and knit around for 1¼ in (3 cm). Change to color B and work in k1, p1 ribbing for 1¼ in (3 cm). BO in ribbing on next rnd.

Fold in ribbing and sew down on WS.

CASING

With larger size needle and color A, pick up and knit 3 sts for every 4 rows/sts around hood (on cast-on row at center of hood, pick up 1 st in every st). Work in stockinette for 1¼ in (3 cm). BO knitwise on next row. Fold casing in and sew down on WS., leaving a small opening on each end.

With color B, knit an I-cord (see video at klompelompe.no/en/ or use a knitting mill). Insert cord through casing.

Sew a zipper on front edges.

FACING

Pick up and knit 4 sts along front neck on one side of the zipper (1 st in each of the 3 sts cast on at neck + 1 st). Work in stockinette until facing measures same length as zipper (front opening of onesie). Leave sts on needle.

Do the same on opposite side.

Next Row: K4, CO 2 sts, k4 from holder. Work in stockinette until facing covers entire zipper (if necessary trim zipper to correct length first). Sew facing down so it covers zipper neatly on WS.

FINISHING

Weave in all ends neatly on WS.

Block by laying onesie flat, patted out to finished measurements, on a damp towel until completely dry.

Striped Overalls

Cute overalls with the same striped pattern as the rest of the set.

SKILL LEVEL: 2

SIZES: 0–2 (3, 6, 12, 18 months, 2, 4 years)

FINISHED MEASUREMENTS
Chest: Approx. 17 (17, 19¼, 21, 22, 23¼, 24¾) in [43 (43, 49, 53, 56, 59, 63) cm]
Total Length, from waist down: Approx. 15¼ (17, 18, 22, 24¼, 26, 27¼) in [38.5 (43.5, 45.5, 56, 61.5, 66, 69) cm]

YARN: Sandnes Garn Klompelompe Merinoull [CYCA #3 – DK/light worsted, 100% Merino wool, 114 yd (104 m) / 50 g]

YARN COLORS AND AMOUNTS
Color A, 9871: 100 (150, 200, 200, 200, 250, 300) g
Color B, 2560: 50 (50, 50, 50, 50, 50, 50) g

NEEDLES: U.S. sizes 2.5 and 4 (3 and 3.5 mm): 16 and 32 in (40 and 80 cm) circulars

NOTIONS: 2 buttons, ⅝ in (15 mm) in diameter

GAUGE: 22 sts on larger size needle = 4 in (10 cm). Adjust needle size to obtain correct gauge if necessary.

The overalls begin at the top with a ribbed waistband and worked in the round on a circular needle.

With smaller size circular and color A, CO 94 (94, 108, 116, 124, 130, 138) sts. Join, being careful not to twist cast-on row; pm for beginning of rnd. The rnd begins at center back. Work 10 rnds in k1, p1 ribbing.

BIB
The back of the bib is worked first. With smaller size needle, pick up and knit 36 (36, 40, 40, 44, 46, 48) sts on top of ribbing, at center front. Work 10 (10, 12, 12, 14, 16, 16) rnds in stockinette up on the back (with knit over purl and purl over knit). Make a buttonhole on next row: K3, BO 2 sts, knit until 5 sts rem, BO 2 sts, k3. On the next row, CO 2 sts over each gap. Work 3 rows in stockinette. Knit 1 row on RS as a foldline. Now work down to the ribbing again. Work 3 rows in stockinette and make 2 more buttonholes: P3, BO 2 sts, purl until 5 sts rem, BO 2 sts, p3. On the next row, CO 2 sts over each gap.

Work 15 (15, 17, 17, 19, 21, 21) rows in stockinette.
On next row (RS), increase as follows:
K1, 1, knit until 1 st rem, M1, k1.
Purl 1 row.
Repeat the increase row as above.
Purl 1 row.
On next row, repeat increases.
Purl 1 row = 42 (42, 46, 46, 50, 52, 54) sts.

Now begin working bib and pants together. Begin at center back, at beginning of rnd with larger size needle. K26 (26, 31, 35, 37, 39, 42). To join bib and pants: Join 1 st each from bib and pants with k2tog. Knit 1 rnd and a*t the same time* increase 12 (18, 18, 20, 20, 20 20) sts evenly spaced around = 106 (112, 126, 136, 144, 150, 158) sts.

Lengthen back with German short rows (see video at klompelompe.no/en/) as follows:
K10; turn and p20; turn. K25; turn and p30; turn. K35; turn and p40; turn. Knit to end of rnd.
With color A, knit around for ¾ in (2 cm).

Now work stripes.

STRIPE SEQUENCE
6 rnds color B, 18 rnds color A.
Tip: For a smooth transition between color rnds, change color, knit 1 rnd. On next rnd, slip first st.

Knit around in stockinette until body measures 7½ (9, 9½, 10¾, 11½, 11¾, 12¼) in [19 (23, 24, 27, 29, 30, 31) cm] from top of ribbing, as measured down the side. Pm on each side of the center 6 sts on both front and back. Increase on each side of the 6 sts = 4 sts increased. Rep the increases on every other rnd a total of 4 times.

On next rnd, BO the center 6 sts on both front and back = 55 (58, 65, 70, 74, 77, 81) sts rem for each leg.

LEGS

With larger size needle, continue in stripe sequence. Using magic loop method (see video at klompelompe.no/en/), k55 (58, 65, 70, 74, 77, 81). Pm at join. After ¾ in (2 cm), begin decreasing as follows: k1, k2tog, knit until 3 sts rem, sl 1, k1, psso, k1.

Decrease the same way every 1¼ (¾, ⅝, ¾, ¾, ¾, ¾) in [3 (2, 1.5, 2, 2, 2, 2) cm] until 47 (46, 49, 48, 50, 53, 53) sts rem. Continue around until leg measures 5½ (6, 6¼, 9, 10¼, 11, 12¼) in [14 (15, 16, 23, 26, 28, 31) cm]. Knit 1 rnd decreasing 9 (8, 11, 10, 10, 11, 11) sts evenly spaced around. Change to smaller size needle and continue with color A. Work 9 (9, 9, 11, 13, 15, 15) rnds in k1, p1 ribbing. BO in ribbing on next rnd..

STRAPS

With smaller size needle and color A, pick up and knit 9 sts for the right strap (there should be 8 sts between the straps at center back). Work 12 rows in k1, p1 ribbing. Set first strap aside while you make left strap the same way.

On next row, CO 1 st (center st) at end of row and then knit sts of other strap = 19 sts. Work 4 rows in ribbing. On next row, BO center st and work each strap separately until they measure 7 (7, 8, 8¾, 9½, 10¼, 11) in [18 (18, 20, 22, 24, 26, 28) cm] from row where you picked up sts. BO in ribbing.

FINISHING

Sew a button on end of each strap. Sew sides of bib over ribbing.

Weave in all ends neatly on WS.

Block by laying overalls flay, patted out to finished measurements, on a damp towel until completely dry.

MarMar
COPENHAGEN

Aurora Layette Set

Aurora Baby Cardigan

The leaf pattern on the Aurora cardigan has followed us through the years. It began with a summer top, became a christening dress, and is now the highlight of a sweet little layette set.

SKILL LEVEL: 3

SIZES: 0–1 (3, 6–12, 18–24 months)

FINISHED MEASUREMENTS
Chest: Approx. 17 (18¼, 21½, 23¾) in [43.5 (46, 54.5, 60) cm]
Total Length: Approx. 8¾ (10¼, 11½, 13¾) in [22 (26, 29, 35) cm]

YARN: Sandnes Garn Klompelompe Tynn Merinoull [CYCA #1 – fingering, 100% fine Merino wool, 191 yd (175 m) / 50 g]

YARN COLORS AND AMOUNTS
Color 2650: 100 (100, 150, 200) g

NEEDLES: U.S. sizes 1.5 and 2.5 (2.5 and 3 mm): 24 and 32 in (60 and 80 cm) circulars

NOTIONS: 3 (3, 3, 3) buttons, ⅝ in (15 mm) in diameter

GAUGE: 27 sts on larger size needle = 4 in (10 cm).
Adjust needle size to obtain correct gauge if necessary.

The sweater is worked back and forth on a circular needle, from the top down.

With smaller size circular CO 78 (78, 84, 88) sts. Working back and forth, knit 3 ridges (1 ridge = 2 knit rows) and, *on the 3rd row*, make a buttonhole: knit until 5 sts rem, BO 2 sts, k3. On next row, CO 2 sts over gap. You will make a total of 3 buttonholes with 8 (8, 9, 10) ridges between each. Change to larger size needle.

From this point on, the outermost 5 sts at each side (front bands) are continued in garter stitch. The next 11 sts at each side are worked in the leaf pattern following the chart. The remainder of the sts are worked in stockinette. See chart on page 145. Don't forget the buttonholes!

The yoke is shaped with increases out to the shoulders on each side of the 6 sleeve/shoulder sts as follows:

K5, 11 sts pattern, k1 (1, 2, 3), M1, k1, M1, pm, k6 (sleeve sts), M1, k1, M1, k28 (28, 32, 34), M1, k1, M1, pm, M1, k1, M1, pm, k6 (sleeve sts), M1, k1, M1, k1 (1, 2, 3), 11 sts leaf pattern, k5 = 8 sts increased. The increases are worked only on the front and back; the sleeve stitch count remains unchanged.

Continue, increasing the same way on every RS row (continuing 5-st garter bands and 11-st leaf panels as est):

Work until 1 st before marker, M1, k1, M1, k6, M1, k1, M1, knit until 1 st before next marker, M1, k1, M1, k6, M1, k1, M1, work as est to end of row.

Purl 1 row (with pattern panels and garter-st bands as est).

Knit 1 row with pattern panels and increases as est.

Now raise back with German short rows (see video at klompelompe.no/en/):

NEXT ROW (WS): Purl until 17 sts rem; turn. Knit, including increases, until 17 sts rem; turn and purl until 19 sts rem; turn. Knit, including increases, until 19 sts rem; turn and purl to end of row.

Continue increasing on RS until you've increased a total of 5 (6, 8, 9) times = 118 (126, 148, 160) sts.

Now increase on front, back, and sleeves (raglan shaping) as follows:

Move front markers 1 st in from fronts = 7 sts between markers.

The st after the marker is now a raglan st.

Work to marker, M1, k1, M1; rep *-* a total of 4 times, work to end of row = 8 sts increased.

Purl 1 row (with pattern panels and garter-st bands as est).

Knit 1 row with pattern panels and raglan increases as est.

Purl 1 row (with pattern panels and garter-st bands as est).

SIZES 18–24 MONTHS:

Knit 1 row with pattern panels and raglan increases as est.

Purl 1 row (with pattern panels and garter-st bands as est).

ALL SIZES:
Now increase only for the sleeve sts:

Work to and including raglan st, M1, k2, M1, knit until 2 sts before raglan st, M1, k2, M1; rep *-*, work as est to end of row.

Increase on sleeves the same way on every RS row until there are 42 (46, 54, 62) sts on each sleeve (not including raglan sts).

Next Row (RS): Work as est to sleeve sts, place the 42 (46, 54, 62) sleeve sts on a holder, CO 4 sts for underarm, knit to next sleeve, place the 42 (46, 54, 62) sleeve sts on a holder, CO 4 sts for underarm, work as est to end of row = 122 (130, 152, 168) sts rem for body.

Continue as est with front bands and leaf panels.

Pm on each side of the 4 underarm sts at each side.

After working as est for 1½ in (4 cm), increase 1 st on each side of the 4 underarm sts at each side. Increase the same way every 1½ in (4 cm) a total of 3 (3, 4, 5) times.

Continue until body measures (from shoulders) 8 (9½, 10¾, 13) in [20 (24, 27, 33) cm]. Finish with 5 garter ridges across all sts, binding off knitwise on last row.
Note: Do not change to smaller size needle for the garter edge because this is a flared design.

SLEEVES
With larger size circular, pick up and knit 2 sts, beginning at center of underarm, pick up and knit 1 st in gap between underarm and armhole, knit the 42 (46, 54, 62) held sleeve sts, 1 st in gap between armhole and underarm, and 2 sts along underarm = 48 (52, 60, 68) sts total.

The first st is a marked st and is always purled down the sleeve.

Join and work around in stockinette for ¾ in (2 cm).

Begin sleeve shaping on next rnd: P1, k2tog, knit until 2 sts rem, sl 1, k1, psso.

Decrease the same way every ¾ (¾, ⅝, ⅝) in [2 (2, 1.5, 1.5) cm] until 38 (38, 40, 42) sts rem. Continue without further decreasing until sleeve measures 4¾ (5½, 7, 9½) in [12 (14, 18, 24) cm]. Change to smaller size needle and purl 1 rnd. Knit 1 rnd and a*t the same time* decrease 4 sts evenly spaced around. Purl 1 rnd, knit 1 rnd, BO purlwise on next round.

FINISHING
Stitch to close any holes at underarms. Sew buttons on, spaced as for buttonholes.

Block cardigan flat, patted out to finished measurements, on a damp towel until completely dry or gently steam press it under a damp pressing cloth.

Aurora Baby Cap

A fun project with a lovely lace pattern.

SKILL LEVEL: 2

SIZES: preemie (0–1, 1–3, 3–6, 9–12 months, 1–2 years)

YARN: Sandnes Garn Klompelompe Tynn Merinoull [CYCA #1 – fingering, 100% fine Merino wool, 191 yd (175 m) / 50 g]

YARN COLORS AND AMOUNTS
Color 4331: 50 (50, 50, 50, 50, 50) g

NEEDLES: U.S. sizes 1.5 and 2.5 (2.5 and 3 mm): 16 and 32 in (40 and 80 cm) circulars

GAUGE: 27 sts on larger size needle = 4 in (10 cm).

Adjust needle size to obtain correct gauge if necessary.

Do not work on sizes preemie, 1-3 and 9-12 months

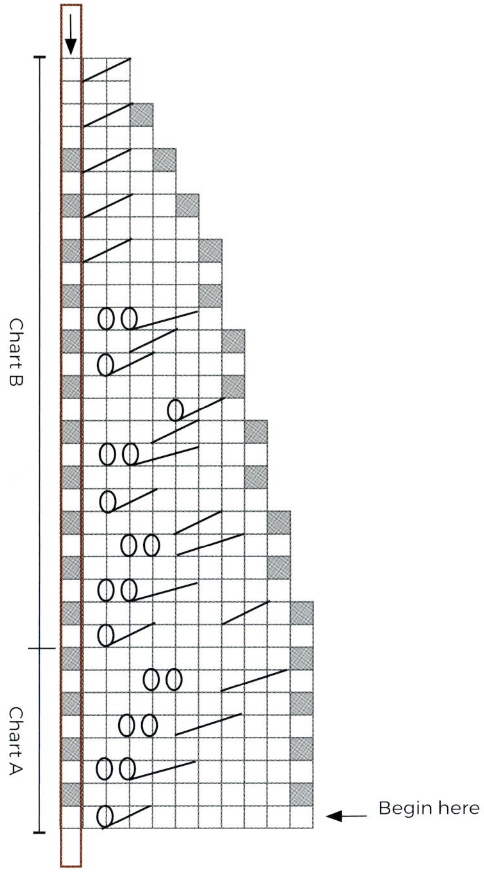

= knit on RS, purl on WS

= knit on WS, purl on RS

= k2tog

= sl 1, k1, psso

= sl 1, k1, psso

= sl 2tog as if to knit, k1, psso (= CDD/centered double decrease)

= yo between 2 sts

With smaller size circular CO 72 (78, 88, 92, 96, 102) sts. Join, being careful not to twist cast-on row; pm for beginning of rnd. Work 10 (10. 12, 12, 14, 14) rnds in k1, p1 ribbing.

Change to larger size needle. Knit 1 rnd increasing 8 (10, 2, 7, 4, 8) sts evenly spaced around = 80 (88, 90, 99, 100, 110) sts.

Begin leaf pattern following chart. Work chart A 2 (3, 4,4, 5, 6) times and then work chart B.

SIZES 0-1, 3-6, AND 9-12 MONTHS:
Next Rnd: *K1, k2tog*; rep *-* until - (1, -, 0, -, 2) sts rem, k - (1, -, 0, -, 2.

ALL SIZES:
Knit 10 rnds in stockinette.

Cut yarn and draw end through rem sts; tighten.

FINISHING
Weave in all ends neatly on WS.

Block by laying cap between two damp towels until completely dry.

Aurora Soakers

It doesn't take more than a pair of sweet soakers and a pretty leotard to dress your baby. Practical and quick to knit.

SKILL LEVEL: 2

SIZES: 0–1 (3, 6, 12, 18–24 months)

YARN: Sandnes Garn Klompelompe Tynn Merinoull [CYCA #1 – fingering, 100% fine Merino wool, 191 yd (175 m) / 50 g]

YARN COLORS AND AMOUNTS
Color 2650: 50 (50, 50, 50, 100) g

NEEDLES: U.S. sizes 1.5 and 2.5 (2.5 and 3 mm): 16 and 32 in (40 and 80 cm) circulars

GAUGE: 27 sts on larger size needle = 4 in (10 cm).

Adjust needle size to obtain correct gauge if necessary.

With smaller size needle, CO 102 (112, 122, 122, 132) sts. Join, being careful not to twist cast-on row; pm for beginning of rnd.

Work around in k1, p1 ribbing for 14 (14, 16, 16, 18) rnds

Change to larger size needle. Knit 1 around increasing 10 (12, 10, 14, 12) sts evenly spaced around = 112 (124, 132, 136, 144) sts.

Raise back with German short rows (see video at klompelompe.no/en/):

K22; turn and p44; turn. K47; turn and p50; turn.

SIZES 6, 12, 18–24 MONTHS:
K53; turn and p56; turn. K59; turn and p62; turn.

ALL SIZES:
Knit around.

Pm on next rnd as follows:

K28 (31, 33, 34, 36), pm, work 11 sts in charted leaf pattern, pm, k34 (40, 44, 46, 50), pm, 11 sts leaf pattern, pm, k28 (31, 33, 34, 36).

Left Side

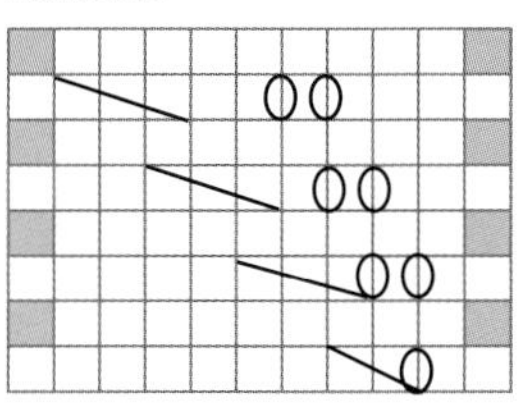

Right Side

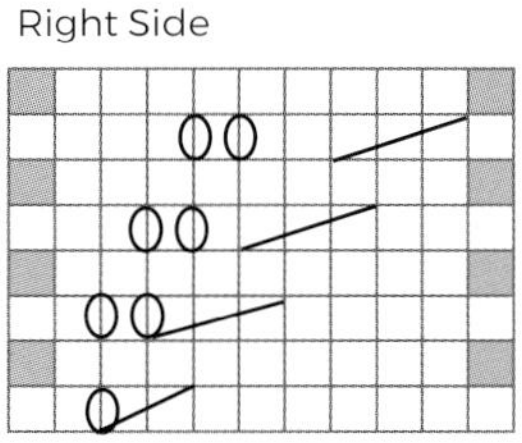

Continue with charted leaf pattern on the 11 sts at each side and stockinette for rem sts.

Work as est until piece measures 4 (4½, 5, 5¼, 5¾) in [10.5 (11.5, 12.5, 13.5, 14.5) cm] down center front.

Cut yarn. Slip last 26 (28, 30, 31, 33) sts to left needle. Work back on backmost 52 (56, 60, 62, 66) sts, 26 (28, 30, 31, 33) sts before and after the beginning of rnd.

Place rem sts on a holder. Now work back and forth. The first row is on RS.

Begin decreasing on next RS row: K2tog, knit until 2 sts rem, sl 1, k1, psso. Decrease the same way on every RS row.

Continue decreases as est until 18 (20, 22, 24, 26) sts rem. BO purlwise on next WS row.

Front: Place the outermost 18 (22, 22, 22, 24) sts at each side on a holder and work the center 24 (28, 28, 30, 30) sts back and forth. Decrease as for back, but, when 18 (20, 22, 24, 26) sts rem, continue without decreasing until front is approx. ⅜ in (1 cm) shorter than back.

Join front and back with Kitchener st.

With smaller size needle, pick up and knit sts around leg with about 3 sts for every 4 sts/rows and knit held sts. Work 6 (6, 7, 7, 9) rnds in k1, p1 ribbing. BO in ribbing on next rnd. Finish second leg the same way.

FINISHING
Weave in all ends neatly on WS.

Block by laying soakers between two damp towels until completely dry.

- □ = knit on RS, purl on WS
- ■ = knit on WS, purl on RS
- = k2tog
- = sl 1, k1, psso
- = k3tog
- = sl 2tog as if to knit, k1, psso (= CDD/centered double decrease)
- = yo between 2 sts

Lilly Baby Socks

Sweet, delicate socks with a darling leaf pattern.

SKILL LEVEL: 2

SIZES: 1–3 (6–9, 12–18 months, 2, 3–4 years)

YARN: Sandnes Garn Klompelompe Tynn Merinoull [CYCA #1 – fingering, 100% fine Merino wool, 191 yd (175 m) / 50 g]

YARN COLORS AND AMOUNTS
Color 1013: 50 (50, 50, 50, 50) g

NEEDLES: U.S. size 1.5 (2.5 mm): 32 in (80 cm) circular

GAUGE: 32 sts on gauge-size needle = 4 in (10 cm). Adjust needle size to obtain correct gauge if necessary.

The rnds begin at center back.

CO 40 (44, 48, 52, 56) sts. Join to work in the round.

Work around in k2, p2 ribbing for 3 (3¼, 3¾, 4, 4) in [7.5 (8.5, 9.5, 10, 10) cm].

On next rnd, make eyelets as follows:

Sizes 1–3, 12–18 months, and 3–4 years: *K2tog, yo, p2*; rep *-* around.

Sizes 6–9 months and 2 years: *K2tog, yo, p2*; rep *-* 5 (6) times, k2, p2, rep *-* 5 (6) times.

Work 3 (4, 5, 5, 6) rnds in ribbing.

Cut yarn. Place backmost 20 (20, 24, 24, 28) sts on needle Place 10 (10, 12, 12, 14) sts at each side of beginning of rnd and front sts on a holder.

Tip: If you are knitting with magic loop (see video at klompelompe.no/en/), you can leave the front sts on one needle while you work the heel back and forth with the other needle.

Work heel with back sts as follows:

HEEL SHAPING

Work back and forth in stockinette.

Row 1 (RS): Knit until 1 st rem; turn.

Row 2 (WS): Sl 1 purlwise, tighten yarn and purl until 1 st rem; turn.

Row 3 (RS): Sl 1 knitwise, tighten yarn and purl until 2 sts rem; turn.

Row 4 (WS): Sl 1 purlwise, tighten yarn and purl until 2 sts rem; turn.

Continue the same way until 8 (8, 10, 10, 12) sts rem at center of row.

Still working back and forth, work 1 more st before turning. To avoid holes at the turns: Sl strand between the sts (before the added st) and place it twisted on needle. Join strand to added st with k2tog or p2tog.

Continue as est until you are once again working across all sts of the heel.

Return to knitting in the round on all sts. The rnd now begins at the side before the heel.

Knit 1 rnd adjusting stitch count to 41 (41, 47, 51, 55) sts. = 21 (21, 21, 25, 25) sts on instep and rem sts on sole.

Before you begin next rnd, slip strand before first st twisted onto needle and k2tog with next st to avoid a hole at beginning of rnd.

Continue sole in stockinette and instep in pattern following chart.

After working charted rows 2 (2.5, 3, 3.5, 4) times, knit 1 rnd and decrease 1 st on instep = 40 (40, 456, 50, 54) sts rem. Move side marker so you have the same number of sts on both instep and sole.

Now shape toe on sole and instep:

K1, sl 1, k1, psso, knit until 3 sts rem before marker (side), k2tog, k1; rep *-* once more = 4 sts decreased around.

Decrease on every other rnd a total of 5 (5, 6, 6, 7) times = 20 (20, 22, 26, 26) sts rem.

Cut yarn, leaving long enough end to seam toe. Lay sock flat and Kitchener stitch the 10 (10, 11, 13, 13) instep sts with the 10 (10, 11, 13, 13) sole sts.

FINISHING

Weave in all ends neatly on WS.

Block by laying socks between two damp towels until completely dry or carefully steam press under a damp pressing cloth.

Make a twisted cord or use an imitation leather cord for ties to insert through eyelet round of each sock.

= knit on RS, purl on WS

= knit on WS, purl on RS

= k2tog

= sl 1, k1, psso

= k3tog

= sl 2tog as if to knit, k1, psso (= CDD/centered double decrease)

= yo between 2 sts

Sizes 1–3, 6–9, 12–18 months

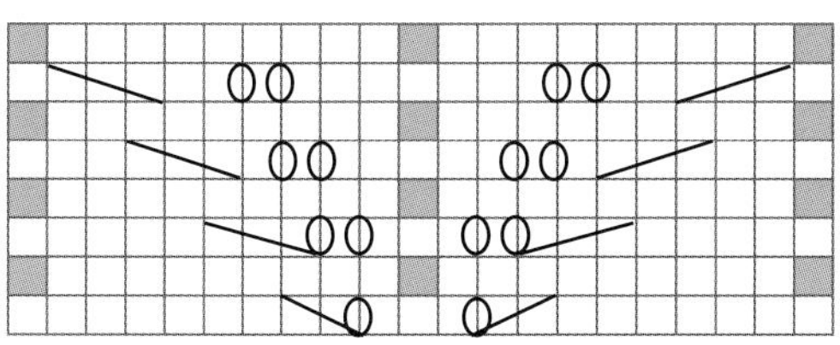

Sizes 2, 3–4 years

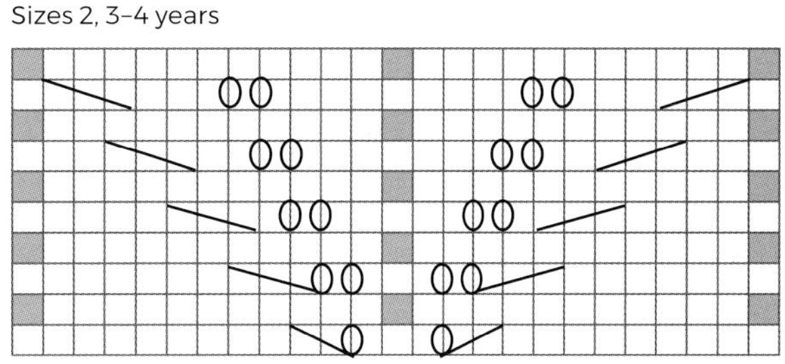

Lilly Playsuit

This fine Lilly lace pattern has been with us since the beginning. This time, we use its charm for a sweet play outfit.

SKILL LEVEL: 2

SIZES: 1–3 (6, 9, 12, 18 months, 2 years)

FINISHED MEASUREMENTS
Chest: Approx. 19¼ (20, 20½, 21, 22½, 22⅝) in [49 (51, 52, 53, 57, 57.5) cm]
Total Length: Approx. 17¾ (19, 20, 22, 24, 28) in [45 (48, 51, 56, 61, 71) cm]

YARN: Sandnes Garn Klompelompe Tynn Merinoull [CYCA #1 – fingering, 100% fine Merino wool, 191 yd (175 m) / 50 g]

YARN COLORS AND AMOUNTS
Color 6033: 150 (200, 200, 250, 250, 300) g

NEEDLES: U.S. sizes 1.5 and 2.5 (2.5 and 3 mm): 16 and 24 in or 32 in for magic loop [40 and 60 cm or 80 cm for magic loop] circulars + sets of 5 dpn for sleeves if preferred

NOTIONS: U.S. C-2 (2.75 mm) crochet hook for button loop, 8 (10, 10, 10, 12, 12) buttons, ⅝ in (15 mm) in diameter

GAUGE: 27 sts on larger size needle = 4 in (10 cm).
Adjust needle size to obtain correct gauge if necessary.

The playsuit begins with the lace pattern panel and is worked back and forth on a circular needle.

With smaller size circular CO 24 (24, 24, 28, 28, 28) sts. Work back and forth following the pattern chart—for the 3 smallest sizes, work version B.

When you've worked the chart rows 22 (23, 24, 21, 22, 22) times = 22 (23, 24, 21, 22, 22) leaves, BO on WS. Steam piece well, under a damp pressing cloth, with steam iron before you pick up and knit sts so you'll have nice results. Seam short ends.

With RS facing and larger size needle, pick up and knit 98 (104, 108, 121, 128, 128) sts along upper edge of lace panel.

Knit 1 row.

Now you'll make an opening at back neck and raise the back with German short rows (see video at klompelompe.no/en/):

Next Row: P38 (40, 42, 44, 46, 46); turn and k38 (40, 42, 44, 46, 46); turn. P34, 36, 38, 40, 42, 42); turn and k34 (36, 38, 40, 42, 42); turn and purl to end of row.

Next Row: K38 (40, 42, 44, 46, 46); turn and p38 (40, 42, 44, 46, 46); turn. K34, 36, 38, 40, 42, 42); turn and p34 (36, 38, 40, 42, 42).

Next Row: *K1, k2tog*; rep *-* across.
Knit 3 rows, binding off on last row.

With RS facing and larger size needle, pick up and knit 210 (216, 222, 234, 245, 250) sts along lower edge of lace panel. Knit 3 (3, 5, 7, 9, 13) rows.

DIVIDE FOR SLEEVES AND BODY:
K29 (30, 30, 32, 34, 34), place next 47 (48, 50, 52, 54, 56) sts on a holder (sleeve sts), CO 7 sts for underarm, k58 (60, 62, 66, 69, 70), place next 47 (48, 50, 52, 54, 56) sts on a holder (sleeve sts), CO 7 sts for underarm, K29 (30, 30, 32, 34, 34) = 130 (134, 136, 144, 151, 152) sts rem for body. Pm on each side of the 7 underarm sts at each side.

Join and knit 1 rnd, adjusting stitch count to 138 (148, 160, 166, 180, 188) sts.

Knit around in stockinette for 1¼ in (3 cm). On next rnd, increase with M1 on each side of the marked 7 sts on each side.

Increase the same way every 1¼ (1½, 1½, 2, 2, 2) in [3 (4, 4, 5, 5, 5) cm] a total of 3 (3, 4, 4, 4, 5) times = 150 (160, 176, 182, 196, 208) sts.

Measuring down center back, continue around until piece measures 11¾ (13½, 14, 14½, 15¾, 16½) in [30 (34, 35.5, 37, 40, 42) cm].

Raise back with German short rows (see video at klompelompe.no/en/):

K20; turn and p40; turn. K43; turn and p46; turn. K49; turn and p52; turn.

SIZES 9, 12, 18 MONTHS, 2 YEARS:
K55; turn and p58; turn.

SIZES 18 MONTHS, 2 YEARS:
K61; turn and p64; turn.

ALL SIZES: Knit around.

Pm on each side of the center 8 sts on both front and back.

Next Rnd: M1 on each side of the 8 marked sts at front and back.

Increase the same way on every 3rd rnd a total of 5 times.

Next Rnd: BO the center 8 sts at front and back. Work each leg separately, back and forth = 77 (82, 90, 93, 100, 106) sts rem for each leg.

LEGS
Purl 1 row.
Next Row: K1, k2tog, knit until 3 sts rem, sl 1, k1, psso, k1.

Decrease the same way on every 4th row a total of 9 (9, 10, 10, 11, 11) times.

Continue back and forth in stockinette until leg measures 6 (7, 7¾, 8¼, 9, 10¼) in [15 (18, 19.5, 21, 23, 26) cm] and next row is WS.

Purl 1 row, adjusting stitch count to 36 (36, 38, 38, 40, 40) sts.

Change to smaller size needle and knit 3 ridges (= knit 6 rows), binding off on last row.

Make second leg the same way.

BUTTON/BUTTONHOLE BANDS
Note: Pick up and knit sts, not just pick up.

With smaller size needle, pick up and knit 3 sts for every 4 sts along crotch opening. <page 151> Where you bound off on crotch, pick up and knit 1 st in every st.

Knit 4 ridges (= 8 knit rows), binding off on last row.

On front, make 7 (9, 9, 9, 11, 11) buttonholes evenly spaced on 2nd row: BO 2 sts and CO 2 sts over each gap on next row.

Charts for Lilly Playsuit and Lilly Rompers

- = knit on RS, purl on WS
- = knit on WS, purl on RS
- = k2tog
- = sl 1, k1, psso
- = k3tog
- = sl knitwise as if to k2tog, k1, psso (= CDD, centered double decrease)
- = yo between 2 sts
- = turn
  Tip for turning without holes: Before you turn, bring yarn around next st and join that wrap and the st tog the next time you come to the stitch.

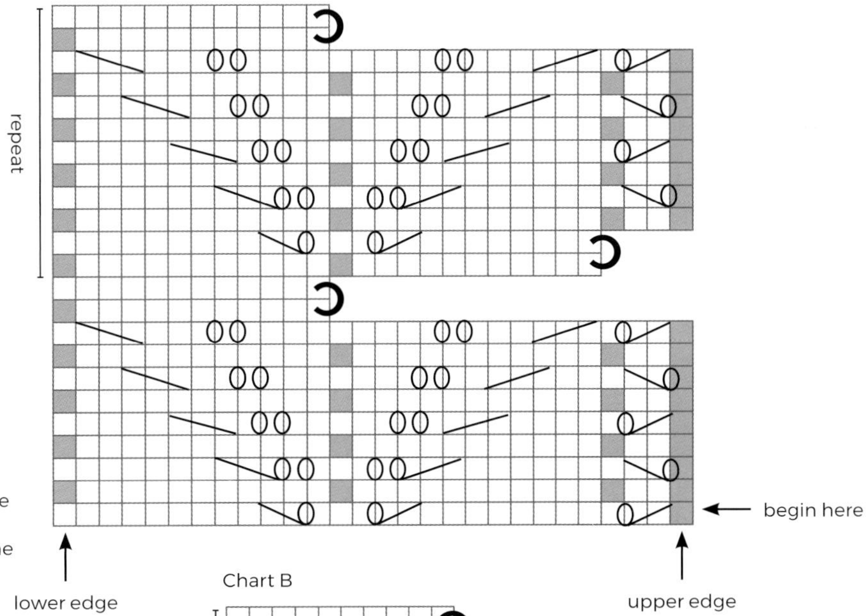

Chart B

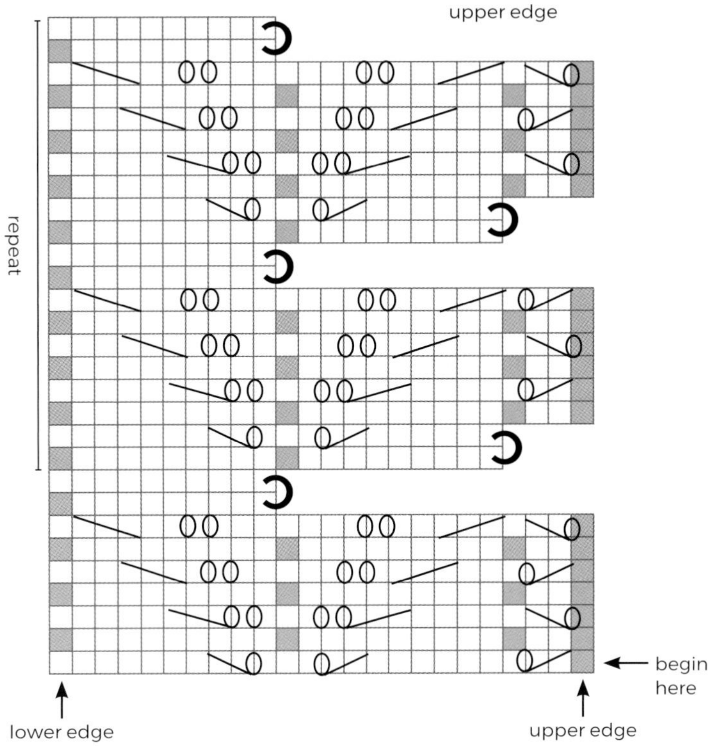

SLEEVES

With larger size magic loop needle or dpn, beginning at center of underarm, pick up and knit 4 sts, pick up and knit 1 st in gap between underarm and armhole, knit the held 47 (48, 50, 52, 54, 56) sts, pick up and knit 1 st in gap between armhole and underarm and 3 sts along underarm. Pm for end of rnd = 56 (57, 59, 61, 63, 65) sts total.

Join and knit sleeves around. The first st is a marked st and always purled.

Knit around until sleeve is ⅝ in (1.5 cm) long and then begin decreasing to shape sleeve as follows:

P1 (marked st), k2tog, knit until 2 sts before marker, sl 1, k1, psso.

Decrease the same way every ⅝ (⅝, ⅝, ¾, ¾, 1) in [1.5 (1.5, 1.5, 2, 2, 2.5) cm] until 40 (41, 43, 43, 45, 49) sts rem.

Continue without further decreasing until sleeve measures 5½ (6¼, 7, 8, 8¼, 9) in [14 (16, 18, 20, 21, 23) cm]. Knit 1 rnd decreasing 5 sts evenly spaced around.

Change to smaller size needle and work 2.5 ridges (= 5 rnds, alternating purl and knit rnds). BO knitwise on next rnd.

FINISHING

With crochet hook, ch 4 on one side of back neck for button loop and attach with 1 sl st. Sew button to opposite side. Weave in all ends neatly on WS. Sew buttons on, spaced as for buttonholes.

Block by laying playsuit flat, patted out to finished measurements, on a damp towel until completely dry.

Lilly Rompers

Sweetly embellished rompers. Pair this with leggings and baby will be ready for a party!

SKILL LEVEL: 2

SIZES: 1–3 (3–6, 9, 12, 18 months, 2 years)

FINISHED MEASUREMENTS
Chest: Approx. 19¼ (20, 20½, 21, 22½, 22⅝) in [49 (51, 52, 53, 57, 57.5) cm]
Total Length: Approx. 17¾ (19, 20, 22, 24, 28) in [45 (48, 51, 56, 61, 71) cm]

YARN: Sandnes Garn Klompelompe Tynn Merinoull [CYCA #1 – fingering, 100% fine Merino wool, 191 yd (175 m) / 50 g]

YARN COLORS AND AMOUNTS
Color 9871 or 1013: 150 (150, 200, 200, 250, 250) g

NEEDLES: U.S. sizes 1.5 and 2.5 (2.5 and 3 mm): 16 and 24 in or 32 in for magic loop [40 and 60 cm or 80 cm for magic loop] circulars or set of 5 dpn for sleeves if preferred

NOTIONS: U.S. C-2 (2.75 mm) crochet hook for button loop, 5 (5, 5, 5, 5, 5) buttons, ⅝ in (15 mm) in diameter

GAUGE: 27 sts on larger size needle = 4 in (10 cm).
Adjust needle size to obtain correct gauge if necessary.

The rompers begin with the lace pattern panel and then worked back and forth on a circular needle.

With smaller size circular CO 24 (24, 24, 28, 28, 28) sts. Work back and forth following the pattern chart—for the 3 smallest sizes, work version B.

When you've worked the chart rows 22 (23, 24, 21, 22, 22) times = 22 (23, 24, 21, 22, 22) leaves, BO on WS. Steam piece well, under a damp pressing cloth, with steam iron before you pick up and knit sts so you'll have nice results. Seam short ends.

With RS facing and larger size needle, pick up and knit 98 (104, 108, 121, 128, 128) sts along upper edge of lace panel.

Knit 1 row.

Now you'll make an opening at back neck and raise the back with German short rows (see video at klompelompe.no/en/):

Next Row: P38 (40, 42, 44, 46, 46); turn and k38 (40, 42, 44, 46, 46); turn. P34, 36, 38, 40, 42, 42); turn and k34 (36, 38, 40, 42, 42); turn and purl to end of row.

Next Row: K38 (40, 42, 44, 46, 46); turn and p38 (40, 42, 44, 46, 46); turn. K34, 36, 38, 40, 42, 42); turn and p34 (36, 38, 40, 42, 42).

Next Row: *K1, k2tog*; rep *-* across.

Knit 2 rows. BO knitwise on next row.

With RS facing and larger size needle, pick up and knit 210 (216, 222, 234, 245, 250) sts along lower edge of lace panel. Knit 3 (3, 5, 7, 9, 13) rows.

DIVIDE FOR SLEEVES AND BODY:

K29 (30, 30, 32, 34, 34), place next 47 (48, 50, 52, 54, 56) sts on a holder (sleeve sts), CO 7 sts for underarm, k58 (60, 62, 66, 69, 70), place next 47 (48, 50, 52, 54, 56) sts on a holder (sleeve sts), CO 7 sts for underarm, K29 (30, 30, 32, 34, 34) = 130 (134, 136, 144, 151, 152) sts rem for body.

Join and knit 6 (6, 6, 8, 8, 10) rnds.

Next Rnd: *K3, M1*; rep *-* until 1 (2, 1, 0, 1, 2) sts rem, k1 = 173 (178, 181, 192, 201, 202) sts.

Knit around in stockinette until piece measures 12¼ (13½, 13¾, 15, 15¾, 17¼) in [31 (34, 35, 38, 40, 44) cm].

Knit 1 rnd decreasing 1 (0, 1, 0, 1, 0) st.

Raise back with German short rows (see video at klompelompe.no/en/):

K50 (50, 52, 52, 55, 54); turn and p100 (100, 104, 104, 108, 108); turn. K98 (98, 102, 102, 106, 106); turn and p96 (96, 100, 100, 104, 104); turn. Knit to end of rnd.

Divide for legs as follows:

K16 (17, 17, 19, 19, 20) (back), knit next 58 (59, 60, 63, 66, 66) sts onto spare needle, k24 (26, 26, 28, 30, 30) (front), knit next 58 (59, 60, 63, 66, 66) sts onto spare needle, k16 (17, 17, 19, 19, 20) (back).

Cut yarn and work back first.

The first row = RS.

Next Row: K2tog, knit until 2 sts rem, sl 1, k1, psso.

Purl 1 row.

Repeat these 2 rows until 14 sts rem on needle. Place sts on a holder.

Work front as follows:

The first row = RS.

Next Row: K2tog, knit until 2 sts rem, sl 1, k1, psso.

Purl 1 row.

Repeat these 2 rows until 14 sts rem.

Work 3 rows in stockinette.

Place sts on a holder.

With smaller size needle, pick up and knit sts for leg edging.

Knit 9 sts along front of leg, *k2tog*; rep *-* a total of 29 (29, 30, 31, 33, 33) times, k0 (1, 0, 1, 0, 0), knit 14 sts of back.

Knit 2 rows. BO knitwise on next row.

Work opposite side the same way.

BUTTON/BUTTONHOLE BANDS ON CROTCH
With smaller size needle, pick up and knit 3 sts on end of garter ridge of leg edge, knit held sts and pick up and knit 3 sts on opposite side. Knit 4 rows. BO knitwise on next row.

On front, make 4 (4, 4, 4, 4, 4) buttonholes evenly spaced on 2nd row: K2 tog, yo.

SLEEVES
With larger size magic loop needle or dpn, beginning at center of underarm, pick up and knit 4 sts, pick up and knit 1 st in gap between underarm and armhole, knit the held 47 (48, 50, 52, 54, 56) sts, pick up and knit 1 st in gap between armhole and underarm, 3 sts along underarm. Pm for end of rnd = 56 (57, 59, 61, 63, 65) sts total.

Join and knit sleeves around. The first st is a marked st and always purled.

Knit around until sleeve is ⅝ in (1.5 cm) long and then begin decreasing to shape sleeve as follows:

P1 (marked st), k2tog, knit until 2 sts before marker, sl 1, k1, psso.

Decrease the same way every ⅝ (⅝, ¾, ¾, ¾, 1) in [1.5 (1.5, 2, 2, 2, 2.5) cm] until 40 (41, 43, 43, 45, 49) sts rem.

Continue without further decreasing until sleeve measures 5½ (6¼, 7, 8, 8¼, 9) in [14 (16, 18, 20, 21, 23) cm]. Knit 1 rnd decreasing 5 sts evenly spaced around.

Change to smaller size needle and purl 1 rnd, knit 1 rnd. BO purlwise on next rnd.

RUFFLE
With larger size needle, pick up and knit 210 (215, 220, 235, 245, 250) sts along lower edge of lace panel.

Next Rnd: *K2, M1, k3, M1*; rep *-* around.

Knit 10 (10, 10, 12, 12, 14) rnds.

Purl 1 rnd, knit 1 rnd, purl 1 rnd, binding off on last rnd.

FINISHING
With crochet hook, ch 4 on one side of back neck for button loop and attach with 1 sl st. Sew button to opposite side.

Weave in all ends neatly on WS.

Sew buttons on, spaced for buttonholes.

Block by laying rompers flat, patted out to finished measurements, on a damp towel until completely dry.

Little Sister's Thick Socks

Thick garter-stitch socks—warm, sweet, and they fit well.

SKILL LEVEL: 2

SIZES: 0–1 (3–6, 9–12 months)

YARN: Sandnes Garn Klompelompe Tynn Merinoull [CYCA #1 – fingering, 100% fine Merino wool, 191 yd (175 m) / 50 g]

YARN COLORS AND AMOUNTS
Color 1013 or 4032: 50 (50, 50) g

NEEDLES: U.S. size 2.5 (3 mm): 32 in (80 cm) circular for magic loop

NOTIONS: 4 decorative buttons, ⅝ in (15 mm) in diameter

GAUGE: 27 sts on gauge-size needle = 4 in (10 cm).

Adjust needle size to obtain correct gauge if necessary.

SOCK CONSTRUCTION

The socks are worked back and forth. Make 2 alike.

CO 31 (35, 37) sts.

Knit 1 row.

Increase Row 1: K1, M1, k14 (16, 17), M1, k1, M1, k14 (16, 17), M1, k1.

Knit 1 row.

Increase Row 2: K1, M1, k15 (17, 18), M1, k3, M1, k15 (17, 18), M1, k1.

Knit 1 row.

Increase Row 3: K1, M1, k16 (18, 19), M1, k5, M1, k16 (18, 19), M1, k1.

Knit 1 row.

Increase Row 4: K1, M1, k17 (19, 20), M1, k1, M1, k5, M1, k1, M1, 17 (19, 20), M1, k1.

Knit 5 rows.

Decrease Row 1: K19 (21, 22), k2tog, k7, k2tog, k19 (21, 22).

Knit 1 row.

Decrease Row 2: K18 (20, 21), k2tog, k7, k2tog, k18 (20, 21).

Knit 1 row.

Decrease Row 3: K17 (19, 20), k2tog, k7, k2tog, k17 (19, 20).

Knit 1 row.

Decrease Row 4: K16 (18, 19), k2tog,k2tog, k3, k2tog, k2tog, 16 (18, 19).

Knit 1 row.

Decrease Row 5: K17 (19, 20), k2tog, k1, k2tog, k17 (19, 20).

Knit 1 row.

Decrease Row 6: K14 (16, 17), k2tog, k2tog, k1, k2tog, k2tog, k14 (16, 17).

Knit 1 row.

Decrease Row 7: K12 (14, 15), k2tog, k2tog, sl 1, k2tog, psso, k2tog, k12 (14, 15) = 28 (32, 34) sts rem.

Join to knit in the round. Work around in k1, 1 ribbing for 30 (34, 34) rnds.

BO loosely.

FINISHING

Seam sole and heel of each sock.

Weave in all ends neatly on WS.

Fold ribbing in half and sew on 2 decorative buttons on side of sock, stitching through both layers of ribbing.

Block by laying socks between two damp towels until completely dry.

Aurora Hairband

Sometimes the sweetest accessory makes the outfit. A fun project you can make in an evening, it will be an adorable touch!

SKILL LEVEL: 2

SIZES: 0–3 (4–12 months, 1–3 years)

YARN: Sandnes Garn Klompelompe Tynn Merinoull [CYCA #1 – fingering, 100% fine Merino wool, 191 yd (175 m) / 50 g]

YARN COLORS AND AMOUNTS
Color 2650: 50 (50, 50) g or leftovers

NEEDLES: U.S. size 1.5 (2.5 mm): 24 or 32 in (60 or 80 cm) circular for magic loop

GAUGE: 30 sts on gauge-size needle = 4 in (10 cm).
Adjust needle size to obtain correct gauge if necessary.

HAIRBAND CONSTRUCTION
The hairband begins with one leaf.

CO 8 (8, 8) sts. Join and work around in magic loop technique (see video at klompelompe.no/en/).

Divide sts 4–4 onto magic loop needle tips and work each side following the chart.

Cut yarn and draw end through rem sts; tighten.

Pick up and knit 8 sts along cast-on edge of leaf.

Work around in stockinette for 1½ in (4 cm).

Next Rnd: K2, M1, k4, M1, k2.

Knit for ⅝ in (1.5 cm).
Next Rnd: *K2, M1, k1, M1, k2* rep *-*.

Knit for ¾ in (2 cm).
Next Rnd: *K3, M1, k1, M1, k3* rep *-*.

SIZE 1–3 YEARS:
Knit for ¾ in (2 cm).
Next Rnd: *K4, M1, k1, M1, k4* rep *-*.

ALL SIZES:
Work in stockinette until piece measures 13 (15½, 16¼) in [33 (39, 41) cm] from row where you picked up sts.

SIZE 1–3 YEARS:
Next Rnd: *K4, sl 2 knitwise as if to knit tog, k1, psso, k4* rep *-*.
Knit for ¾ in (2 cm).

ALL SIZES:
Next Rnd: *K3, sl 2 knitwise as if to knit tog, k1, psso, k3* rep *-*.
Knit for ¾ in (2 cm).

Next Rnd: *K2, sl 2 knitwise as if to knit tog, k1, psso, k2* rep *-*.
Knit for ⅝ in (1.5 cm).

Next Rnd: *K1, k2tog, k2* rep *-*.
Knit for 1½ in (4 cm).
Work following chart on each side. Cut yarn and draw end through rem sts; tighten.

FINISHING
Weave in all ends neatly on WS.

Block by laying hairband between two damp towels until completely dry.

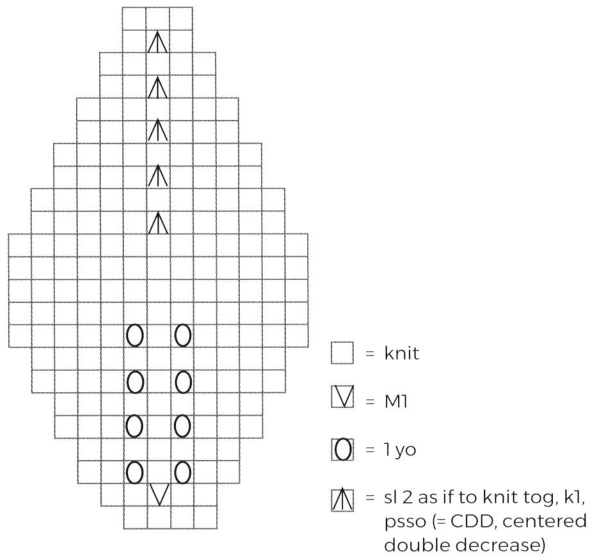

Aurora Coverlet

A charming leaf pattern and fine yarn combine for a delicate coverlet.

SKILL LEVEL: 2

FINISHED MEASUREMENTS: 27½ x 32¼ in (70 x 82 cm)

YARN: Sandnes Garn Klompelompe Tynn Merinoull [CYCA #1 – fingering, 100% fine Merino wool, 191 yd (175 m) / 50 g]

YARN COLORS AND AMOUNTS
Color 4032: 300 g

NEEDLES: U.S. size 2.5 (3 mm): 32 in (80 cm) circular

GAUGE: 27 sts on gauge-size needle = 4 in (10 cm).

Adjust needle size to obtain correct gauge if necessary.

CO 189 sts.

Knit 10 ridges (= 20 rows; 1 ridge = 2 knit rows).

Next Row (RS): K10, work following charted pattern until 10 sts rem, k10.

Continue, following chart with 10-st garter bands at each side.

When coverlet measures approx. 29½ in (75 cm), and you've worked last row on chart, knit 10 ridges, binding off on last row.

FINISHING

Weave in all ends neatly on WS.

Block by laying coverlet flat, patted out to finished measurements, on a damp towel until completely dry.

- = knit on RS, purl on WS
- = knit on WS, purl on RS
- = k2tog
- = k3 tog
- = sl 2 as if to knit tog, k1, psso (= CDD, centered double decrease)
- = 1 yo
- = 1 yo between 2 sts

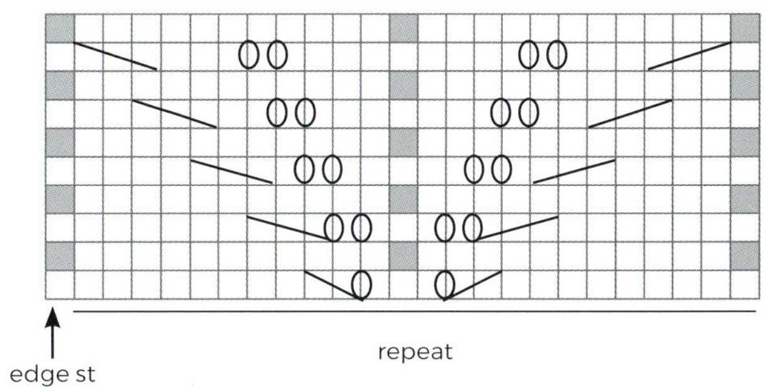

Cutiepie Layette Set

Fishing Net Pullover for Baby

Smart-looking with a simple structure that makes this pullover a very fun project.

SKILL LEVEL: 2

SIZES: 3 (6–9 months, 1, 2, 4 years)

FINISHED MEASUREMENTS
Chest: Approx. 21 (22, 23¾, 25¼, 26½) in [53 (56, 60, 64, 67) cm]
Total Length: Approx. 9½ (10¾, 12¼, 13¾, 15½) in [24 (27, 31, 35, 39) cm]

YARN: Sandnes Garn Klompelompe Merinoull [CYCA #3 – DK/light worsted, 100% Merino wool, 114 yd (104xz m) / 50 g]

YARN COLORS AND AMOUNTS
Color 9871: 150 (200, 200, 250, 300) g

NEEDLES: U.S. sizes 2.5 and 4 (3 and 3.5 mm): 16, 24, and 32 in (40, 60, and 80 cm) circulars

GAUGE: 22 sts on larger size needle = 4 in (10 cm).
Adjust needle size to obtain correct gauge if necessary.

ABBREVIATIONS
wyf: with yarn held in front.
wyb: with yarn held in back.
wf: with float: **k1wf** = lift loose strand (float) lying in front of work and k2tog joining it and next stitch.

The sweater is worked bottom up in the round on a circular needle.

With smaller size circular, CO 116 (124, 132, 140, 148) sts. Join, being careful not to twist cast-on row; pm for beginning of rnd.
Work 12 rnds in k1, p1 ribbing.

Change to larger size needle and knit 1 rnd.

Pattern:
Rnd 1: Work *p1, sl 3 wyf*; rep *-* around.
Rnds 2–3: Knit.
Rnd 4: K2, k1wf, *k3, k1wf *; rep *-* until 1 st rem, sl 1 wyf.
Rnd 5: Sl 2 wyf, p1, *sl 3 wyf, p1*; rep *-* until 1 st rem, k1.
Rnds 6–7: Knit 2 rnds.

Rnd 8: K1wf, *k3, k1 wf* until 3 sts rem, k3.

Rep pattern Rnds 1–8 as est until body measures approx. 6¾ (7½, 8¾, 9¾, 11) in [17 (19, 22, 25, 28) cm] and next rnd is Rnd 4 of pattern (where you catch the float).

On next rnd, shape armholes: BO 4 sts, work 49 (53, 57, 61, 65) sts in pattern, BO 9 sts, work 49 (53, 57, 61, 65) sts in pattern, BO 5 sts.

Set body aside while you make sleeves.

SLEEVES

With smaller size circular, CO 32 (32, 36, 36, 40) sts.

Join, being careful not to twist cast-on row; pm for beginning of rnd (= center of underarm).

Work 12 rnds in k1, p1 ribbing.

Change to large size needle. Knit 1 rnd and *at the same time* increase 4 sts evenly spaced around. Work in pattern.

Continue as est, increasing to shape sleeve every 2½ (1¾, 2½, 2, 2) in [6 (4.5, 6, 5, 5) cm]—increase on rounds that are all knit:

K1, M1, work in pattern until 1 st rem, M1, k1.

Add new sts to pattern when there are enough for a repeat.

Continue in pattern with increases until there are 40 (44, 46, 50, 54) sts. Continue in pattern without increases until sleeve measures approx. 6¼ (8, 8¾, 10¼, 11) in [16 (20, 22, 26, 28) cm] and next rnd is either Rnd 4 or Rnd 8 in pattern.

Right sleeve: On next rnd, BO first 5 sts and last 4 sts.
Left sleeve: On next rnd, BO first 4 sts and last 5 sts.

Arrange sleeves and body on same circular = 160 (176, 188, 204, 220) sts.

Slip first 2 sts of left sleeve to right needle. Begin round here. There are 4 raglan sts in each raglan panel (2 sts on each side of each marker). The raglan sts are worked in stockinette throughout. On rnds with slip sts, slip the sts wyb.

Place markers as follows (on Rnd 1 or 5 in patten: *Pm, sl 2 wyb, work 23 (27, 29, 33, 37) st in pattern, sl 2 wyb, pm, sl 2 wyb, work 49 (53, 57, 61, 65) sts in pattern, sl 2 wyb*; rep *-*.

Next Rnd: Begin raglan shaping as follows:

K1, sl 1, k1, psso, work in pattern until 3 sts before marker, k2tog, k1; rep *-* around.

Decrease the same way on **every other** rnd of pattern (not including pattern rnds where you slip sts for floats) a total of 9 (10, 12, 13, 15) times.

Next Rnd: Work the center 11 (13, 13, 15, 15) front sts and place them on a holder, Work in pattern to end of rnd. Cut yarn.

Begin on WS of front and work 1 row in pattern.

Next Row: K2tog, work in pattern, including raglan decreases, until 2 sts rem, sl 1, k1, psso. Repeat every time you are on RS.

When row with slipped sts is on WS, purl first and last sts.

If you only have 1 st between the raglan panels on the sleeves, decrease at marker: K1, sl 2, k2tog, psso.

On the next decrease, decrease at marker as: sl 1, k2tog, psso.

Decrease until 2 sts rem on front. Work 1 row and *at the same time* k2tog at beginning and end of row. Cut yarn.

NECKBAND

With smaller size circular, work 1 rnd, picking up any float sts in pattern. Work to end of rnd, pick up and knit 8 sts to held sts, work held sts, pick up and knit 8 sts and work to end of rnd.

Work 13 rnds in k1, p1 ribbing. Change to larger size needle and BO in ribbing.

FINISHING

Fold down neckband and sew edge loosely to WS. Make sure neckband is not too tight.

Seam underarms.

Weave in all ends neatly on WS.

Block by laying sweater flat, patted out to finished measurements, on a damp towel until completely dry.

Fishing Net Hipster Cap

This cool-for-baby cap features a distinctive surface and a fun-to-knit pattern.

SKILL LEVEL: 2

SIZES: 3 (6–9 months, 1–3 years)

YARN: Sandnes Garn Klompelompe Merinoull [CYCA #3 – DK/light worsted, 100% Merino wool, 115 yd (105 m) / 50 g]
+ Sandnes Garn Klompelompe Tynn Merinoull [CYCA #1 – fingering, 100% fine Merino wool, 191 yd (175 m) / 50 g]

YARN COLORS AND AMOUNTS
Merinoull, Color 9871: 50 (50, 50) g
Tynn Merinoull, Color 9871: 50 (50, 50) g

NEEDLES: U.S. sizes 2.5 and 4 (3 and 3.5 mm): 16 and 32 in (40 and 80 cm) circulars

GAUGE: 27 sts on larger size needle = 4 in (10 cm).
Adjust needle size to obtain correct gauge if necessary.

The cap is knitted in the round on a circular needle.

With smaller size circular and Tynn Merinoull, CO 90 (98, 98) sts. Join, being careful not to twist cast-on row; pm for beginning of rnd. Knit around in stockinette for 5 (5¼, 5½) in [12.5 (13, 14) cm]. Fold brim with cast-on edge inside and join every 3rd cast-on to a live st with k2tog. Make sure sts align vertically. If you think this is too difficult, you can sew the edge down later.
Knit 4 rnds.
Turn work inside out. The WS is now the RS.

Change to larger size circular and Merinoull. Knit 1 rnd adjusting stitch count to 72 (80, 80) sts [= decrease 18 (18, 18) sts evenly spaced around).
Knit around in stockinette until cap measures 2¾ (3, 3¼) in [7 (7.5, 8) cm] from rnd where you joined cast-on sts.

Fishing Net Pattern:
Rnd 1: *P1, sl 3 wyf*; rep *-* around.
Rnds 2–3: Knit.
Rnd 4: K2, k1wf, *k3, k1wf*; rep *-* until 1 st rem, sl 1 wyf.
Rnd 5: Sl 2 wyf, p1, *sl 3 wyf, p1*; rep *-* until 1 st rem, k1.
Rnds 6–7: Knit.
Rnd 8: K1wf, *K3, k1wf*; rep *-* until 3 sts rem, k3.

ABBREVIATIONS
wyf: with yarn held in front.
wyb: with yarn held in back.
wf: with float: **k1wf** = lift loose strand (float) lying in front of work and k2tog joining it and next stitch.

Rep Rnds 1–8 of pattern until cap measures approx. 3½ (4, 4¾) in [9 (10, 12) cm] from rnd where you turned brim inside out and next rnd is Rnd 5 of pattern.

SHAPE CROWN
Rnd 1: Sl 2 wyf, p1, *sl 3 wyf, p1* rep *-* until 1 st rem, k1.
Rnd 2: K4, k2tog, *K6, k2tog*; rep *-* until 2 sts rem, k2.
Rnd 3: Knit.
Rnd 4: K1wf, *k2, k1wf, k3, k1wf*; rep *-* until 6 sts rem, k2, k1wf, k3.
Rnd 5: P1, *sl 2 wyf, p1, sl 3 wyf*; rep *-* around.
Rnd 6: Knit.
Rnd 7: *K5, k2tog*; rep *-* around.
Rnd 8: K1, k1wf, *k2, k1wf*; rep *-* until 1 st rem, k1.
Rnd 9: Sl 1 wyf, p1, *sl 2 wyf, p1*; rep *-* until 1 st rem, sl 1 wyb.
Rnds 10–11: Knit.
Rnd 12: *K1wf, k2, k1wf, k2tog*; rep *-* around.
Rnd 13: *P1, sl 2 wyf, p1, sl 1 wyf*; rep *-* until 5 sts rem, p1, sl 2 wyf, p1, k1 wyb.
Rnds 14–15: Knit.
Rnd 16: *K1, k1wf, k1, k2tog wf*; rep *-* until 5 sts rem, k1, k1wf, k1, k2tog.
Rnd 17: Knit.
Rnd 18: *K2, k2tog*; rep *-* around.
Rnd 19: Knit.
Rnd 20: *K1, k2tog*; rep *-* around.
Rnd 21: Knit.
Rnds 22–23: *K2tog*; rep *-* around.

Cut yarn and draw end through rem sts; tighten.

FINISHING
Weave in all ends neatly on WS.
Block by gently steam pressing cap brim under a damp pressing cloth.

Cutiepie Onesie

In our very first book, we had a lovely little sweater design, the Go'klompen cardigan. We decided to turn the cardigan into a onesie, with the same precious texture pattern and good fit.

SKILL LEVEL: 3

SIZES: 0–1 (3, 6–9 months, 1, 2, 3 years)

FINISHED MEASUREMENTS
Chest: Approx. 19 (20, 21¾, 22, 23¼, 25¼) in [48 (51, 55, 56, 59, 64) cm]
Total Length: Approx. 16¼ (17¾, 19¾, 23¾, 26¾, 29¼) in [41 (45, 50, 60, 68, 74) cm]

MATERIALS
Yarn: Sandnes Garn Klompelompe Tynn Merinoull [CYCA #1 – fingering, 100% fine Merino wool, 191 yd (175 m) / 50 g]

YARN COLORS AND AMOUNTS
Color 6061: 150 (150, 200, 250, 250, 300, 300) g

NEEDLES: U.S. sizes 1.5 and 2.5 (2.5 and 3 mm): 32 in (80 cm) circulars

NOTIONS: 6 (6, 7, 7, 8, 8) buttons, ⅝ in (15 mm) in diameter; crochet hook US D-3 (3 mm)

GAUGE: 27 sts on larger size needle = 4 in (10 cm).
Adjust needle size to obtain correct gauge if necessary.

The onesie is worked back and forth on a circular needle, from the top down.

With smaller size circular, CO 79 (83, 89, 89, 93, 93) sts. Work back and forth in k1, p1 ribbing. The first row = WS.
Row 4: Make a buttonhole: Rib 3, k2tog, yo, rib to end of row.
Work a total of 7 rows in ribbing.

Buttonhole Note: Make a total of 6 (6, 7, 7, 8, 8) buttonholes approx. 1¾ (2, 1¾, 2, 2, 2) in [4.5 (5, 4.5, 5, 5, 5) cm] apart.

Begin pattern and raglan increases, but, *before you begin knitting, read through next section.*

PATTERN
Row 1: Knit on RS, purl on WS.
Row 2: Knit on WS, purl on RS.
Row 3: *P1, k1*; rep *-*.
Row 4: *K1, p1*; rep *-* (so knit is over knit and purl over purl).

RAGLAN STITCH PATTERN
(marked sts)
Row 1: K3.
Row 2: K3.
Row 3: K1, p1, k1.
Row 4: P1, k1, p1.
Change to larger size needle.

Begin pattern (Row 1) and increase for raglan shaping as follows:

K14 (14, 16, 16, 16, 16) (left front), yo, k3 (marked raglan sts), yo, k9 (9, 9, 9, 11, 11) (sleeve), yo, k3 (marked raglan sts), yo, k21 (25, 27, 27, 27, 27) (back), yo, k3 (marked sts), yo, k9 (9, 9, 9, 11, 11) (sleeve), yo, k3 (marked raglan sts), yo, k14 (14, 16, 16, 16, 16) (right front) = 8 sts increased.

Continue in pattern. On WS, knit yarnovers through back loop on Row 2 of pattern and either twisted knit or twisted purl as appropriate in pattern on Row 4.

Note:
On Row 3 of pattern, the first st or yarnover in each pattern section (not the marked raglan sts) should be purled. This is so the pattern will continue to match.

Continue as est by making a yarnover on each side of marked raglan sts panel on every RS row (Rows 1 and 3) until you've increased 17 (18, 19, 20, 22, 25) times = 215 (227, 241, 249, 269, 293) sts.

Next Row: Work in pattern including the first 2 marked sts, place next marked st, the 43 (45, 47, 49, 55, 61) sleeve sts and next marked st on a holder. CO 5 sts for underarm, work 2 marked sts, back sts, and next marked st, place next marked st and the 43 (45, 47, 49, 55, 61) sleeve sts and next marked st on a holder. CO 5 sts for underarm, work in pattern to end of row = 135 (143, 153, 157, 165, 177) sts rem for body.

Continue in pattern as est until onesie measures approx. 10¼ (11, 12¼, 13¾, 15½, 16¼) in [26 (28, 31, 35, 39, 41) cm] and you've just worked pattern Row 2.

Next Row (RS): Hold last 5 sts behind the first 5 sts and knit the the sets of sts tog. Pm on each side of these 5 sts and on each side of the 5 center back sts.

Now begin working in the round.

Next Rnd: Increase 1 st on each side of the 5 center front and back sts.

Increase the same way on every other rnd a total of 4 times. On next rnd, BO the 5 sts at center front and back = 68 (72, 77, 79, 83, 89) sts rem for each leg.

Work around in texture pattern as est and, on first rnd, decrease 0 (0, 1, 1, 1, 1) st.

When leg measures 4 (4¾, 5½, 8, 9½, 11) in [10 (12, 14, 20, 24, 28) cm], work 1 rnd, adjusting stitch count to 44 (44, 46, 46, 48, 48) sts.

Change to smaller size needle and work in k1, p1 ribbing for 2½ in (6 cm). BO in ribbing on next rnd.

Make second leg the same way.

SLEEVES

With larger size circular, beginning at center of underarm, pick up and knit 3 sts, work held 45 (47, 49, 51, 57, 63) sleeve sts, pick up and knit 2 sts on underarm; pm for beginning of rnd. Work around in pattern.

After ¾ in (2 cm) begin shaping sleeve with decreases: K2tog, work until 2 sts before marker, sl 1, k1, psso.Decrease the same way every ¾ in (2 cm) until 38 (38, 40, 42, 42, 44) sts rem. Continue in pattern without further decreasing until sleeve measures 4¾ (5½, 6¼, 7½, 9, 10¼) in [12 (14, 16, 19, 23, 26) cm]. Change to smaller size needle.

Work around in k1, p1 ribbing for 1¼ in (3 cm). BO in ribbing on next rnd.

Make second sleeve the same way.

FINISHING

Make a row of single crochet along edge of each front band. Seam crotch. Sew on buttons.

Weave in all ends neatly on WS.

Block by laying onesie flat, patted out to finished measurements, on a damp towel until completely dry or stretch garment to size as you dampen it.

Coziest Cutiepie Cap

With two strands of yarn held together, this is a quick-knit cap. It's perfect for cold days and to wear at nursery school.

SKILL LEVEL: 2

SIZES: 3–5 (6–12 months, 1–3, 3–6 years)

YARN: Sandnes Garn Klompelompe Merinoull [CYCA #3 – DK/light worsted, 100% Merino wool, 114 yd (104 m) / 50 g]
+ Sandnes Garn Mini Alpakka [CYCA #1 – fingering, 100% alpaca, 164 yd 9150 m) / 50 g]

YARN COLORS AND AMOUNTS
Merinoull, Color 1013: 50 (50, 50, 100) g
Mini Alpakka, Color 1015: 50 (50, 50, 50) g

NEEDLES: U.S. size 8 (5 mm): 16 in (40 cm) circular and U.S. 6 (4 mm): 32 in (80 cm) circular

GAUGE: 17 sts with 1 strand of each yarn held together on larger size needle = 4 in (10 cm).

Adjust needle size to obtain correct gauge if necessary.

The cap begins with the cords on the earflaps.

With smaller size needle and Mini Alpakka, CO 4 sts. Knit an I-cord (see video at klompelompe.no/en/) until it's 7 in (18 cm) long.

EARFLAPS

Change to larger size needle and one strand of each yarn held together..

Row 1 (WS): P1, k1, M1, k1, p1.

Row 2 (RS): P1 in front loop and k1 in back loop of first st, p1, k1, p1, in last st: k1 in front loop and p 1 in back loop.

Row 3: Work in k1, p1 ribbing across.

Row 4 (RS): K1 in front loop and p1 in back loop of first st, k1, p1, k1, p1, k1, in last st: p1 in front loop and k1 in back loop.

Row 5: Work in k1, p1 ribbing across.

Continue as est, increasing until there are 15 (17, 17, 19) sts. Work last row on WS. Set earflap aside and make a second one the same way.

CO 3 sts, work in ribbing over one earflap, CO 19 (21, 25, 25) sts, work in ribbing over second earflap.

CO 2 sts = 54 (60, 64, 68) sts. Join and work 7 (8, 8, 9) rnds in k1, p1 ribbing.

Knit 1 rnd increasing 6 (6, 8, 4) sts evenly spaced around = 60 (66, 72, 72) sts.

PATTERN

Rnds 1–2: K1, p1 around.
Rnd 3: Knit around.
Rnd 4: Purl around.
Rep Rnds 1–4.

Begin working around in pattern.
After working 5 (6, 7, 9) pattern repeats, continue as follows:
Work in pattern, but, on Rnd 3 (all knit sts), decrease: *K4, k2tog*; rep *-* around.

Continue in pattern, but, on Rnd 3 (all knit sts), decrease: *K3, k2tog*; rep *-* around.
Work 2 rnds.
Next Rnd: *K2, k2tog*; rep *-* around.
Work 2 rnds.
Next Rnd: *K1, k2tog*; rep *-* around.
Work 1 rnd.
Next Rnd: *K2tog*; rep *-* around.
Next Rnd: *K1, k2tog*; rep *-* until 4 (2, 0, 0) sts rem, k4 (2, 0, 0) = 8 sts rem.

Knit around on rem 8 sts for 4 in (10 cm). Cut yarn and draw end through rem sts; tighten.

FINISHING

Weave in all ends neatly on WS.

Block by laying cap between two damp towels until completely dry.

Cutiepie Cozy Coverlet

One of our most loved texture patterns from our first book, it stands the test of time. This coverlet is large, soft, and wonderful.

SKILL LEVEL: 1

SIZES: One size

FINISHED MEASUREMENTS: 39½ x 47¼ in (100 x 120 cm)

YARN: Sandnes Garn Kos [CYCA #5 – bulky, 62% alpaca, 29% polyamide, 9% wool, 164 yd (150 m) / 50 g]

YARN COLORS AND AMOUNTS
Color 2611: 700 g

NEEDLES: U.S. size 11 (8 mm): 32 in (80 cm) circular

GAUGE: 12 sts with 2 strands of yarn held together on gauge-size needle = 4 in (10 cm).

Adjust needle size to obtain correct gauge if necessary.

Pattern:
Row 1: *K1, p1*; rep *-* until 1 st rem, k1.
Row 2: *P1, k1*; rep *-* until 1 st rem, p1.
Rows 3–4: Knit across.
Rep Rows 1–4.

With 2 strands of yarn held together, CO 121 sts. Work back and forth in pattern until coverlet measures 47¼ in (120 cm).

BO in pattern.

FINISHING
Weave in all ends neatly on WS.

Block by laying coverlet flat, patted out to finished measurements on a damp towel until completely dry.

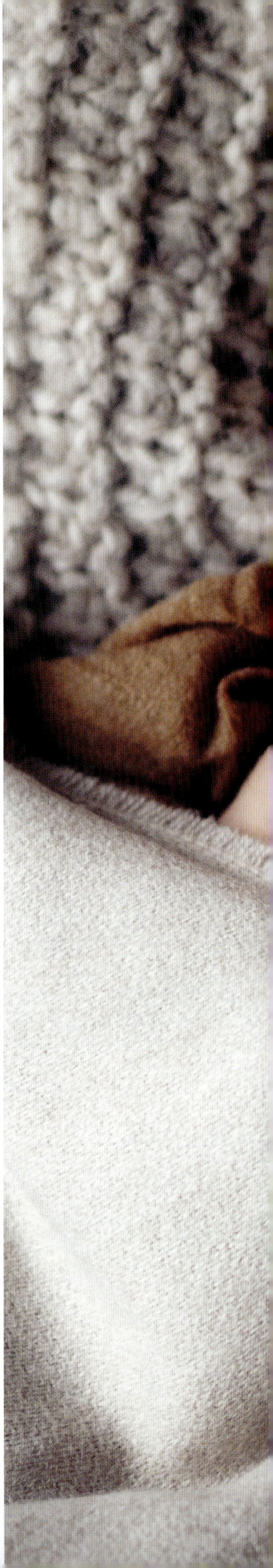

Fishing Net Baby Socks

Easy baby socks that fit well and have the same standout texture pattern as the rest of the set.

SKILL LEVEL: 2

SIZES: 0–4 (4–12, 18 months, 2–3 years)

YARN: Sandnes Garn Klompelompe Tynn Merinoull [CYCA #1 - fingering, 100% fine Merino wool, 191 yd (175 m) / 50 g]

YARN COLORS AND AMOUNTS
Color 2652: 50 (50, 50, 50) g

NEEDLES: U.S. size 2.5 (3 mm): 32 in (80 cm) circular

GAUGE: 27 sts on gauge-size needle = 4 in (10 cm).
Adjust needle size to obtain correct gauge if necessary.

The socks begin at the top and are worked around on a long magic loop circular needle.

CO 40 (48, 48, 56) sts. Join and work 5 rnds in k1, p1 ribbing.
Now work in pattern as follows:

ABBREVIATIONS
wyf: with yarn held in front.
wf: with float: **k1wf** = lift loose strand (float) lying in front of work and k2tog joining it and next stitch.

Fishing Net Pattern:
Rnd 1: *P1, sl 3 wyf*; rep *-* around.
Rnds 2–3: Knit.
Rnd 4: K2, k1wf, *k3, k1wf;*; rep *-* until 1 st rem, sl 1 wyf.
Rnd 5: Sl 2 wyf, p1, *sl 3 wyf, p1*; rep *-* until 1 st rem, k1.
Rnds 6–7: Knit.
Rnd 8: K1wf, *K3, k1wf*; rep *-* until 3 sts rem, k3.

After working pattern Rnds 1–8, 4 (4, 5, 5) times, you've completed the pattern section.
Knit 2 rnds, and a*t the same time* on 2nd rnd, decrease 0 (6, 2, 8) sts evenly spaced around = 40 (42, 46, 48) sts rem.

EYELETS
Size 0–4 months: *K2tog, yo, k2*; rep *-* around.
Size 4–12 months: *K2tog, yo, k2*; rep *-* 5 times, k2, rep *-* 5 times.
Size 18 months: *K2tog, yo, k2*; rep *-* 5 times, k6, rep *-* 5 times
Size 2–3 years: *K2tog, yo, k2*; rep *-* around.

Knit 3 rnds. Cut yarn.
Place the first 12 (13, 14, 14) sts and the last 12 (13, 14, 14) sts on a holder and work the center 16 (16, 18, 20) sts separately.

FRONT (INSTEP)
Work back and forth in stockinette.
Work in stockinette for approx. 1⅜ (1¾, 2¼, 2½) in [3.5 (4.5, 5.5, 6.5) cm]. On next row (RS), decrease as follows:
K2tog, knit until 2 sts rem, sl 1, k1, psso.
Decrease the same way on every RS row a total of 3 (3, 4, 4) times. BO on next row (WS). Cut yarn.

Attach yarn at center back, where the rnd began previously.
Knit held sts, pick up and knit approx. 3 sts for every 4 sts around instep, knit rem held sts = 62 (68, 74, 80) sts. Work around in garter ridges (1 ridge = purl 1 rnd, knit 1 rnd).

When you've worked 3.5 (3.5, 4.5, 5.5) ridges and next rnd is a knit rnd, decrease as follows:
Decrease Rnd 1: K1, k2tog, k22 (25, 28, 31), k2tog, k8, k2tog, k22 (25, 28, 31), k2tog, k1.
Purl 1 rnd.

Decrease Rnd 2: K1, k2tog, 18 (21, 24, 27), k2tog, k2tog, k8, k2tog, k2tog, k18 (21, 24, 27), k2tog, k1.

Purl 1 rnd.

Decrease Rnd 3: K1, k2tog, k2tog, k17 (20, 23, 26), k2tog, k1, k2tog, k1, k2tog, k17 (20, 23, 26), k2tog, k2tog, k1.

Purl 1 rnd.

Decrease Rnd 4: K1, k2tog, k16 (19, 22, 25), k2tog, k3, k2tog, k16 (19, 22, 25), k2tog, k1.

Purl 1 rnd.

BO knitwise on next rnd.

FINISHING

Seam soles. Weave in all ends neatly on WS.

Make two twisted cords and draw through eyelet rnds.

Block by laying socks between two damp towels until completely dry.

Fine Lillemor Pants

Fancy pants! They hold up perfectly to baby's joyful explorations.

SKILL LEVEL: 3

SIZES: preemie (0–1, 3, 6, 9, 12, 18 months)

FINISHED MEASUREMENTS
Chest: Approx. 17¼ (19, 19, 20½, 20½, 21¾, 21¾) in [44 (48, 48, 52, 52, 55.55, 55.5) cm]
Total Length, excluding straps: Approx. 11½ (12¾, 14¾, 15½, 17½, 19, 20¾) in [29.5 (32.5, 37.5, 39.5, 44.5, 48.5, 52.5) cm]

YARN: Sandnes Garn Klompelompe Tynn Merinoull [CYCA #1 – fingering, 100% fine Merino wool, 191 yd (175 m) / 50 g]

YARN COLORS AND AMOUNTS
Color 2652: 100 (100, 100, 150, 150, 150, 150) g

NEEDLES: U.S. sizes 1.5 and 2.5 (2.5 and 3 mm): 16 and 32 in (40 and 80 cm) circulars

NOTIONS: 2 (2, 2, 2, 2, 2, 2) buttons, ⅝ in (15 mm) in diameter

GAUGE: 27 sts on larger size needle = 4 in (10 cm).
Adjust needle size to obtain correct gauge if necessary.

With smaller size circular, CO 120 (130, 130, 140, 140, 150, 150) sts. Join, being careful not to twist cast-on row; pm for beginning of rnd. Work 19 rnds in k1, p1 ribbing and, on 8th rnd, make 2 buttonholes at the front:

Rib 49 (52, 52, 56, 56, 59, 59), k2tog, yo, rib 18 (22, 22, 24, 24, 28, 28), yo, sl 1, k10, psso, rib 49 (52, 52, 56, 56, 59, 59.

Change to larger size needle and knit 1 rnd.

Raise the back with German short rows (see video at klompelompe.no/en/):

K10; turn and p20; turn. K25; turn and p30. K35; turn and p40. Knit to end of rnd.

Now work around in pattern:

STITCH NOTES: lk = long knit (also called a "dip stitch"): see *lang rett* video at klompelompe.no/en/. **K1lk** = Knit 1 in the space between the k2tog and k2tog tbl 2 rnds/rows below, lengthening new st to reach sts on needle as you place it on right needle. Work next k1lk into same hole.

Rnds 1–8: Knit around.
Rnd 9: K3, *k2tog, k2tog tbl, k6*; rep *-* until 7 sts rem, k2tog, k2tog tbl, k3.
Rnd 10: Knit around.
Rnd 11: K3, k1lk, k2, k1lk, k6*; rep *-* until 5 sts rem, k1lk, k2, k1lk, k3.
Rnds 12–19: Knit around.
Rnd 20: K2tog tbl, *k6, k2tog, k2tog tbl*; rep *-* until 8 sts rem, k6, k2tog.
Rnd 21: Knit around.
Rnd 22: K1, k1lk, *k6, lk, k2, k1lk*; rep *-* until 7 sts rem, k6, k1lk, k1.
Rep these 22 rnds throughout.

When piece measures 6¼ (7, 8¾, 9, 10¼, 11, 11½) in [16 (18, 22, 23, 26, 28, 29) cm], pm on each side of the center 6 sts at both front and back.

Increase 1 st with M1 on each side of the marked 6 sts on every other rnd = 4 sts increased per rnd.

Increase the same way a total of 4 times.

Next Rnd: BO the center 6 sts at front and back = 62 (67, 67, 72, 72, 77, 77) sts rem for each leg.

LEGS
Continue in pattern as est until leg measures 3½ (4, 4¼, 4¾, 5½, 6¼, 7½) in [9 (10, 11, 12, 14, 16, 19) cm], but, when leg measures approx. ⅝ in (1.5 cm) (all sizes),

Color 9871

decrease as follows: K1, k2tog, work in pattern until 3 sts rem, sl 1, k1, psso, k1. Continue in pattern. When sts no longer fit in pattern, knit those sts.

Decrease the same way every ⅝ (⅝, ⅝, ⅝, ¾, 1, 1¼) in [1.5 (1.5, 1.5, 1.5, 2, 2.5, 3) cm] until 52 (55, 55, 58, 58, 65, 65) sts rem.

Knit 1 rnd, adjusting stitch count to 38 (40, 40, 42, 42, 44, 44) sts.

Change to smaller size needle and work in k1, p1 ribbing for 19 rnds. BO in ribbing on next rnd. Make second leg the same way.

STRAPS

With smaller size needle, pick up and knit 19 sts across center back. Work 12 rows in k1, p1 ribbing. On next row, BO center st.

Work each side separately until each strap measures 6¼ (7, 7, 8, 8¾, 8¾, 9½) in [16 (18, 18, 20, 22, 22, 24) cm] from pick up row.

RUFFLE

With larger size needle, pick up all the sts of first rnd after ribbing. Knit 1 rnd.

Next Rnd: *K2, M1*; rep *-* around.

Knit 7 (7, 8, 8, 9, 9, 10) rnds. Purl 1 rnd, knit 1 rnd. BO purlwise on next rnd.

FINISHING

Sew a button on end of each strap. Weave in all ends neatly on WS.

Block by laying pants flat, patted out to finished measurements on a damp towel until completely dry or gently steam press under a damp pressing cloth.

Toys

Rattle

YARN: Sandnes Garn Duo [CYCA #3 - DK/light worsted 55% Merino wool/45% cotton, 126 yd (115 m) / 50 g]

YARN COLORS AND AMOUNTS
Color 2650: 50 g + small amounts of 2 colors for embroidering face

NEEDLES: U.S. size 1.5 (2.5 mm): 32 in (80 cm) circular for magic loop

NOTIONS: 2 small bells; fiberfill

GAUGE: 26 sts on gauge-size needle = 4 in (10 cm).
Adjust needle size to obtain correct gauge if necessary.

Note: Fill ball with fiberfill as you knit and place two bells at the center of the ball.

CO 6 sts. Join to work in the round.

Increase Rnd 1: *Kf&b*; rep *-* around.
Increase Rnd 2: *K1, kf&b*; rep *-* around.
Increase Rnd 3: *K2, kf&b*; rep *-* around.
Increase Rnd 4: *K3, kf&b*; rep *-* around.
Increase Rnd 5: *K4, kf&b*; rep *-* around.
Increase Rnd 6: *K5, kf&b*; rep *-* around.
Knit 15 rnds.
Decrease Rnd 1: *K5, k2tog*; rep *-* around.
Decrease Rnd 2: *K4, k2tog*; rep *-* around.
Decrease Rnd 3: *K3, k2tog*; rep *-* around.
Decrease Rnd 4: *K2, k2tog*; rep *-* around.
Knit 3 rnds.
Increase Rnd: *K2, M1*; rep *-* around.
Knit around until handle measures 5¼ in (13 cm).
Decrease Rnd *K2tog *; rep *-* around.
Cut yarn. Draw end through rem sts; tighten.

BEAR EARS
Make 2 alike.
CO 18 sts. Join and knit 2 rnds on magic loop circular (see video at klompelompe.no/en/).
Rnd 1: *K4, M1, k1, M1, k4*; rep *-* around.
Rnds 2–5: Knit.
Rnd 6: *K2, k2tog*; rep *-* until 2 sts rem, k2 = 17 sts rem.
Rnd 7: K2tog, *k1, k2tog*; rep *-* until 1 st rem, k1 = 11 sts rem.
Rnd 8: *K2tog*; rep *-* until 1 st rem, k1.
Cut yarn. Draw end through rem sts; tighten.

FINISHING
Sew ears firmly onto rattle, spaced 1¼ in (3 cm) apart. Embroider on eyes, nose, and eyebrows.

Ball

YARN: Sandnes Garn Duo [CYCA #3 - DK/light worsted 55% Merino wool/45% cotton, 126 yd (115 m) / 50 g]

YARN COLORS AND AMOUNTS
Color A: 2650: 50 g or small amounts
Color B: 1015: 50 g or small amounts

NEEDLES: U.S. size 1.5 (2.5 mm): 32 in (80 cm) circular for magic loop

NOTIONS: Fiberfill

GAUGE: 26 sts on gauge-size needle = 4 in (10 cm).
Adjust needle size to obtain correct gauge if necessary.

Note: Fill ball with fiberfill as you knit.

With color A, CO 6 sts. Join to work in the round.
If desired, knit stripes: alternate 6 rnds color A, 3 rnds color B throughout.

Increase Rnd 1: *Kf&b*; rep *-* around.
Increase Rnd 2: *K1, kf&b*; rep *-* around.
Increase Rnd 3: *K2, kf&b*; rep *-* around.
Increase Rnd 4: *K3, kf&b*; rep *-* around.
Increase Rnd 5: *K4, kf&b*; rep *-* around.
Increase Rnd 6: *K5, kf&b*; rep *-* around.
Increase Rnd 7: *K6, kf&b*; rep *-* around.
Increase Rnd 8: *K7, kf&b*; rep *-* around.
Increase Rnd 9: *K8, kf&b*; rep *-* around.
Increase Rnd 10: *K9, kf&b*; rep *-* around.
Knit around for 2 in (5 cm).
Decrease Rnd 1: *K9, k2tog*; rep *-* around.
Decrease Rnd 2: *K8, k2tog*; rep *-* around.
Decrease Rnd 3: *K7, k2tog*; rep *-* around.
Decrease Rnd 4: *K6, k2tog*; rep *-* around.
Decrease Rnd 5: *K5, k2tog*; rep *-* around.
Decrease Rnd 6: *K4, k2tog*; rep *-* around.
Decrease Rnd 7: *K3, k2tog*; rep *-* around.
Decrease Rnd 8: *K2, k2tog*; rep *-* around.
Decrease Rnd 9: *K1, k2tog*; rep *-* around.
Decrease Rnd 10: *K2tog*; rep *-* around.

Cut yarn. Draw end through rem sts; tighten and weave in end to inside of ball.

Cozy Comfort Blankie

YARN: Sandnes Garn Duo [CYCA #3 - DK/light worsted 55% Merino wool/45% cotton, 126 yd (115 m) / 50 g]

YARN COLORS AND AMOUNTS
Color 2650: 100 g + small amounts of 2 colors for embroidering face

NEEDLES: U.S. sizes 1.5 and 4 (2.5 and 3.5 mm): 32 in (80 cm) circulars for magic loop

NOTIONS: Fiberfill

GAUGE: 26 sts on smaller size needle = 4 in (10 cm) and 22 sts = 4 in (10 cm) on larger size needle.

Adjust needle size to obtain correct gauge if necessary.

The blankie is worked back and forth on a circular needle.

With larger size needle, CO 75 sts.

Work 5 rows seed st [= (k1, p1) on first row and then work purl over knit and knit over purl throughout]. Continue with 5 seed sts at each side and remainder in stockinette.

When piece measures approx. 11¾ in (30 cm), work 5 rows seed st all across row. On last row, BO in seed st.

KNOTS
With smaller size circular, pick up and knit 5 sts on one corner of blankie, CO 5 sts. Knit these 10 sts around on magic loop circular (see video at klompelompe.no/en/). Knit 20 rnds.

Next Rnd: *K2, M1, k1, M1, k2*; rep *-* around.
Knit 7 rnds.
Next Rnd: K2tog*; rep *-* around.

Cut yarn. Draw end through rem sts; tighten. Sew down the 5 sts you cast on.

Make a knot in each corner.

HEAD
Fill head with fiberfill as you knit. With smaller size circular, CO 6 sts. Join to work in the round.
Increase Rnd 1: *Kf&b*; rep *-* around.
Increase Rnd 2: *K1, kf&b*; rep *-* around.
Increase Rnd 3: *K2, kf&b*; rep *-* around.
Increase Rnd 4: *K3, kf&b*; rep *-* around.
Increase Rnd 5: *K4, kf&b*; rep *-* around.
Knit 15 rnds.
Decrease Rnd 1: *K4, k2tog*; rep *-* around.
Decrease Rnd 2: *K3, k2tog*; rep *-* around.
Decrease Rnd 3: *K2, k2tog*; rep *-* around.
Decrease Rnd 4: *K1, k2tog*; rep *-* around.
Decrease Rnd 5:*K2tog*; rep *-* around.

Cut yarn. Draw end through rem sts; tighten.

EARS
Make 2 alike. With smaller size circular, CO 18 sts. Join and knit 5 rnds on magic loop circular (see video at klompelompe.no/en/).
Rnd 1: *K4, M1, k1, M1, k4*; rep *-* around.
Rnds 2–11: Knit.
Rnd 12: *K2, k2tog*; rep *-* unti 2 sts rem, k2 = 17 sts rem.
Rnd 13: Knit.
Rnd 14: K2tog, *k1, k2tog*; rep *-* until 1 st rem, k1 = 11 sts rem.
Rnd 15: *K2tog*; rep *-* until 1 st rem, k1.
Cut yarn. Draw end through rem sts; tighten.

FINISHING
Sew ears firmly onto head, spaced about 1 in (2.5 cm) apart. Embroider on eyes, nose, and eyebrows.

Sew head firmly to center of blankie.

Weave in all ends neatly on WS.

Mini Rabbit / Mini Cat

YARN: Sandnes Garn Duo [CYCA #3 - DK/light worsted 55% Merino wool/45% cotton, 126 yd (115 m) / 50 g]

YARN COLORS AND AMOUNTS
Color 2650 or 1015: 50 g + small amounts of 2 colors for embroidering face

NEEDLES: U.S. size 1.5 (2.5 mm): 32 in (80 cm) circular for magic loop

NOTIONS: Fiberfill

GAUGE: 25 sts on gauge-size needle = 4 in (10 cm). Adjust needle size to obtain correct gauge if necessary.

The animal begins with the head. Fill animal with fiberfill as you knit.

Note: Decrease with k2tog; but if you have too few stitches and the knitting is tight because of the fiberfill, you can decrease with sl 1, k1, psso instead.

CO 6 sts. Divide sts evenly over magic loop needles (see video at klompelompe.no/en/); join to work in the round.
Increase Rnd 1: *Kf&b*; rep *-* around = 12 sts.
Increase Rnd 2: *K1, kf&b*; rep *-* around.
Increase Rnd 3: *K2, kf&b*; rep *-* around.
Increase Rnd 4: *K3, kf&b*; rep *-* around.
Knit 10 rnds.
Decrease Rnd 1: *K3, k2tog*; rep *-* around.
Decrease Rnd 2: *K2, k2tog*; rep *-* around.

Decrease Rnd 3: *K1, k2tog*; rep *-* around.
Decrease Rnd 4: *K2tog*; rep *-* around.
Knit 1 rnd.
Increase Rnd 1: *K2, M1*; rep *-* around.
Knit 1 rnd.
Increase Rnd 2: *K3, M1*; rep *-* around.
Knit 1 rnd.
Increase Rnd 3: *K4, M1*; rep *-* around.
Knit 1 rnd.
Increase Rnd 4: *K5, M1*; rep *-* around.
Knit 1 rnd.
Increase Rnd 5: *K6, M1*; rep *-* around.
Knit 1 rnd.
Increase Rnd 6: *K7, M1*; rep *-* around.
Knit 8 rnds.
Decrease Rnd 1: *K4, k2tog*; rep *-* around.
Decrease Rnd 2: *K3, k2tog*; rep *-* around.
Decrease Rnd 3: *K2, k2tog*; rep *-* around.
Decrease Rnd 4: *K1, k2tog*; rep *-* around.
Decrease Rnd 5: *K2tog*; rep *-* around.
Cut yarn. Draw end through rem sts; tighten.

RABBIT EARS

Make 2 alike.
CO 14 sts. Divide sts evenly over magic loop circular and join.
Knit 3 rnds.
Next Rnd: *K3, M1, k1, M1, k3*; rep *-* around = 18 sts.
Knit 9 rnds.
Next Rnd: *K1, k2tog*; rep *-* around.
Knit 1 rnd.
Next Rnd: *K2tog*; rep *-* around.
Cut yarn. Draw end through rem sts; tighten.

CAT EARS

Make 2 alike.
CO 14 sts. Divide sts evenly over magic loop circular and join.
Knit 2 rnds.
Next Rnd: *K2, M1, k3, M1, k2*; rep *-* around.
Knit 2 rnds.
Next Rnd: *K1, sl 1, k1, psso, sl 1, k2tog, psso, k2tog, k1*; rep *-* around.
Next Rnd: *K1, sl 1, k2tog, psso, k1*; rep *-* around.
Knit 2 rnds.
Cut yarn. Draw end through rem sts; tighten.

ARMS

Make 2 alike.
CO 6 sts. Divide sts evenly over magic loop circular and join (see video at klompelompe.no/en/).
Next Rnd: *Kf&b*; rep *-* around.
Knit 6 rnds.
Next Rnd: *K1, k2tog*; rep *-* around.
Knit 4 rnds.
Next Rnd, K4, BO 4 sts.
Next Row: K1, k2tog, k1.
BO purlwise on next row.

FEET

CO 6 sts. Divide sts evenly over magic loop circular and join.
Rnd 1: *Kf&b*; rep *-* around.
Rnd 2: *K1, kf&b*; rep *-* around.
Rnds 3–7: Knit.
Turn Heel: K4; turn and p8; turn. K9; turn and p10; turn. K11; turn and p12; turn. K6.
Rnd 1: Knit around.
Rnd 2: K4, sl 1, k1, psso, sl 1, k1, psso, k2, k2tog, k2tog, k4.
Rnd 3: Knit.
Rnd 4: K2, sl 1, k1, psso, sl 1, k1, psso, k2, k2tog, k2tog, k2.
Rnds 5–8: Knit.

RIGHT LEG

BO 5 sts, k5.
BO purlwise on next rnd.

LEFT LEG

K5, BO 5 sts.
BO knitwise on next rnd.

CAT TAIL

CO 3 sts. Make an I-cord (see video at klompelompe.no/en/) 2¼ in (5.5 cm) long. Cut yarn and draw end through rem sts; tighten. Sew tail firmly ⅝ in (1.5 cm) from center of cat's backside.

FINISHING

Sew arms securely at neck between body and head. Sew ears on 1¼ in (3 cm) apart. Sew legs on securely, spaced ¾ in (2 cm) apart.

Embroider on eyes, eyebrows, and nose.

Weave in all ends on WS.

Acknowledgments

We are so fortunate to have published our 16th book! We would not have managed it without the fantastic team at J.M. Stenersens Forlag. We value their work for making our book so good. We especially thank Solveig (our favorite editor), Raymond, Tine, Camilla, Thomas, and Cathrine, all of whom we've come to know so well over the years. Thank you for cheering us on, sharing good advice along the way, and greeting us with an always warm welcome whenever we visited.

Thank you to the fantastic team of test knitters. It was especially great when several of the test knitters produced sweet, small models only a few days old, to pose.

Thank you to designer Anne Vines who put the book together so well.

Thank you to Sandnes Garn for such good collaboration and the lovely quality yarn produced in Norway.

Thank you to Stig Øyvind and Arve for holding out on long work days and holding the fort when we were away.

Thank you to our charming models:
Guro, Ingvild, Sarah, Noah, Elias, Mads, Benjamin, Tobias, Even, Olav, Erle, Oline, Magnus, Mats, Hedda, Iben, Agnes, Sara Oline, Reidun, Gustav, Caspian Matheo, Filippa, and Lotta.

TEST KNITTERS:
Britt Alise K. Stange, Line Tangen, Åse Osmundsen, Kristin Karlsen, Svanhild Andreassen, Marianne Hartwedt, Gunnvor Thulin, Mary Therese Utvik, Lillian H. Johansen, Gro Torunn Utvik, Maria Hjelmaas, Sissel Eikeland, Ingebjørg Thorsen, Aina Pedersen, Solveig Hartwedt, Anna L. Larsen, Lena T. Yrke, Bodhild Bang, Mariann Midtbø, Ingrid H. Hiller, Tove K. Milje, Johanna F. K. Gismervik, Kristine Leirdal, Linneah Hilbig, Helene Aardal, Christine Ulland, Randi Andreassen,